THE LAW OF
BOUNDARIES AND FENCES

THE LAW OF BOUNDARIES AND FENCES

by

VINCENT POWELL-SMITH
LL.B. (Hons.), LL.M., D.Litt.,
Dip. Com., F.R.S.A., F.S.A. Scot.,
F.F.B., F.Ph.S.
Lecturer in Law at the
University of Aston Management Centre

SECOND EDITION

LONDON
BUTTERWORTHS
1975

ENGLAND: BUTTERWORTH & CO. (PUBLISHERS) LTD.
LONDON: 88 Kingsway, WC2 6AB

AUSTRALIA: BUTTERWORTHS PTY. LTD.
SYDNEY: 586 Pacific Highway, Chatsworth, NSW 2067
MELBOURNE: 343 Little Collins Street, 3000
BRISBANE: 240 Queen Street, 4000

CANADA: BUTTERWORTH & CO. (CANADA) LTD.
TORONTO: 2265 Midland Avenue, Scarborough, M1P 4S1

NEW ZEALAND: BUTTERWORTHS OF NEW ZEALAND LTD.
WELLINGTON: 26–28 Waring Taylor Street, 1

SOUTH AFRICA: BUTTERWORTH & CO. (SOUTH AFRICA) (PTY.) LTD.
DURBAN: 152–154 Gale Street

ISBN 0 406 34001 3

Printed in Great Britain by William Clowes & Sons Limited, London, Colchester and Beccles

PREFACE TO THE SECOND EDITION

The call for a second edition of this book has enabled me to deal with several recent developments in the law of boundaries and fences. There have been no really startling or revolutionary changes in the law—with the exception of the Animals Act 1971—but there has been a great number of judicial decisions of considerable interest, clarifying a number of formerly doubtful points.

Considerable alterations have been made in the text, with the result that the book is somewhat longer than its predecessor. In the first place, several important decisions in the Court of Appeal and elsewhere have merited consideration and inclusion. This has meant the revision of much of the earlier text as well as references in footnotes. Secondly, there have been some statutory changes which have had to be noted. Finally, my own views on the subject have developed and this has meant changes by way of expansion and emendation. In this connection, the comments of users and reviewers have been particularly helpful.

New sections are included dealing with the width of the highway in its relation to boundaries and with electrified fences. There have also been considerable other expansions. I hope that my revisions have improved the content and quality of the book and that it will continue to be useful to conveyancers, surveyors, estate agents and others who are concerned with its subject matter.

I am indebted to Mr Michael Barrett, M.Sc., for the useful and interesting Appendix on the land surveying aspects of boundary disputes, and to The Law Society for permission to reproduce parts of The Law Society's General Conditions of Sale (1973 Revision). I must once again thank Butterworths for their help and I am grateful to my wife for her encouragement and support in the preparation of this new edition.

I have endeavoured to state the law as it was on 1st June, 1974, but some developments have been noted at a late stage of production wherever possible.

VINCENT POWELL-SMITH

Leicester
November, 1974

EXTRACT FROM THE PREFACE TO THE FIRST EDITION

The purpose of this book is to present a brief and concise statement of the law governing private boundaries and fences, and to show the subject in its proper setting as an essential feature of conveyancing.

A simple boundary query can involve many points, and the case law on the subject is frightening. I have not hesitated to state what I think the law to be where there is doubt, but all my assertions are backed by judicial or academic authority. Inevitably, there are some repetitions in the text. This is intentional, and may perhaps be forgiven in the interests of ease of reference and use.

Better conveyancing by reference to an adequate and well-drawn plan would considerably reduce the number of boundary disputes. Frequently the client has only himself to blame because he is not willing to go to the expense of having the boundaries checked by a surveyor. In many cases that precaution is essential, and there is room for more co-operation between lawyers and surveyors.

V. P.-S.

TABLE OF CONTENTS

Chapter 7. LIABILITY IN TORT

Chapter 8. PARTY WALLS

Chapter 9. BOUNDARY DISPUTES

Chapter 10. MISCELLANEA

APPENDICES

INDEX

TABLE OF STATUTES

References in this Table to "Statutes" are to Halsbury's Statutes of England (Third Edition) showing the volume and page at which the annotated text of the Act will be found. Page numbers printed in bold type indicate where the Act is set out in part or in full.

TABLE OF CASES

In the following Table references are given to the English and Empire Digest where a digest of each case will be found.

C

PAGE

PAGE

K

L

Q

PAGE

R

S

PAGE

T

U

Z

Chapter 1

INTRODUCTION

"Conveyancers, however, have to do the best they can with the facts supplied to them and it is only now and again that confusion arises".
Per LORD SUMNER in *Eastwood* v. *Ashton,* [1915] A.C. 900, at 916.

DEFINITIONS

Boundary

The term "boundary" has no special meaning in law, but is commonly used to denote the imaginary line which is the ascertainable limit of one person's freehold or leasehold property. A boundary may also be the physical feature by which that limit is marked, *e.g.*, a hedge, a wall, a bank or a stream.[1] A dictionary definition of boundary is "a limit line" or else "that which marks the extreme limits of anything".[2] These definitions sufficiently convey the meaning of the term, and also indicate the subject-matter of this book, which is concerned with private boundaries. No more precise attempt at definition is necessary.[3]

The variable nature of boundary features is apparent from an old treatise[4] where it was said:

> "The term mearing or boundary signifies the ascertained limits of adjacent lands belonging to different proprietors; and fence is properly applicable to the inclosure of lands by walls, drains or hedges, for the purpose of agricultural improvement or preventing trespass.

1. 3 *Halsbury's Laws*, 3rd Edn., 354, defines a boundary as "an imaginary line which marks the confines or line of division of two contiguous estates".
2. *The Concise Oxford Dictionary; The Penguin English Dictionary.*
3. There are many other definitions of boundary. For example, Jowitt's *Dictionary of English Law*, (1959), gives "the imaginary line which divides two pieces of land from one another", while *The Encyclopaedia Britannica*, (1959, Dict. 1), states that a boundary is "any object serving to indicate a limit or confine".
4. 1 Furlong, *Landlord and Tenant*, 696, quoted in part in Hunt, *Boundaries and Fences*, (6th Edn., 1912), p. 1.

> A boundary may be known by taking a line between two fixed points or objects or it may be marked by stakes, erected at intervals, and, at the discretion of the proprietor, may be permanently distinguished or fenced by a wall or a drain, according to the nature of the soil."

The learned author might also have added natural boundary features to this brief catalogue.

Fence

Fence is a composite word covering any kind of barrier, be it a hedge, wall or railing. "A fence may consist of almost any kind of enclosure or division; but a hedge, ditch, bank or wall will be most commonly found to answer that term".[5] "Fence" is used in this broad sense throughout this book, unless otherwise stated.[6]

PRELIMINARY MATTERS

The boundaries of land are a matter of fact and of evidence. The precise boundary line and, indeed, whether or not a particular boundary feature is included in the property depends on the facts of the case. In the absence of documentary or other admissible evidence the court may be guided by certain rebuttable presumptions of law which are applicable in both registered and unregistered conveyancing. These are fully discussed in Chapter 3. Physical features such as walls and fences, together with the description in the parcels, may, and often do, indicate the situation of the boundaries.

Boundary disputes are all too common, perhaps because boundaries are seldom defined in older deeds with any degree of precision. Unhappily some modern conveyancing leaves much to be desired in this respect, especially where land is conveyed by reference to a plan. In registered conveyancing an application can be made for fixed boundaries, but this is rarely done.[7] The conveyancer must always be on guard to see that a conveyance or other instrument describes the property in question with clarity and certainty, but can take heart from LORD SUMNER's sympathetic dictum quoted at the head of this chapter.

---

5. Woolrych, *Party Walls and Fences*, p. 281.
6. For the purpose of liability under the Animals Act 1971, "fencing" is defined in s. 11 so as to include "the construction of any obstacle designed to prevent animals from straying". Clearly this includes cattle grids.
7. Curtis & Ruoff, *Registered Conveyancing*, (2nd Edn.), p. 62. Fixed boundaries are discussed in Chapter 2, *post*, pp. 29–30.

Conveyancing documents are meant to be understood and must be construed in a rational and commonsense way, the idea being to express the legal position in clear terms. Greater clarity of expression in conveyances and unequivocal definition of boundaries would inevitably reduce the number of boundary disputes. The writer believes that in all but the simplest cases, a proper survey and correctly drawn and accurate plan pays dividends, in spite of the additional expense involved. The land surveying aspects of boundary disputes are of intense interest, and Appendix I will be found enlightening. At present, "a conveyancer in this country, who wishes to be absolutely precise as to boundaries, is . . . faced with the impossible task of defining in a document something which has not been determined on the ground".[8]

The common law imposes no obligation upon a landowner to erect and maintain fences around his land; he need not delineate the boundaries of his property in any way. "For the law bounds every man's property and is his fence."[9] Yet it is a convenient and customary practice for property to be bounded in by some physical division, not merely to mark the actual physical limits of ownership but for the more utilitarian purpose of preventing intrusion. "Fences, although they may have been occasionally used as boundaries for the division of property are, nevertheless, treated by our law for the most part as guards against intrusion."[10]

Problems as to boundaries arise not only as between adjoining owners, but between vendor and purchaser and landlord and tenant. The latter relationship imposes on the tenant an obligation to preserve the boundaries of the demised premises.[11] There is no concomitant

---

8. Law Commission, Working Paper No. 45, "Transfer of Land—Land Registration (Third Paper)", July 1972, p. 4. A footnote adds "Unless there has been a recent accurate survey, for example, in the case of a newly developed estate".
9. Theobald, *Law of Land*, (2nd Edn., 1929), p. 345, citing *Star* v. *Rookesby* (1710), 1 Salk. 335; *Boyle* v. *Tamlyn* (1827), 6 B. & C. 329; *Cornwell* v. *Metropolitan Sewers Commissioners* (1855), 10 Exch. 771; *Erskine* v. *Adeane* (1873), 8 Ch. 756; *Jones* v. *Lee* (1912), 106 L.T. 123.
10. Woolrych, *op. cit.*, p. 281.
11. *A.-G.* v. *Fullerton* (1813), 2 Ves. & B. 263; *Brown* v. *Wales* (1872), L.R. 15 Eq. 142. See also *Whitfield* v. *Weedon* (1772), 2 Chit. 685; *Cheetham* v. *Hampson* (1791), 4 Term Rep. 318; *Powley* v. *Walker* (1793), 5 Term Rep. 373; Hill & Redman, *Landlord and Tenant*, (15th Edn.), p. 299; and *post*, p. 168.

obligation on the landlord to repair existing fences, in the absence of an express covenant imposing liability.[12]

TYPES OF BOUNDARIES

Natural and Artificial

Boundaries may be classified in a number of ways. They are either natural or artificial. Natural boundaries are those which are not placed in position by man: natural water-courses, lakes, islands, the seashore and the like. In these cases certain rebuttable presumptions may arise at common law which help to establish ownership of boundary features and the line of demarcation between adjacent properties, in the absence of contrary evidence. There is no room for presumptions if the boundary can be established from the deeds, and any admissible evidence as to construction. Those advising on boundary disputes must first inspect the documents of title, for the court is primarily concerned with title to land. This is to be deduced from such concrete evidence showing the acts and intentions of the parties and their predecessors, *i.e.*, the deeds, and not by presumptions.

Artificial boundaries are man-made. They include such things as fences, canals, railway lines and rights of way. Common law presumptions may similarly come into play. Acts of ownership will always be evidence of the position of boundaries.[13]

Vertical and Horizontal Boundaries

By s. 205 (1) (ix) of the Law of Property Act 1925, "land" is very widely defined:

> " 'Land' includes land of any tenure, and mines and minerals, whether or not held apart from the surface, buildings or parts of buildings, (whether the division is horizontal, vertical or made in any other way), and other corporeal hereditaments . . ."

There is thus no limit to the sub-division except physical impossibility. As a fairly recent development we have the maisonette which is in general a self-contained flat having direct access at ground level.[14]

---

12. *Cheetham* v. *Hampson* (1791), 4 Term Rep. 318; *Erskine* v. *Adeane* (1873), 8 Ch. App. 756.
13. See, *e.g.*, *per* BAYLEY, J. in *Guy* v. *West* (1808), 2 Selwyn's N.P. 1287; *post*, pp. 80–81.
14. See E. F. George, *The Sale of Flats*, (3nd Edn.), which includes useful precedents for the conveyance and lease of maisonettes.

An ordinary flat does not necessarily have a direct entrance from the ground.

Horizontal boundaries include strata of minerals, roads and ways and, very importantly, storey boundaries. In conveying or leasing a floor or storey of a building the grant is merely of a layer or stratum of the building. It follows that the presumption *cujus est solum, ejus est usque ad coelum et ad inferos* does not apply. Dispute exists as to whether the structures dividing the premises conveyed or demised from those above or below are party structures *eo nomine* and therefore subject to normal party rights. The point is of more than academic interest, as it has practical application in the realm of leasehold conveyancing. The problem was left undecided in the modern case of *Sturge* v. *Hackett*,[15] but for reasons which will be advanced later the writer is of the opinion that the dividing structures are "party floors" and subject to the provisions of s. 38 of the Law of Property Act 1925, unless some contrary provision is made.[16]

Mineral strata are a form of horizontal boundary but do not require extensive treatment. Mines and minerals vested in the person conveying will pass with the freehold without express mention, and consequently should be excluded where it is desired to reserve mineral rights to the grantor.[17] On a grant or exception of minerals in general there is no specified boundary of depth below which they may be worked alone. The grant or exception will be subject to the surface owner's right to lateral and subjacent support and will entitle the grantee to work mineral substances in strata.

The general rule regarding the passing of minerals is subject to an exception in the case of purchases by railway and water undertakings in the exercise of their statutory powers. In such cases mines and minerals are excluded from the land acquired, unless they are expressly

15. [1962] 3 All E.R. 166.
16. The matter is discussed at length in Chapter 8, *post*, pp. 146–147.
17. Coal is, of course, vested in the National Coal Board by virtue of s. 3 (3) of the Coal Act 1938, as amended by the Coal Industry Nationalisation Act 1946, with effect from January 1st, 1947. Formerly it was vested in the Coal Commission under the 1938 Act. The Petroleum Production Act 1934, vests petroleum existing in its natural condition in strata in the Crown. See the Atomic Energy Act 1946, as to uranium and allied substances. At common law the Crown is entitled to gold and silver found in a mine: *Case of Mines* (1568), 1 Plowd. 310; *A.-G.* v. *Morgan* [1891] 1 Ch. 432.

mentioned in the conveyance or land registry transfer. There are also restrictions on the working of minerals under such lands.[18]

Vertical boundaries comprise such things as fences, water boundaries and the like. In the absence of contrary provision in a lease or conveyance, the demise or grant of a part of a building divided vertically and horizontally will include the external walls enclosing the part granted or demised.[19]

These introductory remarks are necessary to place the subject in its proper context. It is now proposed to examine the manner in which boundaries may be fixed, varied or determined, and then to give detailed consideration to the various problems arising in this complex branch of the law.

---

18. This rule applies where land is acquired subject to the provisions of s. 77 of the Railways Clauses Consolidation Act 1845, or s. 18 of the Waterworks Clauses Act 1847. The authority may, of course, purchase the minerals after they have acquired the surface, but the statutory limitation that the authority is not entitled to minerals unless "expressly purchased" applies whether the purchase is compulsory or by agreement: *Errington* v. *Metropolitan District Rail. Co.* (1882), 19 Ch.D. 559.

19. *Carlisle Café Co.* v. *Muse Brothers & Co.* (1897), 67 L.J. Ch. 53; *Hope Brothers, Ltd.* v. *Cowan*, [1913] 2 Ch. 312; *Goldfoot* v. *Welch*, [1914] 1 Ch. 213; *Sturge* v. *Hackett*, [1962] 3 All E.R. 166.

Chapter 2

THE FIXING AND VARIATION OF BOUNDARIES

"Cursed is he that removeth his neighbour's landmark." *The Commination Service in the Book of Common Prayer.*

The position of boundaries may be fixed or altered in several ways. The subject may be conveniently divided into three parts:

(A) By act of the parties;
(B) by statutory authority;
(C) by the court.

Boundaries may also be determined by legal presumption in appropriate cases in relation to the ownership of particular boundary features. These cases are discussed at length in Chapter 3.

(A) BY ACT OF THE PARTIES

The parties to a transaction concerning land may of their own volition fix the boundaries of the property in its relation to contiguous estates. Boundaries may be determined by the parties themselves in four ways.

1 BY AGREEMENT

An estate owner who is not under any disability may fix or alter the boundaries of his land by agreement with the adjoining owner, *e.g.*, by selling or exchanging lands. A deed is necessary to give effect to an agreement changing the position of a boundary where this amounts to an assurance of the land involved, *i.e.*, if some land changes hands.[1] It has, however, been held that an agreement fixing bound-

1. Law of Property Act 1925, s. 52 (1): "All conveyances of land or of any interest therein are void for the purposes of conveying or creating a legal estate unless made by deed." See *Hetherington* v. *Galt* (1905), 7 F. (Ct. of Sess.) 706.

aries can be implied from the conduct of the parties, but the facts of the case in question were somewhat unusual.[2]

If the agreement is a genuine attempt to settle a doubtful boundary, neither deed nor writing is necessary as there is no assurance of lands for the purposes of s. 52 of the Law of Property Act 1925. In effect the parties are merely stating what is thought always to have been the position. In practice in a case of this sort there should be a properly drafted memorandum of agreement. The memorandum should incorporate a sufficient and accurate plan made after a survey of the site. *Penn* v. *Lord Baltimore*[3] is authority for the proposition that in such a case the settlement itself is sufficient consideration to make the agreement mutually enforceable. In that case specific performance was ordered of an agreement relating to the boundaries of land in America, although the defendant was in England.

Where registered land is involved the boundaries may be altered by amendment of the register by the Chief Land Registrar.[4] Application for rectification of the register must be made to him, and if necessary he may hold a hearing. There is a right of appeal against his decision to a single judge of the Chancery Division.[5] Alternatively, the appropriate Land Registry form of transfer could be used to change the line of the boundary, *e.g.*, where one owner transfers a strip of land to his neighbour with a view to fixing a fresh boundary.

2 BY TITLE DEEDS

Boundaries are commonly determined by the title deeds themselves for these reveal the acts of the successive owners of the different estates. If the boundaries are clearly and unambiguously defined in the muniments of title, this will normally be conclusive in any dispute,

---

2. *Taylor* v. *Parry* (1840), 1 Man. & G. 604.
3. (1750), 1 Ves. Sen. 444. A form of agreement for the settlement of a boundary dispute is set out in 2 *Encyclopaedia of Forms and Precedents* (3rd Edn.) 294. Precedent clauses for an agreement straightening boundaries between neighbouring properties may also be found in Moore's *Practical Agreements*, (10th Edn.) p. 139.
4. Powers of rectification are given him by s. 82 of the Land Registration Act 1925, which authorises rectification *inter alia* to give effect to an agreement between interested parties. But see *Re Freehold Land in Dances Way, West Town, Hayling Island*, [1962] 2 All E.R. 42, discussed in Chapter 9, *post*, p. 169.
5. Rule 299 of the Land Registration Rules 1925, provides that "any person aggrieved by an order or decision of the registrar may appeal to the Court": see *Re Gilbert's Application*, [1961] 2 All E.R. 313 and Chapter 9, *post*, p. 171.

although it may be that the title deeds of the different owners are in conflict.[6] Parol evidence will be admissible to clarify any ambiguity, or to show what the boundaries were before the grant in question because this is relevant as showing what it was intended to convey.

In registered conveyancing the boundaries are not guaranteed and the boundaries shown on the General Map, filed plan or land certificate do not necessarily show the exact line of the boundary.[7] This can cause practical difficulties but the usual preliminary searches and inquiries should serve to clear up any doubtful points, *e.g.*, the ownership of the bed of a stream forming the boundary of the property. In any event, the usual rebuttable presumptions as to the ownership of boundary features will apply. An instructive case is *Lee* v. *Barrey*[8] for there the boundaries of registered land were shown differently on the transfer and on the General Map and filed plan. The court held that where the boundaries are clearly shown on a plan attached to the transfer itself, this will not be defeated because something different is shown on the General Map. The lesson of *Lee* v. *Barrey* is the need for an accurately drawn and dimensioned plan of suitable scale in both registered and unregistered conveyancing. The case could be regarded as exceptional because in practice the Land Registry maps show the boundaries with all available detail.[9] Land Registry plans are not, however, necessarily informative, and sometimes on registration of title information contained in the title deeds is not reproduced on the register or filed plan. The Law Commission is of the view that the pre-registration deeds ought to be retained.[10]

---

6. But note that boundaries may be varied by adverse possession and by estoppel: *post*, pp. 15–22.
7. Land Registration Rules 1925, r. 278, *post*, p. 29. The plan bound up with the land certificate does not define precisely the legal boundaries of the property except in the very rare case of fixed boundaries.
8. [1957] Ch. 251; [1957] 1 All E.R. 191; see also *Re Boyle's Claim*, [1961] 1 All E.R. 620. Cases like *Lee* v. *Barrey* are rare, but see Appendix 1.
9. Where monetary loss is suffered due to a mistake by the Registry in its maps, a claim for compensation would lie under s. 83 of the Land Registration Act 1925, which provides a right of indemnity for persons suffering loss: see *Re Chowood's Registered Land*, [1933] Ch. 574; *Re Boyle's Claim*, [1961] 1 All E.R. 620. See Chapter 9, *post*, p. 169 ff.
10. Working Paper No. 45, July 1972, p. 26. The Law Commission add:

    "It may be that in the vast majority of cases they will never again have to be referred to. There may, however, be cases where the ownership of a boundary of a property registered with general boundaries is in dispute, and the manner in which the property has developed in the past may be relevant".

It is obviously of great importance that title deeds be drawn up with care, and in Chapter 4 the matter is considered in detail. The deeds are not necessarily conclusive because the boundaries there set out and defined may be altered in a number of ways, notably by adverse possession or estoppel.[11] In general, however, if the descriptive parcels are clear the client can be advised with confidence. In a boundary dispute where the roots of title of the parties are different, the plaintiff's documents of title will not bind the defendant. In order to defeat the plaintiff's claim, however, the defendant will have to show a better title than that established by the plaintiff. He can only do that by referring to his own root of title.

Rectification

It may happen that a conveyance or other instrument contains an error so that it does not accurately represent the agreement of the parties to it. In such circumstances the court has power to order rectification of the document. So in the well-known case of *Craddock Brothers Ltd.* v. *Hunt*[12] two adjoining plots of land were purchased by the same person at different dates. The owner built a dwelling-house on one plot, using the remainder of that plot and the vacant plot as a builder's yard. After his death, his executors put the property up for sale in two lots. The particulars described the lots as a house and a yard adjoining. The yard was sold to the plaintiff and the house to the defendant. The vendors' solicitors prepared the contracts of sale taking the description of the properties sold from the parcels in the conveyances to the original purchaser, the testator. These descriptions were afterwards embodied in the separate conveyances to the plaintiff and the defendant. The Court of Appeal held that there had been a mutual mistake entitling the plaintiff to have his contract and conveyance rectified so as to include the whole instead of part of the yard, that being what he intended to purchase.[13] The right to claim rectification can be asserted against a purchaser with notice of the mistake, as in *Craddock Brothers Ltd.* v. *Hunt*, but not against a bona fide purchaser for value without notice.[14]

---

11. See *post*, pp. 15–22.
12. [1923] 2 Ch. 136. See also *United States* v. *Motor Trucks, Ltd.*, [1924] A.C. 196.
13. YOUNGER, L. J. in a dissenting judgment took the view that the evidence was insufficient to establish mutual mistake.
14. *Smith* v. *Jones*, [1954] 2 All E.R. 823. See also *Garrard* v. *Frankel* (1862), 30 Beav. 445.

Generally the court will only rectify an instrument if it fails to record the intention of both parties: there must be a mutual mistake. "The essence of rectification," it has been said,[15] "is to bring the document which was expressed and intended to be in pursuance of a prior agreement into harmony with that prior agreement. It presupposes a prior contract and it requires proof that by common mistake the final completed instrument as executed fails to give proper effect to the prior contract. For this purpose evidence of what took place prior to the execution of the completed document is obviously admissible and indeed essential."

Rectification may also be ordered on the ground of unilateral mistake, "on the principle that a party is entitled to rectification of a contract on proof that he believed a particular term to be included in the contract and the other party concluded the contract with the omission or variation of that term in the knowledge that the first party believed the term to be included."[16] Such instances are likely to be rare.

The person seeking rectification must satisfy a heavy burden of proof; he must establish his case by evidence which leaves "no fair and reasonable doubt upon the mind that the deed does not embody the final intention of the parties."[17] Rectification is an equitable remedy, and the plaintiff may disentitle himself to relief, *e.g.*, by laches. If rectification is ordered the document need not be executed afresh. A copy of the order is endorsed on the rectified document, which is then read accordingly. The effect of rectification is that the document "is to be read as if it had been originally drawn in its rectified form".[18]

15. *Per* COZENS-HARDY, M.R. in *Lovell and Christmas, Ltd.* v. *Wall* (1911), 104 L.T. 85. See also *Crane* v. *Hegeman-Harris Co., Inc.*, [1939] 4 All E.R. 68, C.A., and *Joscelyne* v. *Nissen*, [1970] 2 Q.B. 86; [1970] 1 All E.R. 1213, C.A.
16. *Per* PENNYCUICK, J. in *A. Roberts & Co., Ltd.* v. *Leicestershire County Council*, [1961] 2 All E.R. 545, at 551, citing with approval the following statement from Snell's *Principles of Equity*, (25th Edn.), p. 569: "By what appears to be a species of equitable estoppel, if one party to a transaction knows that the instrument contains a mistake in his favour but does nothing to correct it, he (and those claiming under him) will be precluded from resisting rectification on the ground that the mistake is unilateral and not common". See also *Whiteley* v. *Delaney*, [1914] A.C. 132; *George Cohen, Sons & Co., Ltd.* v. *Docks and Inland Waterways Executive* (1950), 84 Ll.L.R. 97, at 111; and *Clark* v. *Girdwood* (1877), 7 Ch.D. 9.
17. *Per* LORD CHELMSFORD, L.C. in *Fowler* v. *Fowler* (1859), 4 De G. & J. 250, at 265.
18. *Per* LORD STERNDALE, M.R. in *Craddock Brothers, Ltd.* v. *Hunt*, [1923] 2 Ch. 136, at 151. See also *White* v. *White* (1872), L.R. 15 Eq. 247; *Hanley* v. *Pearson* (1879), 13 Ch.D. 545.

Technical words

Conveyancing practice has established that certain words have a technical meaning and as a form of legal short-hand such words can assist in defining boundaries when used in the written parcels.[17] An erroneous addition to an otherwise clear description of the property in the parcels will be disregarded, applying the maxim *falsa demonstratio non nocet.*[20] By the same rule a description by physical objects will prevail where the boundaries are defined by reference to them but the parcels go on to give a conflicting description by area.[21]

The following are the more usual technical words which may be helpful in defining boundaries. They are arranged alphabetically.

Adjacent used in contrast to "adjoining" means lying near to the land, no actual contact being necessary.[1]

Adjoin or adjoining denotes contiguity but not necessarily physical contact.[2] In *Buckinghamshire County Council* v. *Trigg*[3] a Divisional Court (LORD PARKER, C.J., SALMON and WINN, JJ.) considered the meaning of both "adjoin" and "abut" in the context of the Highways Act 1959. The court there held that an upper maisonette having access to the street only by a right of way across the garden of the lower maisonette did not "adjoin" the street so as to make its owner liable for road charges. The court cited with approval a dictum of BOWEN, L.J. in *Lightbound* v. *Higher Bebington Local Board*[4] where the learned Lord Justice said:

> "You cannot define 'adjoin' as meaning benefit of access, or vice versa, but in considering whether houses adjoin which are placed in close proximity to the part of the street which is to be paved, it is a most

---

19. See, *e.g.*, Gibson's *Conveyancing*, (19th Edn.), p. 183.
20. So in *Maxted* v. *Plymouth Corporation* [1957], C.L.Y. 243 the verbal description stated that the property was bounded by the centre line of a hedge adding "which said piece of land is delineated on the plan drawn hereon". The plan showed the boundary line along the foot of the hedge and was ignored.
21. *Manning* v. *Fitzgerald* (1859), 29 L.J.Ex. 24.
1. *Mayor of Wellington* v. *Mayor of Lower Hutt*, [1904] A.C. 773; *Re Ecclesiastical Commissioners for England's Conveyance*, [1936] Ch. 430.
2. *Wakefield Local Board* v. *Lee* (1875), 1 Ex.D. 336; *Lightbound* v. *Higher Bebington Local Board* (1885), 16 Q.B.D. 577; *Ware U.D.C.* v. *Gaunt*, [1960] 3 All E.R. 778, especially *per* ASHWORTH, J., at 788.
3. [1963] 1 All E.R. 403.
4. (1885), 16 Q.B.D. 577, at 584, also considered and applied in *Ware U.D.C.* v. *Gaunt*, [1960] 3 All E.R. 778.

important fact, and in many cases a dominant fact, to see whether there is substantial access and advantage which the houses enjoy from that portion of the street which is to be paved, and a substantial access and advantage of that kind, coupled with close proximity, may bring the case within the word 'adjoin' though there is no actual touch . . ."

The Divisional Court stated that in the context of road charges it is beyond doubt that the words "adjoin" and "abut" envisage some contact between part of the premises and the street. In the earlier case of *Ware U.D.C.* v. *Grant*[5], however, it was held that land may adjoin the highway even though it is separated from it by a public right of way which is not part of the street.

Bounded by is a neutral expression and does not include or exclude the named feature.[6]

Farm passes both the farmhouse and farm lands.

House and messuage apparently mean the same thing,[7] and pass the dwellinghouse and its curtilage, buildings forming part of it and any gardens attached to it. Curtilage means "a garden, yard, field or piece of voide ground, lying near and belonging to the messuage".[8] It has, however, been held not to include an orchard behind a house and its outbuildings.[9]

There is a special definition of "house" in the Leasehold Reform Act 1967, which also contains a provision for the adjustment of boundaries on enfranchisement.[10] The statutory definition states that, for the purposes of the Act, "house" includes any building designed or adapted for living in and reasonably so called, notwithstanding that the building is not structurally detached, or was or is not solely designed or adapted for living in, or is divided horizontally into flats or maisonettes. However, for the purposes of the Act, where a building is divided horizontally, the flats or maisonettes into which it is so divided are not separate houses, and where a building is divided vertically the building as a whole is not a "house" although any of the units into

5. [1960] 3 All E.R. 778.
6. *Re Belfast Dock Act 1854, Ex parte Ranfurly* (1867), 1 Ir. Eq. Rep. 128, at 140; see also *per* COLERIDGE J. in *Lord* v. *Commissioners of Sydney* (1859), 12 Moore P.C.C. 473 at 497, quoted *infra* p. 15. It is a question of common-sense whether or not a named feature is included.
7. See *per* ASHURST, J. in *Doe d. Clements* v. *Collins* (1788), 2 Term Rep. 502.
8. *Termes de la Ley* (1708).
9. *Asquith* v. *Griffin* (1884), 48 J.P. 724; *Brass* v. *London County Council*, [1904] 2 K.B. 336.
10. Leasehold Reform Act 1967, s. 2.

which it is divided may be.[11] There is a further complication in that references in Part I of the Leasehold Reform Act 1967 (which deals with enfranchisement and extension of long leaseholds) to a house "do not apply to a house which is not structurally detached and of which a material part lies above or below a part of the structure not comprised in the house".[12]

In *Parsons* v. *Viscount Gage*,[13] the House of Lords decided that the words "structurally detached" in s. 2(2) of the Act meant detached from any other structure. In that case, therefore, where a material part of a mews property laid above part of the structure not comprised in the dwelling, the property was not a "house" for the purposes of s. 1(1). The fact that the property had its own separate entrance and was separated by walls, ceiling and floors from the rest of the structure did not mean that it was "structurally detached". LORD WILBERFORCE dealt with the question in this way:[14]

> "From s. 2(1) it appears . . . that the 1967 Act was intended to provide 'enfranchisement' for dwelling houses but not for flats. Flats, as are 'strata' in other systems, are units which arise by horizontal division of a building, and by this criterion they are excluded . . .On the other hand, the Act evidently intended to allow enfranchisement of terrace houses and dwellings arising by vertical division . . ."

His Lordship's view of "structurally detached" meant that the mews property did not fall within the statutory definition. He added that the exemption was confined to cases of structural attachment, in order not to include within it cases of mere projection, over or under another structure, without attachment.

Premises are strictly the operative part of a deed before the habendum but "gradually by common acceptance 'premises' became applied, as it generally is now, to houses, land, shops or whatever it may be, so that the word has come to mean generally real property of one sort or another".[15] Being such an imprecise word its use is best avoided, as there are better alternatives, *e.g.*, dwellinghouse.

Water passes only the right to the water itself and fishing rights

---

11. Leasehold Reform Act 1967, s. 2(1).
12. *Ibid.*, s. 2(2).
13. [1974] 1 All E.R. 1162.
14. *Ibid.*, at p. 1165.
15. *Per* LORD GODDARD, C. J. in *Gardiner* v. *Sevenoaks R.D.C.* [1950] 2 All E.R. 84, at 85. See also *Whitley* v. *Stumbles*, [1930] A.C. 544.

and not the land covered by water. "Covered by water" or "pool" pass the water and its bed.

There is one general canon of construction which should be borne in mind in connexion with the drafting of the parcels. It was put in this way by COLERIDGE, J. in *Lord* v. *Commissioners of Sydney*: [16]

> "Words in an instrument of grant, as elsewhere, are to be taken in the sense which the common usage of mankind has applied to them, in reference to the context in which they are found. If lands granted are described as bounded by a house, no one can suppose the house is included in the grant; but if the land granted is described as bounded by a highway, it would be equally absurd to suppose that the grantor has reserved to himself the right to the soil *ad medium filum* [which is] in the far greater majority of cases wholly unprofitable."

3 BY ADVERSE POSSESSION

Title to land may be acquired by adverse possession under the provisions of the Limitation Act 1939. Rights acquired or in the course of acquisition under the Act are overriding interests.[17] Boundaries are frequently varied in this way by minor encroachments upon neighbouring property, often when walls are rebuilt or wooden fences re-erected. Title by adverse possession may be registered at the Land Registry[18] although such registration is not common in practice.

The encroachment must last for twelve years and fulfil the requirements of the 1939 Act for adverse possession inconsistent with the title of the original owner. So, for example, in *Marshall* v. *Taylor*[19] a hedge and ditch separated two properties. The defendant laid out the ditch as part of his garden, planting trees and shrubs there, and enjoyed it as such for more than twelve years. During this time the original owner had not done anything except discharging sewage into a drain which ran along the ditch. This filling in of the ditch was held sufficient to establish dispossession of the original owner and acquisition by the defendant.

---

16. (1859), 12 Moore P.C.C. 473, at 497.
17. Land Registration Act 1925, s. 70(1)(f).
18. The owner of title by adverse possession may be granted an absolute title (Land Registration Act 1925, s. 75(2)) and there is also a special form of possessory title: Land Registration Act 1925, s. 8 (1) (iii).
19. [1895] 1 Ch. 641. See also *Norton* v. *London and North Western Rail Co.* (1879), 13 Ch.D. 268.

In *Kynoch, Ltd.* v. *Rowlands*,[20] on the other hand, in an action for trespass, the defendant claimed title to the land in question by adverse possession. The only evidence of such possession was that cattle belonging to the defendant's tenants had been allowed to graze on the land. JOYCE, J. rejected the defendant's claim, saying:[1]

> "... if I own the fence with a ditch on the other side between my land and my neighbour's field, my neighbour will not, by lapse of time, acquire the ownership of the ditch merely because his sheep or cattle may have cropped such herbage, if any, as grew upon the sides of the ditch or in the bottom of the hedge. I do not lose my hedge simply because I do not maintain another fence or place a line of barbed wire on the outer edge of it. In order to acquire any property in the ditch as against me, my neighbour must take actual possession of it, as, for instance, by cultivating the ground, building upon or paving it ... or something of that kind ... He must, in my opinion, at least do something for which if I knew of it I could reasonably maintain an action for trespass or ejectment."

During the limitation period the squatter must not acknowledge the true owner's right to the land. Undisturbed and adverse possession for the statutory period completely extinguishes the former owner's rights in the land, except where the title is registered.

In exceptional cases the limitation period is extended, *e.g.*, the period is generally thirty years against the Crown. If the true owner is under a disability at the time when the right of action for possession first accrued, *i.e.*, when he was dispossessed, he may bring his action after the limitation period has expired, provided he does so within six years of the time the disability ceases, and not more than thirty years after the right of action first accrued.[2] Time does not begin to run where there has been fraud or concealment until the plaintiff discovers or ought reasonably to have discovered the facts. The onus of proving discontinuance of possession lies on the squatter.[3]

Similarly, time does not run against the owner until he has been dispossessed or has discontinued his possession and adverse possession

20. [1912] 1 Ch. 527.
1. *Ibid.*, at p. 531.
2. The Limitation Act 1939, s. 22. This is one of the risks in accepting a possessory title: s. 31 (2) (3) provides that a person is deemed to be under a disability if he is a minor or is of unsound mind. For a definition of "person of unsound mind" see Sched. 7 of the Mental Health Act 1959. For a classic exposition of the subject of adverse possession see G. C. Cheshire, *Modern Law of Real Property*, (11th Edn.), pp. 871–897.
3. *Kingston Race Stand, Ltd.* v. *Kingston Corporation*, [1897] A.C. 509.

has been taken by someone else.[4] Both elements are necessary.[5] To be adverse the squatter's possession must be inconsistent with the rights and intentions of the true owner. In the case of minor encroachments of the sort likely to be encountered in boundary disputes the fencing in and subsequent use of the land is normally sufficient.[6]

However in the classic case of *Leigh* v. *Jack*[7] a strip of land was used as a dump for foundry refuse by a stranger who enclosed part of the strip and fenced off its ends. It was held that this did not amount to adverse possession because it was not inconsistent with the owner's only intention which was to dedicate the land to the public as a highway. In reaching this conclusion, BRAMWELL, L.J. said, "acts must be done which are inconsistent with (the owner's) enjoyment of the soil for the purposes for which he intended to use it." The headnote to *Leigh* v. *Jack* enunciates the principle in the following way: "Acts of user committed upon land, which do not interfere and are consistent with the purpose to which the owner intends to devote it, do not amount to 'dispossession' of him, and are not evidence of 'discontinuance of possession' by him" for the purposes of the Limitation Act.[8] In most cases the act of fencing off and cultivating or otherwise using the land will be enough. This is the only sort of boundary dispute in which a claim of this nature will be advanced. A typical case was *Bell* v. *Marsh*[9] where a greenhouse had been built so as to encroach on neighbouring property. A claim based on adverse possession was upheld.

The subject of adverse possession has been before the courts on several occasions in recent years.[10] In a case in 1958, *Williams*

---

4. 1939 Act, ss. 5 (1) and 10 (1). A licensee in occupation cannot acquire title: *Cobb* v. *Lane*, [1952] 1 All E.R. 1199.
5. *Searby* v. *Tottenham Rail. Co.* (1868), L.R. 5 Eq. 409.
6. See *Bell* v. *Marsh*, [1903] 1 Ch. 528.
7. (1879), 5 Ex. D. 264. See also *Plumstead Board of Works* v. *British Land Co.* (1874), L.R. 10 Q.B. 16; reversed on other grounds (1875), L.R. 10 Q.B. 203: intention to lay out as roads.
8. See Megarry and Wade, *Law of Real Property*, (3rd Edn.), p. 1006, and *per* HODSON, L.J. in *Williams Brothers Direct Supply Stores, Ltd.* v. *Raftery*, [1958] 1 Q.B. 159; *Wallis's Cayton Bay Holiday Camp, Ltd.* v. *Shell-Mex & B.P., Ltd.*, [1974] 3 All E.R. 575.
9. [1903] 1 Ch. 528.
10. *Williams Brothers Direct Supply Stores, Ltd.* v. *Raftery*, [1958] 1Q.B. 159; [1957] 3 All E.R. 593; *Fairweather* v. *St. Marylebone Property Co., Ltd.*, [1963] A.C. 510; [1962] 2 All E.R. 288 and *Tickner* v. *Buzzacot*, [1965] Ch. 426 and *Wallis's Cayton Bay Holiday Camp, Ltd.* v. *Shell-Mex & B.P., Ltd.*, [1974] 3 All E. R. 575 are the major cases.

Brothers Direct Supply Stores, Ltd. v. *Raftery*[11] fencing did not avail the squatter. The land in question was behind the defendant's house, and from 1943 to 1949 he cultivated it and later erected a shed on part of the land for breeding dogs. He marked off the boundary with bricks and erected a fence which was not, however, in position for the whole of the statutory period. The plaintiffs had bought the land in 1937 for future development and, despite refusal of planning permission, had never abandoned their intention to develop it. The Court of Appeal gave judgment for the plaintiffs, holding that nothing Raftery had done was sufficient to dispossess the plaintiffs. It never entered his head that he was dispossessing anyone and he had done no more than work the land as he was permitted to do.

A successful squatter obtains a new title; he has a possessory title determinable only by someone other than the person dispossessed who can show a better right to possession.[12] If he bars a tenant under a lease, time does not begin to run against the reversioner until the lease comes to an end. An interesting point fell to be decided in *Fairweather* v. *St. Marylebone Property Co., Ltd.*[13] where the House of Lords held that if a tenant is barred by a squatter, and then surrenders his tenancy to the freeholder, the latter may evict the squatter because the surrender of the tenancy has removed the only interest which prevents the reversioner claiming possession.[14] Once the limitation period has run, the original owner's rights are extinguished. This is so even if his right to recover possession is restricted as will normally be the case to-day.[15]

Encroachment by a tenant

As a general rule if a tenant in possession encroaches on neighbouring land and the requirements of the Limitation Act are fulfilled,

---

11. [1958] 1 Q.B. 159. See also *Bligh* v. *Martin*, [1968] 1 All E.R. 1157.
12. *Re Nisbett and Pott's Contract*, [1905] 1 Ch. 391.
13. [1963] A.C. 510; [1962] 2 All E.R. 288.
14. The squatter is a trespasser against the landlord and so not "lawfully residing" in the premises for the purposes of the Rent Acts. See also *Tickner* v. *Buzzacott*, [1965] Ch. 426, [1965] 1 All E.R. 131 where a mistress went to live with a tenant and after his death stayed on for 19 years paying the rent. It was decided that she did not hold under the lease and was merely a squatter. A squatter who has acquired a possessory title against a leaseholder cannot apply for relief against forfeiture if the lease is forfeited, *e.g.*, for nonpayment of rent.
15. *Moses* v. *Lovegrove*, [1952] 2 K.B. 533; [1952] 1 All E.R. 1279 (statutory tenancy).

it is the landlord who will benefit from the land so acquired.[16] This presumption arises from the tenant's obligation to preserve the boundaries of the demised property; the presumption is a rebuttable one. So it is rebutted if the tenant took possession contrary to the wishes of the landlord,[17] or if he evinced an intention to hold the land so acquired for his own benefit.[18] It has been held that the presumption arises only in the case of waste land[19] but *Tabor* v. *Godfrey*[20] suggests otherwise. There a tenant for years under a lease encroached upon and occupied a piece of land belonging to his landlord for more than 12 years. The landlord's action for an injunction and damages for trespass failed, the court holding that the tenant must be deemed to have occupied the piece of ground as part of his holding, and he was entitled to so occupy it during the remainder of his lease.

In the old case of *Doe d. Croft and Skinner* v. *Tidbury*,[1] JERVIS, C.J. summarised the position in this way:

> "Where a tenant who holds under the lord of a manor encroaches upon the waste, he is presumed to have approved against the commoners for the benefit of the lord; in other cases, when the power to encroach is derived from the occupation of the premises held from a landlord and the encroachment is occupied as if it was a part of the holding, then, at the end of the tenancy, the presumption as between the landlord and the tenant is that it is part of the holding and it belongs to the landlord".

It seems, therefore, that all depends on the facts of the case, but in the commonest sorts of encroachment, namely where land is taken in when a fence is resited, there is no doubt that title accrues to the landlord. On the other hand, if a tenant takes adverse possession of a piece of land and occupies it separately, *e.g.*, where it is physically separated from the holding, it is thought that title would accrue to the tenant.

The position of a tenant who squats *against* his landlord was considered by the Court of Appeal quite recently in *Hayward* v. *Challoner*.[2]

---

16. *Whitmore* v. *Humphries* (1871), L.R. 7 C.P. 1; *A.-G.* v. *Tomline* (1877), 5 Ch.D. 750; *Lisburne* v. *Davies* (1866), L.R. 1 C.P. 259; *King* v. *Smith*, [1950] 1 All E.R. 553; *Smirk* v. *Lyndale Developments, Ltd.*, [1974] 2 All E.R. 8.
17. *Doe d. Baddeley* v. *Massey* (1851), 17 Q.B. 373.
18. *Doe d. Lewis* v. *Rees* (1834), 6 C. & P. 610.
19. *Hastings* v. *Saddler* (1898), 97 L.T. 355.
20. (1895), 64 L.J.Q.B. 245; and see *J. F. Perrott & Co., Ltd.* v. *Cohen*, [1950] 2 All E.R. 939.
1. (1854), 14 C.B. 304, at 324.
2. [1968] 1 Q.B. 107; [1967] 3 All E.R. 122; *Smirk* v. *Lyndale Developments, Ltd.*, [1974] 2 All E.R. 8.

There, before 1938 a small piece of land, belonging to an estate, was let to the rector of the parish for use as a garden, with only a nominal rent. No rent was paid after 1942, when a year's rent was paid in advance. There were intervals when the living was vacant. The land was used as the garden of glebe cottages. In 1955 the plaintiff's bought a farm including the piece of land. The defendant was inducted in 1962. The plaintiffs brought an action for possession of the land in 1966. The Court of Appel held (LORD DENNING, M.R. dissenting) that the action must fail. There had been a periodic oral tenancy to the rector as such; he ceased to be tenant when the period covered by the last payment of rent expired and his subsequent possession became adverse possession. The plaintiff's right of action to recover the land was therefore barred by s. 4(3), s. 9(2) and s. 10(1) of the Limitation Act 1939, by reason of more than twelve years' adverse possession.

Subsequent acknowledgment

It sometimes happens that a person in adverse possession acknowledges that his possession is wrongful. It is then provided[3] that time may be started running afresh by a written and signed acknowledgment of the plaintiff's claim. This would be an unusual state of affairs. "Possession by itself gives a good title against all the world, except someone having a better legal right to possession"[4] and in most boundary cases time will have run continuously.

Registered land

Where the squatter occupies adversely land with a registered title the former owner remains the registered proprietor, but holds the land in trust for the squatter.[5] The register will be rectified upon application to show the squatter as proprietor. Any purchaser from the legal owner before rectification is entitled to such indemnity as the Chief Land Registrar thinks just.[6] However, a prospective purchaser should take the precaution of inspecting the property in the usual way.

---

3. 1939 Act, ss. 23 (1) (a) and 24.
4. *Megarry & Wade*, Law of Real Property, (3rd Edn.), p. 997. On limitation of actions generally see *Preston and Newson*, Limitation of Actions, (3rd Edn.).
5. Land Registration Act 1925, s. 75.
6. *Ibid.*, s. 83.

4 BY ESTOPPEL

Estoppel is an evidentiary rule[7] whereby someone is estopped or prevented from denying the existence of a state of things when by his acts or conduct he has caused someone else to believe in the existence of those facts and to act upon the belief to his detriment. Boundaries may be varied by estoppel where an encroachment has taken place to the knowledge of the owner or his predecessors and he or they have acquiesced in the encroachment. This arises independently of adverse possession. Estoppel may operate against a vendor as a result of recitals in a conveyance, for:

> "If a distinct statement of a particular fact is made in the recital of a bond or other instrument under seal, and a contract is made with reference to that recital, it is unquestionably true that as between the parties to that instrument and in an action upon it, it is not competent for the party bound to deny the recital."[8]

Variation of boundaries by estoppel was illustrated recently in *Hopgood* v. *Brown*[9] where the owner of one of two adjacent plots agreed with his neighbour that the latter could build a house and garage in such a way that the garage wall formed an apparent boundary between the two plots. This apparent boundary was continued to the back by a wall and wooden fence, but did not run in a straight line parallel with the other boundaries. It included a wedge-shaped strip lying to the north from such a straight line. It was discovered later that the garage encroached fairly substantially on the first owner's land, the common boundary not being precisely indicated in the conveyances, which referred to a plan "for the purpose of facilitating identification only". The Court of Appeal held that the original owner was estopped from asserting that the boundary was anywhere other than as agreed once the garage had been erected by the defendant. The plaintiff, as successor in title, was similarly bound.[10]

---

7. Some judges have referred to it as a rule of substantive law, *e.g.*, LORD WRIGHT in *Canada and Dominion Sugar Co., Ltd.* v. *Canadian National (West Indies) Steamships, Ltd.*, [1947] A.C. 46, at 56.
8. *Per* PARKE, B. in *Carpenter* v. *Buller* (1841), 8 M. & W. 209.
9. [1955] 1 All E.R. 550. *Cf., Inwards* v. *Baker*, [1965] 2 Q.B. 29; [1965] 1 All E.R. 446.
10. See also *Cairncross* v. *Lorimer* (1860), 3 L.T. 130; *Bell* v. *Marsh*, [1903] 1 Ch. 528; *Re William Porter & Co., Ltd.*, [1937] 2 All E.R. 361.

An owner who stands by and permits an encroachment may therefore prejudice his position[11] and a purchaser may find that he has got less than he has bargained for. Nonetheless he will be estopped by his predecessor's acquiescence. This emphasises the desirability of having a surveyor check the position of the boundaries on purchase in all but the simplest cases.

(B) BY STATUTORY AUTHORITY

Statute may affect the position of boundaries. Thus in former times the boundaries of the Royal forests were settled by the Delimitation of Forests Act 1640. Since then many Royal forests have been disafforested by statute, letters patent or private Inclosure Acts, *e.g.*, the Hainult Forest Act 1851.[12] The only statutory authority of importance in this context to-day is the Land Registration Act 1925, and the system of registered conveyancing based on it. For sake of completeness two other procedures ought to be mentioned.[13] Where boundaries have been varied by statutory authority, this fact should be recorded by endorsement on the deeds.

The definition of boundaries by statutory authority may be considered as follows:

(1) Agricultural boundaries.
(2) Extinguishment of manorial incidents.
(3) Registered land.

1 AGRICULTURAL BOUNDARIES

Formerly the Minister of Agriculture, Fisheries and Food had power under s. 87 of the Agriculture Act 1947, to adjust compulsorily

11. Even if the encroachment does not amount to adverse possession for the purposes of the Limitation Act 1939: see *Bell* v. *Marsh*, [1903] 1 Ch. 528.
12. See further 8 *Halsbury's Laws*, 4th Edn., paras. 1476 *et seq.*
13. There is also an obsolescent procedure under s. 45 of the Inclosure Act 1845 whereby a Valuer appointed under the Act has power to define new boundaries, etc., on the inclosure of commons. The Inclosure Acts 1845–1878 contain many provisions relating to boundaries and fences but these are no longer of practical importance. With the coming into force of the Commons Registration Act 1965 they will be even less so. There are various alternative procedures possible on the inclosure or regulation of common land. Inquiries about such matters should be addressed to The Secretary, Department of the Environment, Marsham Street, London S.W.1. It is generally unlawful to fence common land without the consent of the Secretary of State: Law of Property Act 1925, s. 194.

the boundaries between agricultural units. The procedure was for the Agricultural Land Commission to consider the boundaries in an area and if necessary to submit a draft scheme for Ministerial confirmation. By s. 18 of the Agriculture (Miscellaneous Provisions) Act 1963, the Agricultural Land Commission, together with its Welsh sub-commission, was dissolved upon the making of an Order by the Minister of Agriculture, Fisheries and Food. The appropriate Order came into force on January 1st, 1964[14] and as a result s. 87 of the 1947 Act, and other now superfluous provisions, are repealed by the Act of 1963. The Agricultural Land Commission only prepared one report proposing the adjustment of farm boundaries and that was not accepted by the Minister of the day.

Part II of the Agriculture Act 1967 contains provisions dealing with boundary adjustments, backed up by financial incentives, but detailed consideration is outside the scope of this book.[15]

2 EXTINGUISHMENT OF MANORIAL INCIDENTS

One of the features of the old law of copyholds was the existence of a great many manorial incidents.[16] By ss. 128 and 129 of the Law of Property Act 1922, manorial incidents were extinguished either with or without payment of compensation. The procedure was set out in the Manorial Incidents (Extinguishment) Rules 1925, which contained the relevant provisions of the Copyhold Act 1894, as modified and applied by Part VI of the 1922 Act.

Although copyhold tenure ceased to exist on January 1st, 1926, it was provided that a further period of fifteen years, *i.e.*, until December 31st, 1940, should be allowed during which compensation for loss of manorial rights might be assessed. This period was later extended, owing to the war, to November 1st, 1950.[17] This provision applied only to those incidents temporarily saved, and these could be extinguished voluntarily by either party serving notice requiring the amount of compensation to be ascertained.[18] The incidents ceased on

14. The Agricultural Land Commission Dissolution Order 1963 (S.I. 1963 No. 1241).
15. See (1967) 31 *Conveyancer* 405–423 for a discussion of the Act's provisions as they affect conveyancers.
16. The standard text is Scriven on *Copyhold*, (3rd Edn., 1833).
17. Postponement of Enactments (Miscellaneous Provisions) Act 1939, s. 3; and S.I. 1949 No. 836.
18. The lord of the manor could not serve notice until 1931.

service of the notice and compensation became payable on a scale fixed by the Minister of Agriculture. Where there was doubt as to the identity of the land, the Minister had power to define its boundaries. The Minister's determination was conclusive as between the lord and tenant[19] and the vestigial remanants of this procedure in relation to boundaries may sometimes come to light in deducing the title of former copyhold land.

It may be noted that among the manorial rights or incidents which continue indefinitely unless abolished by written agreement between the parties is liability for the construction, upkeep, cleansing or repair of dykes, ditches, canals, sea walls, bridges and the like.[20]

3 REGISTERED LAND[1]

In view of the rapid extension of compulsory registration of title the definition of boundaries in the case of registered land is of considerable importance. Formerly it was necessary for the actual boundaries to be defined by substantial boundary posts along unmarked boundaries, if they were not clearly defined by physical features. This is no longer insisted upon[2] but it is desirable on first registration to define external boundaries by means of substantial fences.[3]

When a title is first registered, care must be taken to see that the extent of the land is accurately defined on the ground itself, and Rule 279 of the Land Registration Rules 1925, provides as follows[4]

> "Where, and so far as, physical boundaries or boundary marks do not exist, the fullest available particulars of the boundaries shall be added to the filed plan or General Map."

On subsequent transfer if there is a discrepancy between the filed plan and the plan on the transfer, the plan will have to be altered. The parties to the transaction will have to sign the new or amended plan as representing their intentions, and of course registration cures minor defects.

---

19. Rule 34 (5).
20. See Megarry & Wade, *Real Property*, (3rd Edn.), pp. 37–38.
1. See Appendix 3 for Practice Notes.
2. See (1952) 16 Conv. (N.S.) 160.
3. Curtis & Ruoff, *Registered Conveyancing*, (2nd Edn.)., p. 269.
4. Later references to the Rules are by Rule number alone in the text, *e.g.*, Rule 272, and in footnotes to L.R.R., r. 272.

The description of boundaries for registration purposes is not necessarily conclusive. The filed plan and General Map only indicate the *general boundaries* unless the proprietor has made an application for the boundaries to be fixed. Where the boundaries have been fixed this fact will be noted on the property register.[5] Rule 272 provides that "the Ordnance Survey Map shall be the basis of all registered descriptions of land", but this must be read in conjunction with the provisions of s. 76 of the Land Registration Act 1925.

That section provides that land may be described in any of the following ways:

(a) By verbal description and a filed plan or General Map, based on the Ordnance survey map of the area.

(b) By reference to a deed or other document, containing a sufficient description or plan of the property. A copy or extract of the document must be filed in the Registry.

(c) In any other way desired by the applicant and approved by the Chief Land Registrar. Alternatively, if the applicant prefers, in such a way as the court may approve. Regard must be had to the ready identification of the parcels, correct description of the boundaries and so far as may be to uniformity of practice.

Although s. 76 permits land to be described in the register by these different methods, the usual practice is to do this by a short verbal description and a filed plan based on the Ordnance Survey Map. The important point is, however, that, "whatever method is adopted, the boundaries of all registered freehold land and all requisite details in relation to it must, whenever practicable, be entered on the Register or filed plan, or the General Map."[6] The prescribed forms of transfer of registered freehold land include a parcels clause. The registrar has power to "decide any conflict between the verbal particulars and the filed plan or General Map".[7]

A plan is not normally necessary for the contract of sale where the vendor is selling the whole of the land in a particular title which he

5. L.R.R., r. 277; r. 279: see *post*, p. 29. The general boundaries rule does not apply in Scotland where the purchaser generally expects to be given a fixed boundary which can be plotted on the ground. It is guaranteed by the vendor.
6. Curtis & Ruoff, *op. cit.*, p. 53.
7. L.R.R., r. 285.

owns. However, an official search of the Index Map and Parcels Index should always be made by the purchaser's solicitor. This is of particular importance as the only way of establishing that unregistered land in an area of compulsory registration is not registered. In areas of compulsory registration a copy of the plan is sent by the Registry with the result of the search. The search should be made before contracts for the sale are exchanged.

Land Registry maps in general are accurate, being based on the Ordnance Survey, and a leading authority[8] asserts that on first registration "and sometimes also on the registration of dealings with registered land, a clear and reliable plan is substituted for a vague, inaccurate and often completely meaningless map endorsed upon an unregistered title deed or attached to a transfer of part".[9] Nonetheless, it must be remembered that it is not possible, in general, to ascertain the precise boundaries from the filed plan. The filed plan is based on the Ordnance Survey Map, which is topographical.

Building estates comprising registered land are in a special position. This has been authoritatively summarised in the leading text on registered practice, to which reference should be made.[10] In brief, special arrangements are made in regard to registered estates of building plots, and searches on form 94B may describe the land by reference to its number on a special layout plan, previously approved by the Registry. This makes for much simpler practice.

As a general rule a special plan must be incorporated into a transfer or *part* of a registered title.[11] It may also be mentioned that by Rule 284 the registered proprietor may at any time apply for the revision and correction of the Land Registry maps and plans. Such applications are unusual, and the costs involved can be prohibitive.

Ordnance Survey practice is to draw boundary lines down the centre of physical features such as hedges, although as such the Ordnance Survey has no effect on private boundaries. But since the Land Registry maps are based on the Ordnance Survey, this can give

---

8. Curtis & Ruoff, *op. cit.*, p. 53.
9. But see *Lee* v. *Barrey*, [1957] Ch. 251; [1957] 1 All E.R. 191; *Re Boyle's Claim*, [1961] 1 All E.R. 620.
10. Curtis & Ruoff, *op. cit.*, p. 399. See also Ruoff, *Concise Land Registration Practice*. (2nd Edn.), p. 118.
11. L.R.R., Form 20. The plan may be dispensed with if the verbal description is sufficient to enable the land to be identified on the Land Registry maps and plans.

rise to inconsistencies which, in appropriate cases, can only be settled by the use of presumptions. The scales used by the Registry for its maps and plans are 1/1056 (88 ft. to 1 in.) for the former administrative county of London, 1/1250 for built-up areas, estates and building plots elsewhere, 1/2500 for undeveloped areas and 1/10560 (6 in. to 1 mile) for vast undeveloped areas. This does not make for the greatest accuracy, and quite a small draftsman's error could be material.[12] Any inconsistencies between verbal and plan descriptions would have to be settled by reference to the court and not by the registrar.[13]

Land Registry practice concerning the use of the familiar "T" marks (used to denote ownership of fences on plans) is curious. Normally they are not reproduced because of the general boundaries rule.[14] When expressly referred to in a deed supporting an application for first registration, it appears to be practice for this to be reproduced on the register, thus giving an indication as to the position and ownership of such features as party walls. However, the document lodged for registration must contain a statement as to the ownership of the feature in question.

On first registration the applicant may request the Registry to reproduce any "T" marks shown on the plan attached to the deed supporting the application, but a cautionary note is added to the filed plan stating that the "T" marks "are not otherwise referred to in that deed".[15]

Metric Measurements and Ordnance Survey Maps

Since January 1969 metric land measurements have been gradually replacing imperial measurements, and the Ordnance Survey produced its first entirely metric 1/2500 map in 1969. Land registry practice is inevitably affected, and the Chief Land Registrar issued a notice in July 1968 giving details of the revised procedures. It provides:

---

12. See the observations of HILBERY, J. in *Bellotti* v. *Chequers Developments, Ltd.*, [1936] 1 All E.R. 89. Scale 1/1250, which is the scale most commonly used, is approximately 50 inches to the mile.
13. L.R.R., r. 285 provides only that the registrar "shall decide any conflict between the verbal particulars and the filed plan or General Map" and here there is no such conflict.
14. The general boundaries rule has its parallel in the General Conditions of Sale, 1925 (1928 Edn.), cl. 18 (3); Law Society's Conditions of Sale (1973 Edn.), cl. 12.
15. Land Registry Practice Note No. 34.

(i) There will be no complete or automatic retrospective substitution of metric measurements for imperial measurements on existing title plans.

(ii) On all new plans attached to conveyances, transfers, and other instruments lodged for registration, either imperial or metric measurements will be acceptable. Both forms of dimensions should not be used in the same deed.

(iii) When it is necessary to show figured dimensions on official title plans, they will be reproduced in the same form (whether imperial or metric) as those shown on the deed plan.

(iv) When figured dimensions are shown on title plans, the imperial or metric equivalent will not be shown in addition, nor will a conversion factor be added to the plan.

(v) When metric linear dimensions are shown on official plans these will be in the form of metres and decimal parts of a metre. The degree of accuracy will not be more than three places of decimals, but the Chief Land Registrar suggests that two decimal places will be sufficiently precise in most instances.

(vi) When estate developers decide to change over to the metric system when they are in the course of developing a registered building estate, both imperial and metric dimensions may come to be shown on the vendor's filed plan and there will be other instances in which this somewhat undesirable situation may occur. However to avoid confusion, the Land Registry will place a warning note on the face of the filed plan.[16]

The following changes are being introduced into the metric maps:

1/1250 and 1/2500 Scales—On new and revised sheets the heights of bench marks are shown to two decimal places of a metre and spot heights to one decimal place. The mereings of administrative boundaries will be shown in metres to two decimal places. On the 1/2500 map areas of parcels of land are given in hectares to three decimal places and also in acres as hitherto.

1/10,000 Scale—on the 1/10,000 scale maps now being published metric contours are shown either at 5 metre or 10 metre intervals. On some sheets contoured at the 25 ft. interval, the contour values are given in metres to the nearest metre.

---

16. Land Registry Notice (Introduction of Metrication), July 1968.

General boundaries

The general boundaries rule is expressed in Rule 278 in the following terms:

"(1) Except in cases in which it is noted in the Property Register that the boundaries have been fixed, the filed plan or General Map shall be deemed to indicate the general boundaries only.

(2) In such cases the exact line of the boundary will be left undetermined—as, for instance, whether it includes a hedge, or wall and ditch, or runs along the centre of a wall or fence, or its inner or outer face, or how far it runs within or beyond it; or whether or not the land registered includes the whole or any portion of an adjoining road or stream.

(3) When a general boundary only is desired to be entered in the Register, notice to the owners of adjoining lands need not be given.

(4) This rule shall apply, notwithstanding that a part or the whole of a ditch, wall, fence road, stream or other boundary is expressly included in or excluded from the title or that it forms the whole of the land comprised in the title."

This supposes that the usual presumptions will apply as to the boundaries of registered land. If there are no physical features or boundary marks such as hedges, the general boundaries will be shown by dimensions on the land certificate plan. A broken line is used on Land Registry plans to show the boundary where no physical feature exists, but despite Rule 278 (2), in the case of unadopted roads, the boundary line will be indicated to the far side of the unadopted road which is, of course, marked by broken lines.

Fixed boundaries

The fixing of boundaries is dealt with in Rules 276 and 277 which provide as follows:

"276. If it is desired to indicate on the filed plan or General Map, or otherwise to define in the register, the precise position of the boundaries of the land or any parts thereof, notice shall be given to the owners and occupiers of the adjoining lands, in each instance, of the intention to ascertain and fix the boundary, with such plan, or tracing, or extract from the proposed verbal description of the land as may be necessary, to show clearly the fixed boundary proposed to be registered; and any question of doubt or dispute arising therefrom shall be dealt with as provided by these rules.

277. When the position and description of the boundaries of the land have been thus ascertained and determined, the necessary particulars shall be added to the filed plan or General Map, and a note shall be made in the Property Register to the effect that the boundaries have been

fixed. The plan or General Map shall then be deemed to define accurately the fixed boundaries."

Fixed boundaries, as opposed to general boundaries, are guaranteed, in the sense that the position of the legal boundary as it exists at a particular point in time is fixed. However, the boundary is not necessarily fixed for ever, and even fixed boundaries may be varied by adverse possession. Rights acquired or in the course of acquisition under the Limitation Act 1939, are overriding interests.[17] Where there are fixed boundaries any rectification of them would give rise to a claim under s. 83 of the Land Registration Act 1925.[18] There is no prescribed form of application for fixed boundaries, but, largely because of the expense involved, these applications are not usual. Upon receipt of an application for the boundaries to be fixed, the registrar must give notice of the proposal to all owners and occupiers of adjoining land. The notice must be accompanied by a plan.[19] Registration with fixed boundaries involves a much more detailed and accurate survey, and the titles of all adjoining unregistered properties must be deduced. The applicant for the registration is responsible for all the costs involved in serving notices, deducing the titles and surveying. He can be required to deposit money by way of security in advance. When a dispute arises, there will be the usual hearing before the registrar, and the possibility of an appeal to the High Court.[20]

---

17. Land Registration Act 1925, s. 70(1)(f).
18. Subject to certain exceptions as to adverse possession: see *Re Boyle's Claim*, [1961] 1 All E.R. 620.
19. L.R.R., r. 276.
20. The procedure is described in Curtis & Ruoff, *Registered Conveyancing*, (2nd Edn.), pp. 68–69. The Law Commission in Working Paper 45 of July 1972 is on the whole against fixed boundaries and adopts a somewhat complacent view of registration with general boundaries.

    Para. 31 of the Working Paper is worth quoting:

    "[The] 'fixing' of a boundary under these provisions involves two distinct processes. The first is the ascertainment of the position of the boundary. It is only when that has been done that the second step can be taken, namely the fixing of the boundary so ascertained as a matter of record. But fixing in this context means more than just recording the position of a boundary by reference to physical features in the vicinity of the land in question. If the operation is to have any real virtue, it is necessary for the position of the boundary to be recorded in such a way that it can always be reconstructed even if the whole surrounding terrain changes as the result, for example, of enemy action or flooding. This, in practice, is done by fixing the boundary by reference to National Grid co-ordinates supplied to the Registry by the Ordnance Survey Department. From these co-ordinates the position of a boundary could always be reconstructed".

(C) BY THE COURT

At common law the only remedy available to a person whose boundaries had become confused was to bring an action for ejectment or trespass *de ejectione firmae*,[1] and this was a most unsatisfactory remedy.[2] The court, said GRAHAM, B. in the leading case on the subject,[3] "has no power to grant a commission to set out boundaries; it has no power to establish old boundaries, to direct intermingled lands to be separated, or an equivalent set out, and old inclosures to be restored: it can only direct possession to be given after the land in dispute is recovered in an action of ejectment".

This gap in the common law was filled by the courts of equity, and at one time they appear to have exercised a very wide jurisdiction which is of very ancient origin.[4] The origin of this equitable jurisdiction is shrouded in obscurity, but in *Speer* v. *Crawter*[5] GRANT, M.R. said:

> "There are two writs in the register concerning the adjustment of controverted boundaries, from one of which it is probable that the exercise of the jurisdiction of the Court of Chancery took its commencement. The first is the writ *de rationabilibus divisis*; the other, the writ *de perambulatione facienda*. Both LORD NORTHINGTON and LORD THURLOW, without referring to this writ or commission as the origin of the jurisdiction of the court, have yet expressed an opinion that consent was the ground on which it had been at first exercised. The next step would probably be to grant the commission on the application of one party who showed an equitable ground for obtaining it, such as that a tenant or copyholder had destroyed or not preserved the boundaries between his own property, and that of his lessor or lord; and to its exercise on such equitable ground no objection has ever been made."[6]

---

1. *A.-G.* v. *St. Aubyn* (1811), Wight. 167.
2. *Hardcastle* v. *Shafto* (1794), 1 Anst. 184.
3. *A.-G.* v. *St. Aubyn* (1811), Wight 167, at p. 229.
4. See, *e.g.*, *Mullineux* v. *Mullineux* (1617), Toth. 39; *Peckering* v. *Kimpton* (1630), Toth. 39.
5. (1816), 2 Mer. 410, at 416.
6. There is exhaustive case law on the topic, the greater part of it of old vintage. The following is a selection: *Harding* v. *Suffolk* (1632), 1 Rep. Ch. 61; *Norris* v. *Le Neve* (1744), 3 Atk. 82; *Calmady* v. *Calmady* (1795), 2 Ves. 568; *Holder* v. *Chambury* (1734), 3 P. Wms. 256; *Grierson* v. *Eyre* (1804), 9 Ves. 341; *Speer* v. *Crawter* (1816), 2 Mer. 410; *Mullineux* v. *Mullineux* (1617), Toth. 39.

The present position is that "the court has no jurisdiction to fix the boundaries of legal estates, unless some equity is superinduced by the act of the parties".[7] It is thought that the same principles are still applicable. In the absence of consent a mere confusion of boundaries is not of itself sufficient to support a claim for a commission. A commission would only be granted where some equity arises as a result of inequitable conduct of one of the parties.

As an example, where there is a boundary dispute between landlord and tenant application may be made to the Chancery Division and an inquiry in chambers to ascertain the boundaries may be directed.

One may also bring an action for a declaration in the High Court under R.S.C. Ord. 15, r. 17, the application being by way of originating summons under Ord. 5, r. 3. The High Court may make a declaration independently of other relief[8] the only qualification being that there must be some disturbance of the right in respect of which the court is asked to make a declaration. Ord. 15, r. 17, gives the court a very wide jurisdiction:

> "No action or other proceeding shall be open to objection on the ground that a merely declaratory judgment or order is sought thereby, and the court may make binding declarations of right whether or not any consequential relief is or could be claimed."

There must, however, be a justiciable dispute on a matter of a legal right.[9]

The jurisdiction of the county court is somewhat different and more limited. A declaration can only be sought in the county court as "ancillary relief" under s. 74 of the County Courts Act 1959. There is no jurisdiction to make a declaration independent of other relief.[10]

---

7. *Per* LORD KEEPER HENLEY in *Wake* v. *Conyers* (1759), 1 Eden 331.
8. *Llandudno U.D.C.* v. *Woods*, [1899] 2 Ch. 705; *Dysart* v. *Hammerton*, [1914] 1 Ch. 822.
9. See, for example, *Cox* v. *Green*, [1966] Ch. 216; [1966] 1 All E.R. 268, PLOWMAN J. holding that the court had no power to make a declaration on a matter of professional ethics. The power is discretionary and is sparingly used: *Guaranty Trust Co. of New York* v. *Hannay & Co.*, [1915] 2 K.B. 536.
10. *De Vries* v. *Smallridge*, [1928] 1 K.B. 482; *R.* v. *Cheshire County Court Judge, ex parte Maloney*, [1921] 2 K.B. 694, and SCRUTTON, L. J. in *Humber Conservancy Board* v. *Federated Coal and Shipping Co., Ltd.*, [1928] 1 K.B. 492, at 496.

In practice, therefore, an action for trespass should be brought, claiming as ancillary relief a declaration as to the true boundaries. In an action concerning registered land, the court may direct that the Register be rectified under s. 82 of the Land Registration Act 1925.[11]

---

11. See Chapter 9, *post*, p. 169.

Chapter 3

PRESUMPTIONS ABOUT BOUNDARIES

Rebuttable presumptions "are the result of the general experience of a connection between certain facts or things, the one being usually found to be the companion, or the effect, of the other". Taylor, *Law of Evidence*, (12th Edn.), vol. 1, p. 105.

THE USE OF PRESUMPTIONS

The primary evidence as to the position of a boundary is in the documents of title to the properties concerned. If these are clear and unequivocal they are conclusive, subject to what has been said about variation of boundaries. Parol evidence is admissible to clarify an ambiguity, and "when the construction of a deed is doubtful, great weight is to be given to the construction put upon it by the parties, especially in doubtful questions of boundary which must be presumed to be within their knowledge. When both parties, therefore, agree as to the boundaries and lines of a lot, they must be taken to be the true boundaries and lines, unless the contrary appear".[1] In appropriate cases other evidence such as acts of ownership and public documents may be admissible to clarify the position.[2]

In other cases legal presumptions as to particular features may be helpful in determining the position of boundaries. The principles governing the use of these presumptions have been stated with great clarity by GREENE, M.R.[3] The initial question for the court or the practitioner, he said, is:

> "What, on the true construction of the conveyances to the parties, is the boundary of their respective land. If an examination of those conveyances coupled with any evidence that is admissible for the purposes of construing them shows what the boundary is, there is no room at all for the operation of" presumptions.

---

1. *Stone* v. *Clarke* (1840), 1 Met. 378.
2. See Chapter 5, *post*, pp. 76–88.
3. In *Fisher* v. *Winch*, [1939] 1 K.B. 666, at 669.

The presumptions apply where the boundary is defined by reference to, or follows, certain physical features. They may be rebutted by evidence to the contrary.[4]

Boundary presumptions *may* be excluded or modified where the title to the land is registered. In general, however, when interpreting a land certificate plan conveyancers must apply the rebuttable presumptions which may be applicable in unregistered conveyancing in the case of certain boundary features because of the operation of the general boundaries rule.[5] Thus where there is a lack of precision in the written parcels or relevant plan, boundaries may be fixed by legal presumption. The various presumptions will now be considered in detail. Consideration will also be given to problems allied with the particular boundary features discussed.

1 THE SEASHORE

The boundary of land adjoining the sea lies at the top of the foreshore in the absence of contrary evidence. The foreshore is that part of the shore lying between the ordinary high and low water marks occurring between the spring and neap tides.[6] This point was finally settled in 1854 in *A.-G.* v. *Chambers*,[7] and the speech of LORD CRANWORTH, L.C. is worth quoting at length:

"The principle which gives the shore to the Crown is that it is land

---

4. *Duke of Beaufort* v. *Swansea Corporation* (1849), 3 Ex. 413; *Mappin Brothers* v. *Liberty & Co., Ltd.*, [1903] 1 Ch. 118; *Rouse* v. *Gravelworks, Ltd.*, [1940] 1 K.B. 489, at 493; *Davey* v. *Harrow Corporation*, [1958] 1 Q.B. 60. On evidence generally see, *e.g.*, Taylor's *Evidence*, (12th Edn.), 2 vols; 15 *Halsbury's Laws*, 3rd Edn., 257.
5. See L.R.R. 1925, r. 278, *ante* p. 29.
6. *Blundell* v. *Catterall* (1822), 5 B. & Ald. 268; *Mellor* v. *Walmseley*, [1905] 2 Ch. 164, distinguished in *Government of State of Penang* v. *Beng Hong Oon*, [1972] A. C. 425; [1971] 3 All E.R. 1163, P.C. Foreshore has the same meaning as seashore in law: *Lowe* v. *Govett* (1832), 3 B. & Ad. 863; *A.-G.* v. *Chambers* (1854), 4 De M. & G. 206. In *Government of State of Penang* v. *Beng Hong Oon*, [1972] A.C. 425; [1971] 3 All E.R. 1163, P.C., it was taken as settled law that the word "seashore" when used to describe the boundary of land comprised in a conveyance means prima facie the foreshore. The Privy Council said that there was no reason why the same prima facie meaning should not be attributed to the words "sea beach". This has long been the position in Scots law: *Cameron and Gunn* v. *Ainslie* (1848), 10 Dunl. (Ct. of Sess.) 446.
7. (1854), 4 De M. & G. 206; *A.-G.* v. *Chambers and Rees* (1859), 4 De G. & J. 55, at 58; *Mellor* v. *Walmsley*, [1905] 2 Ch. 164, *per* ROMER, L. J.

> not capable of ordinary cultivation or occupation, and so is in the nature of unappropriated soil. LORD HALE gives as his reason for thinking that lands only covered by the high spring tides do not belong to the Crown, that such lands are, for the most part, dry and maniorable; and taking this passage as the only authority at all capable of guiding us, the reasonable conclusion is that the Crown's right is limited to land which is, for the most part, not dry or maniorable. The learned judges whose assistance I had in this very obscure question, point out that the limit indicating such land is the line of the medium high tide between the springs and the neaps. All land below that line is more often than not covered at high water, and so may justly be said, in the language of LORD HALE, to be covered by the ordinary flux of the sea. This cannot be said of any land above that line; I therefore concur with the able opinion of the judges whose valuable assistance I had, in thinking that the medium line must be treated as binding the right of the Crown."[8]

The application of this rule was demonstrated in *Mellor* v. *Walmesley*,[9] a decision of the Court of Appeal. There the defendant's predecessors in title had conveyed to the plaintiff's predecessors in title a piece of land described as bounded "on or towards the west by the seashore" and more particularly delineated in the plan drawn on the back of the conveyance. There was a strip of land between the western boundary of the land conveyed as shown on the plan and what was there defined as seashore. Since the date of the grant, the sea had gradually receded and left a piece of land on the western side of the property uncovered.

The court held that the "seashore" in the conveyance meant that portion of the land adjacent to the sea which was ordinarily and *prima facie* vested in the Crown. A declaration was granted that the plaintiffs were entitled to free access and egress to and from the sea from and to their premises. VAUGHAN WILLIAMS and STIRLING, L.JJ., also held that the defendants were estopped from saying that any part of the land on the western boundary was anything else than seashore.

---

8. (1854), 4 De G. M. & G. at 217–218. The reference is to Hale's *De Jure Maris*, c. 4, p. 12. CRANWORTH, L. C. was assisted by MAULE, J. and ALDERSON, B. The presumption also applies to sea inlets and the shore of a tidal river: *Bridgwater Trustees* v. *Bootle-cum-Linacre* (1866), L.R. 2 Q.B. 4. *Cf.*, *Malcolmson* v. *O'Dea* (1863), 10 H.L. Cas. 593.
9. [1905] 2 Ch. 164. See also *Scratton* v. *Brown* (1825), 4 B. & C. 485.

In the result, where the sea imperceptibly[10] advances or recedes so that the high water mark is changed, the boundary between the seashore and the adjacent land moves accordingly. It is a moveable freehold,[11] it being held in *Mercer* v. *Denne*[12] that at common law the boundary at the line of mean high tide at any time will be treated as having existed throughout legal memory. In *Crook* v. *Seaford Corporation*[13] an interesting aspect of this point was considered. In 1860 the defendants passed a resolution agreeing to let to the plaintiff "the flat part of the beach opposite to" his field, for a term of 300 years at a nominal rent. The plaintiff claimed all the beach comprised in a prolongation of the sides of the field, and he built a wall and terrace on the land so claimed. The court held, ordering specific performance of the agreement, that the grant included only that part of the beach within straight lines perpendicular to the high water mark. The field was triangular in shape, its base being parallel to the seashore.

There is an important difference between gradual and sudden accretions. In the latter case the land will go to the Crown and not to the adjoining owner.[14] In the Irish case of *A.-G.* v. *McCarthy*[15] it was emphasised that the decision of the House of Lords in *R.* v. *Lord Yarborough*[16] conclusively determined that where land is added to the foreshore by the natural and imperceptible action of natural causes, the owner of the adjoining land acquires a good title against the Crown, even if there is evidence by which the former high water mark can be ascertained. The real question is whether or not the progress of the accretion can be ascertained.

The law on this subject is well stated by Blackstone[17]

> "As to lands gained from the sea, either by alluvion, by washing up of sand and earth, so as in time to make *terra firma*, or by dereliction,

---

10. *I.e.*, imperceptible in its progress: *per* LORD TENTERDEN, C. J. in *R.* v. *Yarborough* (1824), 3 B. & C. 91; affirmed by the House of Lords (1824), 2 Bligh. N.S. 147. The dicta of LORD CHELMSFORD, L. C. in *A.-G.* v. *Chambers* (1859), 4 De G. & J. 55 are not supported by authority: *Brighton and Hove General Gas Co.* v. *Hove Bungalows, Ltd.*, [1924] 1 Ch. 372.
11. *Scratton* v. *Brown* (1825), 4 B. & C. 485; *Smart & Co.* v. *Suva Town Board*, [1893] A.C. 301.
12. [1905] 2 Ch. 538.
13. (1871), 6 Ch. App. 551.
14. *Hayes* v. *Hayes* (1897), 31 I.L.T. 392; Hale, *De Jure Maris*, c. 14, 30.
15. [1911] 2 Ir. Rep. 260.
16. (1824), 2 Bligh N.S. 147.
17. 2 Bl. Comm. 262.

> as when the sea shrinks back below the usual water mark; in these cases the law is held to be, that if this gain be by little and little, by small and imperceptible degrees, it shall go to the owner of the land adjoining. For *de minimis non curat lex*, and besides, these owners being often losers by the breaking in of the sea, or at charges to keep it out, this possible gain is therefore, a reciprocal consideration for such possible charge or loss; but if the alluvion or dereliction be sudden and considerable, in this case it belongs to the King, for as the King is lord of the sea, and so the owner of the soil while it is covered with water, it is but reasonable that he should have the soil when the water has left it dry."[18]

A most instructive case was *Brighton and Hove General Gas Co.* v. *Hove Bungalows, Ltd.*[19] There groynes were provided for the purpose of preventing erosion, and the groynes assisted a gradual and imperceptible accretion. This was held to be a natural accretion going to the adjoining owners. Where an addition is caused artificially, *e.g.*, by carrying out reclamation works, the common law doctrine would not apply. It is not, however, excluded where the adjoining land is described in the parcels clause with specific measurements.[20] As was said recently by the highest authority:[21]

> "It is . . . well settled that if the boundary of land conveyed is the line of medium high tide the mere fact that the acreage of the land conveyed is given and that the position of the line of the medium high tide at the date of the conveyance can be established—whether or not it is delineated on a plan—will not prevent land which subsequently becomes dry land through the gradual and imperceptible recession of the sea from being added to the land conveyed."

It is quite clear that the foreshore, the bed of the sea, of estuaries and sea inlets and of navigable rivers belong to the Crown,[1] and a

18. See *Doe d. Seebkristo* v. *East India Co.* (1824), 10 Moo. P.C.C. 140. Hale (*De Jure Maris*, c. 14, 28) says "This *ius alluvionis* is *de iure commune* by the law of England the King's, *viz.*, if by any marks or measures it can be known what is so gained; for if the gain be so insensible and indiscernible by any limits or marks that it cannot be known, *idem est non esse et non apparere*, as well as in maritime increases as in the increases by inland rivers." See also the comments on this passage *per* LORD CHELMSFORD, L. C. in *A.-G.* v. *Chambers* (1859), 4 De G. & J. 55, at 71.
19. [1924] 1 Ch. 372.
20. *A.-G. of Southern Nigeria* v. *John Holt & Co. (Liverpool), Ltd.*, [1915] A.C. 599.
21. *Government of State of Penang* v. *Beng Hong Oon*, [1971] 3 All E.R. 1163, at 1171, *per* LORD CROSS.
1. See the cases cited in note 6, *ante*, p. 35.

subject can only claim rights therein by express or implied grant.[2] In some cases the Crown has granted away the foreshore or leased it to a subject. If a person and his predecessors have been in long possession of the foreshore or have exercised acts of ownership over it, an ancient grant from the Crown may be presumed.[3] Acts of ownership include fetching gravel, enclosing against the sea and other uses but not, it seems, merely pasturing cattle.[4] In *Port of London Authority* v. *Canvey Island Commissioners*[5] the defendants had carried out protection works on the shore of the Thames, which is subject to the same principles since it is a tidal and navigable river. The Court of Appeal held that their doing the works did not operate to vest ownership of the soil of the shore in them. This remained vested in the riparian owners. The rules about accretion apply only to the seashore and tidal rivers: they do not extend to lakes.[6]

Tidal waters are those affected by a lateral or horizontal flow of water as distinct from a vertical rise and fall. They are not necessarily confined to the area between high and low water marks.[7]

To-day the foreshore is generally in the control of the Crown Estate Commissioners, although actual control has in many cases been delegated to the local authority. Those desiring to carry out works on the foreshore should, therefore, make inquiry of both the local authority and the Commissioners.[8]

The Coast Protection Act 1949, enables specified local authorities of coastal areas to carry out necessary works of coast protection, against erosion and encroachment. The Act contains its own definition of "seashore":[9]

---

2. *A.-G.* v. *Emerson*, [1891] A.C. 649; *Lord Advocate* v. *Blantyre* (1879), 4 App. Cas. 770.
3. See, *e.g.*, *A.-G.* v. *Jones* (1862), 2 H. & C. 347; *Hastings Corporation* v. *Ivall* (1874), L.R. 19 Eq. 558.
4. *A.-G.* v. *Chambers* (1859), 4 De G. & J. 55. This could be explained on the grounds that the user was by tolerance.
5. [1932] 1 Ch. 446.
6. *Nesbitt* v. *Mablethorpe U.D.C.*, [1918] 2 K.B. 1; *Trafford* v. *Thrower* (1929), 45 T.L.R. 502.
7. *Ingram* v. *Percival*, [1969] 1 Q.B. 548; [1968] 3 All E.R. 657. *Quaere* whether waters would be tidal if the movement was vertical rather than lateral as when water passes between cliffs: see LORD PARKER, C.J. at p. 659.
8. The address of the Commissioners is: Whitehall, London, S.W.1.
9. Section 49. See Roddis, *Law of Coast Protection.*

> " 'Seashore' means the bed and shore of the sea and of every channel, creek, bay or estuary, and of every river so far up that river as the tide flows, and any cliff, bank, barrier, dune, beach, flat or other land adjacent to the shore."

By s. 18 it is an offence to excavate or remove materials, other than minerals more than 50 ft. below the surface on any part of the seashore, without licence. "Minerals" includes coal and stone and any metallic or mineral substance, and "materials" includes minerals and growing seaweed. The Act does not relieve any person or public body from any existing liability as to coast protection works arising by prescription or otherwise.[10]

It has not been decided where the boundary lies between the foreshore and the high seas, a point of some importance where the foreshore has been granted or leased to a subject. In *R.* v. *Howlett*,[11] counsel for the appellant submitted that in such circumstances the boundary was the average low tide, but the point was not expressly decided.

The public have certain common law rights in relation to the seashore. They have a right of navigation over the foreshore when it is covered by water, a right to moor and anchor boats there, and a right to fish thereover.[12] A right to land on privately owned land adjoining the sea exists only in case of peril or necessity.[13] Other rights of user may be acquired by custom or prescription.[14]

In 1966 the extent of the public's rights fell to be considered by the Court of Appeal in *Alfred F. Beckett, Ltd.* v. *Lyons*.[15] The plaintiffs were licensees of a stretch of the foreshore in the County of Durham, under a licence for value granted them by the local authority which held the rest of the foreshore under a Crown lease. The defendants claimed a right to remove sea-coal from the foreshore. The court granted the plaintiffs a declaration that none of the defendants were entitled to enter on any part of the foreshore otherwise than in exercise of their common law rights or such other rights as they might be

---

10. Prescriptive liability to maintain a sea wall is shown by *Hudson* v. *Tabor* (1877), L.R. 1 Q.B.D. 225.
11. *Times*, (1967), February 4th.
12. *A.-G.* v. *Tomline* (1880), 14 Ch.D. 58; *Free Fishers of Whitstable* v. *Gann* (1866), 11 H.L.Cas. 192.
13. *Brinckman* v. *Matley*, [1904] 2 Ch. 313, at 316.
14. See the examples given in Theobald, *Law of Land*, (2nd Edn., 1929), p. 75.
15. [1967] Ch. 449; [1967] 1 All E.R. 833.

granted by the owners of the foreshore, and injunctions restraining them from removing sea-coal and from going on to the shore other than in exercise of their common law rights.

The nature of those rights was thus explained by HARMAN, L.J.:

> "It is notorious that many things are done on the sea shore by the public which they have no legal right to do. The only clear right of the public on the foreshore is the right to pass over it in boats when it is covered with water, for the purpose of fishing. Bathing, for instance, is not a public right, but goes by tolerance. I can find no clear decision that the public have the right to walk on the foreshore when the tide is out, nor to land from boats or embark except in cases of emergency. It seems also clear enough that there is no public right of way along the foreshore."

WINN, L.J. in his concurring judgment said:

> "After considerable research I have failed to find, (elsewhere than in a partisan essay by a Mr. Hall 'On the Rights of the Crown in the Seashores of the Realm', published in 1830) any support for the view that there has ever been a right in the inhabitants of the United Kingdom, or any county or town or district comprised in it, elsewhere than in Devon and Cornwall, to have access to any foreshore to collect what may be found there by 'beachcombing'."

However, in practice where the foreshore is leased by the Crown to seaside authorities or put to commercial use, the lease reserves for the Crown's licensees rights over the foreshore, including where possible the right for the general public to have access for recreational purposes. It remains the policy of the Crown Estate Commissioners to ensure as far as possible the privilege of public recreation.[16] It is the practice of the Crown to reserve when appropriate a right for the general public to have access for recreational purposes in leases of the foreshore. It may be noted that the Report of the Special Committee on Footpaths and Access to the Countryside said:[17]

> "Since it is evident that a general right of roaming over the foreshore and the land immediately behind is a right unknown in law, we recommend that this land referred to as beach and shore should be subject to access designation."

Moreover, local planning authorities have power to make agreements

---

16. *Times*, (1966), December 1st, p. 6.
17. Cmnd. 7207, para. 208.

or orders giving the public rights of access to "open country", which is defined[18] as land appearing to the planning authority "to consist wholly or predominantly of mountains, moor, heath, down, cliff or foreshore (including any bank, barrier, dune, beach, flat or other land adjacent to the foreshore)".

2 LAKES

A lake is generally a pool of stagnant water, although it may have an inflow and an outflow.[19] There is no truth in the idea that the soil of large inland lakes belongs to the Crown.[20] The bed of a lake belongs to the owner of the surrounding land when the lake is entirely within the boundaries of one piece of land. Consequently the bed will pass on a conveyance without express reference. The lake and its *alveus* or soil could be sold separately, in which case the boundary would be the edge of the water at normal level, unless precisely defined.

There is no settled authority as to where the boundary lies when a lake is bounded by properties in different ownership. In many cases the title deeds will show clearly that one owner is entitled to exclusive possession. There is certainly no settled presumption on the subject. The point was left open in *Marshall* v. *Ulleswater Steam Navigation Co.*[1] In the Irish case of *Johnston* v. *Bloomfield*[2] five years later, the question was again canvassed, and many American authorities were cited to the court.[3] It was there held that the bed did not pass *ad medium filum.*[4] On the other hand, in the Scottish case of *Mackenzie* v. *Bankes*[5] LORD SELBORNE suggested that the boundary

---

18. National Parks and Access to the Countryside Act 1949, s. 59. The power to make access agreements or orders is contained in ss. 64 and 65.
19. "A large body of water entirely surrounded by land" is the definition of lake given in *The Concise Oxford Dictionary*.
20. *Bristow* v. *Cormican* (1878), 3 App. Cas. 641.
1. (1863), 3 B. & S. 732; subsequent proceedings (1871), L.R. 7 Q.B. 166.
2. (1868), I.R. 8 C.L. 68.
3. For example, *Canal Commissioners* v. *The People* (1830), 5 Wendell, N.Y. Rep. 423: where it was said: "Our large fresh water lakes or inland seas are wholly unprovided for by the law of England. As to these, there is neither flow of the tide, nor thread of the stream; and our local law appears to have assigned the shores down to the ordinary low water mark to the riparian owners, and the beds of the lakes, with the islands therein, to the public".
4. See also, *O'Neil* v. *Johnston* (1908), 1 I. R. 358; [1911] A.C. 552; *Bristow* v. *Cormican* (1878), App. Cas. 641.
5. (1878), 3 App. Cas. 1324, at 1338.

line between two properties separated by a lake must be drawn along the centre of the lake, and where there are several riparian owners lines must be drawn radially to the centre. The application of this principle could cause difficulties, but in the absence of more conclusive authority it seems to be a reasonable solution.

The adjoining owners will have rights of fishing and navigation so far as they own the bed. The public may acquire a right of navigation over inland lakes, but there is no inherent right vested in them as there is in the case of tidal rivers.

3 NON-TIDAL RIVERS AND STREAMS

Where two properties are separated by a natural non-tidal river or stream, the boundary line between the two is *prima facie* presumed to coincide with the centre of the stream, so each owner has half the bed.[6]

> "The natural presumption is, that a man whose lands abut on a river owns the bed of the river up to the middle of the stream, and, if he owns the land on both sides, the presumption is that the whole bed of the river belongs to him unless it is a tidal river. There is also a presumption that the owner of the bed of the river has the right to fish in the stream, and to prevent other persons from fishing there. But these are presumptions of fact, which may be rebutted."[7]

COTTON, L.J. expressed the matter in similar terms in *Micklethwait* v. *Newlay Bridge Co.*:[8]

> "The rule of construction is now well settled, that where there is a conveyance of land, even although it is described by reference to a plan, and by colour, and by quantity, if it is said to be bounded on one side by a river or by a public thoroughfare, then on the true construction of the instrument half the bed of the river or half of the road passes, unless there is enough in the circumstances or enough in the expression of the instrument to show that that is not the intention of the parties."

There is no distinction in law between a river, a stream, and a brook "Though the word 'stream' in its more usual application does imply water running between defined banks, it is not confined to that meaning—its essence being that it is water in motion as distinguished from

6. *Wright* v. *Howard* (1823), 1 Sim. & St. 190, at 203; *R.* v. *Landulph* (*Inhabitants*) (1834), 1 Mood. & R. 393; *Edleston* v. *Crossley & Sons, Ltd.* (1868), 18 L.T. 15.
7. *Per* BOWEN, L.J. in *Blount* v. *Layard*, [1891] 2 Ch. 681n., at 689n.
8. (1886), 33 Ch. D. 133. See also *Thames Conservators* v. *Kent*, [1918] 2 K.B. 272.

stagnant water."[9] However, surface water flowing over an undefined area and not following any definite course is not a stream.[10]

The bed means the land covered with water at its average and mean state throughout the year.[11] The centre line is ascertained by reference to so much of the bed as is adequate to contain the water at its average state throughout the year. In the unreported House of Lords decision in *Gooldon* v. *Thames Conservators*[12] "bed" was also defined as the soil under water between the banks, which accords with popular usage.

The presumption may be rubutted in a number of ways. For example, in *Jones* v. *Williams*[13] the plaintiff claimed the whole bed of the river, while the defendant contended that each was entitled *ad medium filum*. Evidence of acts of ownership by the plaintiff on the banks of the river lower down the stream where it flowed between his land and that of a third party was admitted to rebut the presumption. It has been held[14] that it applies where land is described in a conveyance by reference to a plan, described as bounded by a towpath. The presumption applies to both freehold and leasehold land.[15]

Accretions cause the boundary to be adjusted automatically, the accretion belonging to the riparian owner(s).[16] The position has been summarised judicially:[17]

> "The soil of the *alveus* is not the common property of the two proprietors, but the share of each belongs to him in severalty, so that, if from any cause, the course of the stream should be permanently diverted, the proprietors on either side would have a right to use the soil of the

---

9. Per LORD HALSBURY, L.C. in *McNab* v. *Robertson*, [1897] A.C. 129. See also *Taylor* v. *St. Helen's Corporation* (1877), 6 Ch. D. 264; *R* v. *Oxfordshire* (*Inhabitants*) (1830), 1 B. & Ad. 289.
10. *Rawstron* v. *Taylor* (1855), 11 Exch. 369.
11. *Hindson* v. *Ashby*, [1896] 2 Ch. 1, at 25 *per* A. L. SMITH, L.J. A river or stream does not cease to be such merely because it dries up at times: *Stollmeyer* v. *Trinidad Lake Petroleum Co.*, [1918] A.C. 485.
12. Noted at (1955) 19 *Conveyancer* (N.S.) 172.
13. (1836), 2 M. & W. 326.
14. *Thames Conservators* v. *Kent*, [1918] 2 K.B. 272.
15. Although a stream may be a public sewer within the meaning of s. 20 of the Public Health Act 1936, and as such vested in the local authority, this does not affect the ownership of the bed.
16. *Foster* v. *Wright* (1878), 4 C.P.D. 438; and it is immaterial that the original boundary can still be ascertained: *Re Hull and Selby Rail. Co.* (1839), 5 M. & W. 327.
17. *Per* LORD CRANWORTH, L.C. in *Bickett* v. *Morris* (1868), L.R. 1 Sc. & Div. App. 47, at 58.

alveus, each of them up to what was the *medium filum aquae* in the same way as they were entitled to the adjoining land."

This rule does not apply where there is a sudden change; the boundary then remains where it was.[18] It is undecided what the position is where the boundary is shown by some clear physical feature such as a wall, and accretions become perceptible on the other side. The point was left open by LINDLEY, L.J. in *Hindson* v. *Ashby*[19] but it would seem that the boundary remains unchanged because the physical boundary marker provides clear evidence of the boundary line, when considered in conjunction with the parcels, and there is then no basis for the rule.

Running water being *res nullius* is incapable of ownership, but the owner of land abutting on to a private river or stream enjoys quite extensive rights in relation to the water.[20] These arise as part and parcel of the natural rights of ownership and do not depend on grant or prescription.[1] There is a natural servitude vested in every owner of land on the banks of a natural stream, which entitles him to the continued flow of the stream in its natural condition. The position was well summarised by PARKE, B. in *Embrey* v. *Owen*[2] when he observed that the riparian owner's right is "to the flow of the water and the enjoyment of it subject to the similar rights of all the proprietors of the banks on each side to the reasonable enjoyment of the same gift of Providence".

Each owner, then, is entitled to the flow of the stream through his land unaltered in volume or quality. He has the right to extract water from the stream for normal riparian purposes, such as watering his cattle.[3] This is so even though his abstracting the water completely exhausts the stream. He has the right to use the water for any other

---

18. *Ford* v. *Lacey* (1861), 7 H. & N. 151.
19. [1896] 2 Ch. 1, at 13.
20. See, for example, Megarry & Wade, *Real Property*, (3rd Edn.), pp. 73–74; "The rights and duties of riparian owners" by J. F. Garner, (1950) *Conveyancer* (*N.S.*) 388; "The right to take flowing water" by P. Brett, (1950) *Conveyancer* (*N.S.*) 154.
1. *Miner* v. *Gilmour* (1859), 12 Moo. P.C. 131; *Chasemore* v. *Richards* (1859), 7 H.L. Cas. 349; *John White & Sons* v. *White*, [1906] A.C. 72.
2. (1851), 6 Exch. 353, at 369.
3. *McCartney* v. *Londonderry and Lough Swilly Rail. Co.*, [1904] A.C. 301. For the distinction between "ordinary" and "extraordinary" use of water in a stream and the riparian owner's rights to make use of it, see *Rugby Joint Water Board* v. *Walters*, [1966] 3 All E.R. 497.

purpose, provided it is restored to the stream substantially the same in volume and character.[4] These rights extend to the tenants and licensees of the riparian owner.[5]

There is no common law obligation to repair the banks,[6] but such an obligation may be imposed by statute, prescription, custom or tenure. There is similarly no obligation to keep the stream clear of obstruction[7] even to the extent of removing a natural shoal. A riparian proprietor can fortify his own bank against the water. He can also raise it against flooding, provided the operations are confined to the bank on his own side. He must not, however, interfere with the flow of the stream so that the rights of lower owners are affected.[8] As was said in *Nield* v. *London and North Western Rail. Co.*:[9]

> "Reasonable selfishness is permissible in a man who tries to protect himself from a common enemy, such as a flood."

This is so even if as a result of one man's precautions, there is an increased flow of water over his neighbour's land in time of flood. This common law right must now be read in the light of the restriction contained in s. 31 (3) of the Land Drainage Act 1961:

> "No person shall erect or alter any structure designed to contain or divert the floodwaters of any part of the main river except with the consent of and in accordance with plans and sections approved by the river authority."[10]

---

4. *Kensit* v. *Great Eastern Rail. Co.* (1883), 23 Ch.D., 566.
5. Law of Property Act 1925, s. 62 (1) (4) and *Marshall* v. *Ulleswater Steam Navigation Co.* (1871), L.R. 7 Q.B. 166.
6. *Hudson* v. *Tabor* (1877), L.R. 1 Q.B.D. 225; see *Jones* v. *Mersey River Board* (1956), 8 P. & C.R. 103. *Cf.*, Public Health Act 1936, ss. 262, 264.
7. *Hodgson* v. *York Corporation* (1873), 37 J.P. 725; *Withers* v. *Purchase* (1889), 60 L.T. 819. See also [1951] 1 K.B. 115; *Neath R.D.C.* v. *Williams*, [1950] 2 All E.R. 625, a case turning on the provisions of s. 259 of the Public Health Act 1936. But note the provisions of s. 28 of the Land Drainage Act 1961, under which the appropriate authority can serve notice requiring the removal of obstructions.
8. *Trafford* v. *R.* (1832), 1 L.J. Ex. 90.
9. (1874), 44 L.J. Ex. 15.
10. Note also that any mooring placed in a navigable river must not obstruct the right of navigation: *Orr-Ewing* v. *Colquhoun* (1877), 2 App. Cas. 839. The riparian owner is entitled to access to his property at any point along the river: *Marshall* v. *Ulleswater Steam Navigation Co.* (1871), 36 J.P. 583.

4 TIDAL RIVERS AND SEA INLETS

The *alveus* and foreshore of a tidal river or sea inlet *prima facie* are vested in the Crown, between the medium high and low water mark,[11] subject to the public's rights of navigation and fishing.[12] Waters are tidal if they are subject to the regular ebb and flow of the ordinary highest tides,[13] and in *Horne* v. *Mackenzie*.[14] the importance of the degree of salinity was emphasized. A tidal river will cease to be so when fresh water prevails. In *Ingram* v. *Percival*[15] the extent of tidal waters was considered by a Divisional Court. It was emphasised that tidal waters do not necessarily only include waters where there is a lateral ebb and flow. "It may well be", said LORD PARKER, C.J., "as when water passes between cliffs or high ground, that there will not be a lateral movement but a vertical movement." A navigable river is a public highway and in *R.* v. *Ward*[16] the right of navigation was held to include ancillary acts such as mooring in the stream. The boundary is the line of the medium high tides throughout the year.[17]

The Crown's right extends up to the point where the tide ebbs and flows. The non-tidal part of the river,

> "is in exactly the same position as a road running between two properties, and though the public may by dedication acquire the right of navigation thereon, it must be proved in case of dispute that this has been established by long enjoyment or by Act of Parliament. Such a right of navigation if once established prevails over the ordinary rights of a riparian owner, and he cannot make any use of the bed of the river or of its water which will prejudice its enjoyment by the public; . . ."[18]

---

11. *Constable's Case* (1601), 5 Co. Rep. 106a; *Lyon* v. *Fishmonger's Co.* (1875), 1 Ch. App. 662, at 689; *Fitzhardinge* v. *Purcell*, [1908] 2 Ch. 139. Under the Coast Protection Act 1949, the foreshore is managed by the Crown Estate Commissioners except in the case of the rivers Thames and Tees.
12. *Lord Advocate for Scotland* v. *Hamilton* (1852), 1 Macq. 46; *Williams* v. *Wilcox* (1838), 8 A. & E. 333.
13. *Reece* v. *Miller* (1882), 8 Q.B. P. 626; *Micklethwait* v. *Vincent* (1892), 67 L.T. 225.
14. (1839), 6. Cl. & Fin. 628. See also *Calcraft* v. *Guest*, [1898] 1 Q.B. 759.
15. [1969] 1 Q.B. 548; [1968] 3 All E.R. 657.
16. (1835), 4 Ad. & El. 384.
17. *A.-G.* v. *Chambers* (1854), 4 De G.M. & G. 206.
18. Cheshire, *op. cit.*, p. 133, citing *Orr-Ewing* v. *Colquhoun* (1877), 2 App. Cas. 839 and *A.-G.* v. *Terry* (1874), 9 Ch. App. 423.

In other respects the rights of riparian proprietors are the same as in the case of non-tidal rivers, and subject to what has been said, above the flow of the tide the boundary of lands on opposite sides of the river will be presumed to be the *medium filum.*[19]

5 ISLANDS

An island arising in the sea or in a tidal and navigable river belongs to the Crown. An island in a lake will belong to the owner if the lake is entirely on his land, but there are no other relevant presumptions. If, as is thought, the *medium filum* rule applies to lakes[20] it is clear that the same rules as are applicable in private rivers will be in force.

An island arising in the middle of a non-tidal river will belong equally to the adjoining owners, or in such proportion as the centre line of the stream bisects it. An island appearing entirely on one side of the stream will not affect the boundary, and will belong to the near-side owner.[1]

An existing island in a stream provides one of the banks, and consequently the boundary will be presumed to be midway between the two banks in accordance with the normal presumption, *i.e.*, the boundary is in the middle of the stream between the island and the bank.[2] "And if a watercourse divides itself and encircles a field, and thereby forms an island, the property of the field is not altered, but continues in him to whom it belonged before."[3]

There is no settled presumption about the problem of the boundary on the sides of an island facing up and down stream, and the question is of little practical importance.

6 ARTIFICIAL WATER-COURSES

(a) *Canals and conduits*

There is no presumption as to the ownership of the bed of a canal or other artificial stream. However, for the purposes of the Building Regulations 1972, boundary is defined as including "any abutting

---

19. *Bickett* v. *Morris* (1868), L.R. 1 Sc. & Div. App. 47; see also *Great Torrington Commons Conservators* v. *Moore Stevens*, [1904] 1 Ch. 347.
20. See *ante*, p. 42.
1. *Wedderburn* v. *Paterson* (1864), 2 Macph. 902; *Lord Zetland* v. *Glover Incorporation of Perth* (1870), L.R. 2 Sc. & D. 70.
2. *Great Torrington Commons Conservators* v. *Moore Stevens*, [1904] 1 Ch. 347.
3. Angell on *Watercourses*, 50.

part of any street, *canal* or river but only *up to the centre line thereof*".[4] Rights in artificial watercourses are not necessarily the same as those in natural rivers, since they cannot arise *iure naturae* but must depend upon grant, prescription or agreement. Thus in *Rameshur Pershad Narain Singh* v. *Koonj Behari Pattuk*,[5] Sir Montagu Smith remarked that in the case of an artificial watercourse, "any right to the flow of water must rest on some grant or agreement, either proved or presumed, from or with the owners of the lands from which the water is artificially brought or on some other legal origin. In the absence of express grant it may be very difficult to establish that an easement has been acquired in respect of an artificial watercourse, and the question of the intention of the person responsible for construction is particularly important.[6] It has however, been suggested that where the origin of an artificial watercourse is unknown,

> "the proper inference from the use of the water and from other circumstances may be that the channel was originally constructed upon condition that all the riparian owners should have the same rights as they would have had if the stream had been a natural one".[7]

However, land bordering on a canal or other artificial watercourse is bounded by it, and the bed will not pass unless expressly conveyed.[8] It follows that in most cases the bed of artificial water-ways will be vested in one or other owner, or in a third person, and ownership will be a matter of evidence. Once an easement has been established in respect of an artificial watercourse, the dominant owner has the right to carry out any acts essential for securing the enjoyment of his ease-

---

4. Reg. A2 (1) (italics supplied). See further Whyte and Powell-Smith, *The Building Regulations Explained and Illustrated*, 4th Edn., 1973.
5. (1878), 4 App. Cas. 126.
6. *Wood* v. *Waud* (1849), 3 Exch. 748; *Baily & Co.* v. *Clark, Son and Morland*, [1902] 1 Ch. 649. *Schwann* v. *Cotton*, [1916] 2 Ch. 459; *Bartlett* v. *Tottenham*, [1932] 1 Ch. 114.
7. 39 *Halsbury's Laws*, 3rd Edn., 518, citing *Sutcliffe* v. *Booth* (1863), 32 L.J. Q.B. 136. As to the acquisition of prescriptive rights in artificial watercourses see *Whitmores (Edenbridge), Ltd.* v. *Stanford*, [1909] 1 Ch. 427, where it was suggested that in the case of an artificial watercourse constructed for the benefit of several riparian owners the presumption may arise as in the case of a river and *Arkwright* v. *Gell* (1839), 5 M. & W. 203; *Gaved* v. *Martyn* (1865), 13 L.T. 74; *Burrows* v. *Lang*, [1901] 2 Ch. 502; *Baily & Co.* v. *Clark, Son and Morland*, [1902] 1 Ch. 649; *Whitmores (Edenbridge), Ltd.* v. *Stanford*, [1909] 1 Ch. 427.
8. *Chamber Colliery Co.* v. *Rochdale Canal Co.*, [1895] A.C. 564.

ment, including the right to enter on to the servient tenement to carry out repairs.[9]

(b) *Pipe-lines*[10]

Pipe-lines are not strictly boundary features, but may be found along boundaries. In most cases the owner of the pipe-line will merely have an easement, and will not own the site of the line. The Pipe-lines Act 1962 provides that any person wishing to construct a pipe–line across country must obtain authorisation from the Secretary of State for Energy. Pipe-lines are of two kinds:

(i) *Cross-country pipe-lines*, which are those more than ten miles in length. These require ministerial authorisation but not planning permission.

(ii) *Local pipe-lines*, of a lesser length. These require the grant of planning permission but no ministerial authorisation.

Ministerial authorisation may be granted—normally after a public inquiry if there are objections to the advertised proposal—but it does not empower the applicant to disregard private rights. He will need to obtain an easement from the landowners in question or, failing that, a compulsory right order granted under s. 12 of the Act. This involves the payment of compensation to those affected, the procedure being analogous to ordinary compulsory acquisition. No wayleave rental is payable under a compulsory rights order.

Pipe-lines do not have to be registered as an incumbrance in the local land charges register. However, a map showing the route of all pipe-lines laid under the Act must be deposited with the local authority and is available for inspection without fee.[11] This enables purchasers to discover whether there is a pipe-line in or under any property.

7 ROADS AND RIGHTS OF WAY

There are two presumptions relevant to the ownership of the soil of a roadway. The first presumption is that the sub-soil of the highway

---

9. See *per* TWYSDEN, J. in *Pomfret* v. *Ricroft* (1669), 1 Wms. Saund. 321.
10. A useful book is H. W. Wilkinson, *Pipes, Mains, Cables & Sewers*.
11. Section 35.

ad medium filum viae belongs to the owners of adjoining properties,[12] whether in the town or the country.[13] The same presumption arises in the case of a private right of way.[14] Each adjoining owner is entitled to the subsoil absolutely but "they cannot use the soil, or deal with it by breaking it open or in any other manner so as to interfere with the use of it by the public for the purpose of a highway."[15] Where a highway has become vested in the highway authority, *i.e.*, where the authority have become liable for its maintenance, its surface vests in them:

> "The right of the original owner of the land remains untouched, and he remains the owner in fee simple of the land, but subject to there being vested in the road authority the actual road itself and so much of the soil as is necessary to enable the road authority to perform its statutory duties of repairing and maintaining the road as a highway."[16]

The decision of the Court of Appeal in *Tithe Redemption Commissioners* v. *Runcorn U.D.C.*[17] confirms that the legal interest of the highway authority in the topsoil is a fee simple determinable on the land ceasing to be a highway. The short judgment of DENNING, L.J., as he then was, indicates the depth to which the ownership of the highway authority goes. He said[18] that certain statutes have,

> "vested in the local authority the top spit, or perhaps I should say the top two spits, of the road for a legal estate in fee simple determinable in the event of its ceasing to be a public highway."

Accordingly, as an "owner of land" within the meaning of s. 17 (1) (a) of the Tithe Act 1936, in the *Runcorn* case the highway authority was liable to bear an apportioned share of the tithe redemption annuity payable in respect of the land of which the road formed part.[19]

---

12. *Stevens* v. *Whistler* (1809) 11 East 51; *Cooke* v. *Greene* (1823), 11 Price 736; *Frost* v. *Richardson* (1910), 103 L.T. 416.
13. *Re White's Charities*, [1898] 1 Ch. 659.
14. Even if it leads to a close belonging to one of the adjoining owners: *Smith* v. *Howden* (1863), 14 C.B. N.S. 398.
15. *Per* LORD SELBORNE, L.C., in *Goodson* v. *Richardson* (1874), 9 Ch. App. 221.
16. *Per* FARWELL, J. in *Hertfordshire County Council* v. *Lea Sand, Ltd.* (1933), 98 J.P. 109, at 112.
17. [1954] Ch. 383; [1954] 1 All E.R. 653.
18. [1954] 1 All E.R. 653, at 661.
19. See also, s. 226 of the Highways Act 1959: "Subject to the provisions of this section, every highway maintainable at the public expense, together with the materials and scrapings thereof, shall vest in the . . . highway authority. . . ."

The presumption is allowed to prevail, it has been said:[20]

> "upon grounds of public convenience, and to prevent disputes as to the precise boundaries of property, and it is based on the supposition, that when the road was originally formed the proprietors on either side each contributed a portion of his land for the purpose."

The presumption only operates, therefore, when the conveyancing history is unknown. It cannot apply where the conveyancing history is known from the time of common ownership.[1]

There is a second presumption (or canon of construction) that the soil up to the centre of the highway will pass in a conveyance without express mention, for it is reasonable to assume that the grantor would not wish to reserve a strip under the road.[2]

The highway authority have vested in them only sufficient air space above the highway to enable it to be used for traffic and for telephone wires, etc., and other objects lawfully erected in the highway.[3] The presumption may be rebutted by express provision to the contrary in the conveyance or by the surrounding circumstances and in *Giles* v. *County Building Constructors (Hertford), Ltd.*,[4] BRIGHTMAN, J. concluded that the presumption, if it applied at all to a conveyance of a plot of land forming part of a building estate by a grantor who owned both land and road, was one which readily yielded to indications of a contrary intention, in this case, a plan. However, it is not rebutted by the land being described as bounded on one side by a road or by the land being referred to as described by colour on a plan, and half of the road is not

---

20. *Per* COCKBURN, C.J. in *Holmes* v. *Bellingham* (1860), 29 L.J.C.P. 132. *Cf. Pryor* v. *Petre* (1894), 69 L.T. 795. *Doe d. Pring* v. *Pearsey* (1827), 7 BC 304.
1. See *Giles* v. *County Building Constructors (Hertford), Ltd.*, (1971), 218 *Estates Gazette* 851, where the presumption was displaced by a plan in the conveyance.
2. *London and North Western Rail Co.* v. *Mayor of Westminster*, [1902] 1 Ch. 269; *City of London Land Tax Commissioners* v. *Central London Rail Co.*, [1913] A.C. 364. It is undecided whether the presumption applies to leases. In *Doe d. Pring* v. *Pearsey* (1827), 7 B. & C. 304, at 307. HOLROYD J. said that it does, but the point has since been expressly reserved: *Landrock* v. *Metropolitan District Rail Co.*, [1886] W.N. 195. On balance, the presumption probably does not apply: see Emmett on *Title*, 14th Edn., vol. 1, p. 447.
3. *New Towns Commission* v. *Hemel Hempstead Corporation*, [1962] 3 All E.R. 183.
4. (1971), 218 *Estates Gazette* 851.

so hatched.[5] In *Mappin Brothers* v. *Liberty & Co., Ltd.*[6] it was rebutted where a new street was laid out under statutory authority, which imposed a duty inconsistent with the presumption. As a result, it has been suggested that the presumption would not apply to streets laid out on building estates.[7]

Adopted highways are excluded from registered titles. The Land Registry records do not show the ownership of the sub-soil to the centre of the road, even where there is an express conveyance *ad medium filum.* Land Registry practice is to show basements, vaults and cellars under the highway for obvious practical reasons.[8] For the purposes of liability for road charges under the relevant street works codes in the Highways Act 1959, the fact that the street is separated from the property by a public right of way not itself forming part of the street does not prevent the land "adjoining" the street. This follows from *Ware U.D.C.* v. *Gaunt*[9] where ASHWORTH, J. said:

> ". . . the inclusion of the three types of chargeable premises, namely those fronting, adjoining and abutting on, suggests that something more than mere physical contiguity was in the mind of the legislature."[10]

At common law a landowner is entitled to access to the highway from any point on his boundary. To-day this right is subject to statutory modification. In particular, the laying out of a means of access to the highway is development requiring planning permission.[11]

It often happens that there is a strip of land or balk lying between the highway proper and the land of adjoining owners. These strips

---

5. Norton on *Deeds*, 2nd Edn., p. 252; *Berridge* v. *Ward* (1861), 10 C.B.N.S. 400; *Micklethwait* v. *Newlay Bridge Co.* (1886), 33 Ch.D. 133; *Pryor* v. *Petre* (1894), 69 L.T. 795.
6. [1903] 1 Ch. 118.
7. See BRIGHTMAN, J. in *Giles* v. *County Building Constructors (Hertford), Ltd*, (1971), 218 *Estates Gazette* 851, and *Plumstead Board of Works* v. *British Land Co.* (1874), L.R. 10 Q.B. 16; *Beckett* v. *Corporation Leeds* (1872), 7 Ch. App. 421; and *Leigh* v. *Jack* (1879), 5 Exch. Div. 264.
8. They would pass in any event as rights enjoyed with the land under L.R.R., 1925, r. 251. In the case of a private way the soil will not be excluded from the registered title.
9. [1960] 3 All E.R. 778. See J. F. Garner, *Road Charges*, 3rd Edn., p. 31; *ante*, Chapter 2, pp. 12–13.
10. [1960] 3 All E.R. 778, at 788.
11. Considered in Chapter 10, *post*, pp. 175–176.

of wayside waste are subject to a curious rule.[12] Where the road is vested in the local authority it will include the top crust of any wayside strips which are part of the highway. However, trees planted in the highway before dedication and those which spring up subsequently without human aid remain the property of the owner of the sub-soil.[13] In general the public right of way will extend over the whole surface of the road, including any wayside strip.[14]

The presumption is, then, that waste land adjoining the road and its sub-soil belong to the adjoining owners. ABBOT, C.J. delivered himself of an interesting historical excursus in *Steel* v. *Prickett*[15] which is worth quoting at length:

> "In remote and ancient times, when roads were frequently made through uninclosed lands, and they were not formed with the exactness which the exigencies of society now require, it was part of the law that the public, where the road was out of repair, might pass along the land at the side of the road. This right on the part of the public was attended by this consequence, that although the parishioners were bound to the repair of the road, yet, if an owner excluded the public from using the adjoining land, he cast upon himself the onus of repairing the road. If the same person was the owner of the land on both sides, and inclosed both sides, he was bound to repair the whole of the road; if he inclosed on one side only, the other being left open, he was bound to repair to the middle of the road; and where there was an ancient enclosure on one side, and the owner of lands enclosed

12. Balks (also called lynches, lanchards or lanchets) are also a very rare boundary feature between private properties. They have their origin in the strip or three-field system of farming. "In some instances, there is the right to have a balk, that is to say, a strip of land outside the boundary of the particular field, which does not belong to the Lord of the Manor, or to the owner of the field, but which is used by the owner of the field for turning the plough, and which cannot be taken into the adjacent land:" Geo. C. Williamson, *Curious Survivals*, (1923), p. 132. There is no presumption about the ownership of balks lying between the lands of two proprietors: *Godmanchester* v. *Phillips* (1836), 4 Ad. Ad. & El. 550, *per* TAUNTON J. Balks may be met in connection with common land: see Harris and Ryan, *The Law relating to Common Land*, (1967) pp. 23–24; Williams, *Rights of Common*, (1886), p. 66; Hunter, *Open Spaces*, (1896), p. 126.
13. *Goodtitle d. Chester* v. *Alker and Elmes* (1757), 1 Keny. 427. *Cf.*, *Stillwell* v. *New Windsor Corporation*, [1932] 2 Ch. 155: the highway authority has a right to cut down trees on "ancient highways" when they have become an obstruction; they may be under a duty to do so: see further, Chapter 7, *post*, p. 136.
14. *Offin* v. *Rochford U.D.C.*, [1906] 1 Ch. 342; *Corsellis* v. *London County Council*, [1908] 1 Ch. 13. The question of the width of the highway is discussed below, p. 55.
15. (1818), 2 Stark. 463. See also *Simpson* v. *Dendy* (1860), 8 C.B.N.S. 433.

on the other, he was bound to repair the whole. Hence it followed as a natural consequence, that when a person inclosed his land from the road he did not make his fence close to the road but left an open space at the side of the road, to be used by the public when occasion required. This appears to be the most natural and satisfactory mode of explaining the frequency of wastes left at the sides of roads; the object was to leave a sufficiency of land by the side of a road when it was out of repair."

Ditches alongside highways may also give rise to disputes between the adjoining landowner and the highway authority. In *Hanscombe* v. *Bedfordshire County Council*[16] FARWELL, J. stated that there is a rebuttable presumption that a ditch alongside a highway is retained by the proprietor when he dedicates the highway. It is not part of the highway.[17] This is so even though the highway authority may acquire a right to drain into the ditch. It followed from this, for the purposes of the case, that the highway authority could not lay pipes in the ditch without the consent of the owners.[18]

8 WIDTH OF HIGHWAY AND ROADSIDE WASTES

The width of a highway is always a question of fact. There is, however, a rebuttable presumption that the rights of the public which derive from dedication are not confined to the metalled portion of the road or way but extend from fence to fence on either side.

This presumption is a rebuttable one.[19] In *Offin* v. *Rochford R.C.*,[1] WARRINGTON, J. dealt with the problem in this way:

> "The mere existence of fences on either side of a highway is not enough . . . You have to find whether these fences are *prima facie* to be taken to have been in reference to the highway, and, therefore, to the boundaries of the highway . . . Further . . . if you find a fence by the side of the highway, then *prima facie* that fence is the boundary of the highway, unless you can find some reason for supposing that it was put up for a different purpose."

This statement was accepted as a concise and accurate summary of the law by SINGLETON, J. in *Hinds and Diplock* v. *Breconshire County*

---

16. [1938] 3 All E.R. 647.
17. See also *A.-G.* v. *Beynon*, [1969] 2 All E.R. 263, at p. 267 *per* GOFF, J., and *Thorne* v. *Field* (1869), 33 J.P. 727.
18. See also *Chorley Corporation* v. *Nightingale*, [1907] 2 K.B. 637.
19. *R.* v. *Wright* (1832), 3 B. & Ad. 681; *Neeld* v. *Hendon U.D.C.* (1899), 63 J.P. 724.
1. [1906] 1 Ch. 342.

Council,[2] and more recently by GOFF, J. in *A.-G.* v. *Benyon*.[3] The material facts of the case were that the Attorney-General claimed a declaration that a grass verge in Leicestershire was part of the highway. The defendant, who owned property on the other side of the road, and who had been using the verge for the storage of vehicles, denied that he was obstructing the highway, which he would be if the verge were part of the highway.

GOFF, J. analysed the cases in a very careful judgment, and held that the mere fact that a road runs between fences does not *per se* give rise to any presumption that the right of way extends to the whole space between the fences. It is necessary to decide the preliminary question whether the fences were put up by reference to the highway, *i.e.*, to separate the highway from the adjoining closes, or for some other reason. That question is to be decided in the sense that the fences do mark the limit of the highway unless there is something in the condition of the road or the circumstances to the contrary. When that has been decided, a rebuttable presumption of law arises, supplying any lack of evidence of dedication in fact, or inferred from user, that the public right of passage and, therefore, the highway itself, extends to the whole space between the fences.[4]

Where a road passes through unenclosed land, however, it seems that the highway is confined to the metalled portion, unless it can be shown that the public have made use of the adjacent land as a highway.[5]

9 RAILWAYS

There is no presumption that an owner of land abutting a railway owns to the centre of the line.[6] There is a statutory obligation placed upon railway companies (and now British Rail) to fence off land used for the railway from adjoining land.[7] It follows that a grant of land described as bounded by a railway does not pass the right to any minerals under the line.[8] The liability to fence imposed on railway undertakings appears to remain until the line is removed.

---

2. [1938] 4 All E.R. 24.
3. [1970] Ch. 1; [1969] 2 All E.R. 263.
4. See also *Harvey* v. *Truro R.C.* [1903] 2 Ch. 638; *Coats* v. *Herefordshire C.C.* [1909] 2 Ch. 579.
5. *Easton* v. *Richmond Highway Board* (1871), L.R.7 Q.B. 69.
6. *Thompson* v. *Hickman*, [1907] 1 Ch. 550.
7. Considered in detail in Chapter 6, *post*, pp. 94–98.
8. *Thompson* v. *Hickman*, *ante*, p. 43.

10 HEDGE AND DITCH

The common law presumption relating to the ownership of a hedge and ditch arises only when the construction of the documents of title has failed to resolve the issue.[9] Where two properties are divided by a hedge *and* ditch or a ditch and bank, the presumption is that the boundary is along the edge of the ditch further from the hedge or bank.

> "The rule about ditching is this. No man, making a ditch, can cut into his neighbour's soil, but usually he cuts it to the very extremity of his own land; he is, of course, bound to throw the soil which he digs out upon his own land; and often if he likes it he plants a hedge on top of it; therefore if he afterwards cuts beyond the edge of the ditch, which is the extremity of his land, he cuts into his neighbour's land, and is a trespasser."[10]

The presumption applies only to an artificial ditch, and not to a natural watercourse.[11] It is a presumption and nothing more.

As was pointed out in *Fisher* v. *Winch*[12] the presumption assumes what is not necessarily a fact, namely that at the time when the ditch was dug there was no common ownership of the lands in question. In any event, it is displaced not only by contrary evidence supplied by conveyances of the lands in question but also, it seems, by the Ordnance Survey Map if the boundary is defined by reference thereto, although modern Ordnance Survey practice is to show the hedge as a topographical feature only.[13] However, where the parcels conveyed are described by reference to the Ordnance Survey, the legal position was stated clearly by the Court of Appeal in *Davey* v. *Harrow Corporation*:[14]

> "The boundary . . . is delineated on the map by a line, and the evidence of an official from the Ordnance Survey Office, . . . was that the line indicated the centre of the existing hedge. This is in accordance with

---

9. *Rouse* v. *Gravelworks, Ltd.*, [1940] 1 K.B. 489; [1940] 1 All E.R. 26; *Fisher* v. *Winch*, [1939] 1 K.B. 666, at 669.
10. *Per* LAWRENCE, J. in *Vowles* v. *Miller* (1810), 3 Taunt. 137, at 138.
11. *Marshall* v. *Taylor*, [1895] 1 Ch. 641, at 647.
12. [1939] 1 K.B. 666; [1939] 2 All E.R. 144.
13. Letter from the Training and Information Division, Ordnance Survey, *Chartered Surveyor*, June 1971, pp. 564–565. Ordnance Survey practice "is to show the hedge as a topographical feature and not to concern itself with any property boundary that might be related to or adjacent to the feature".
14. [1957] 2 All E.R. 305, at p. 307, *per* LORD GODDARD, C.J.

> the invariable practice of the survey as was proved in *Fisher* v. *Winch*, and in our opinion, after that case and this, courts in future can take notice of this practice of the Ordnance Survey as at least *prima facie* evidence of what a line on the map indicates".

It is true that by s. 12 of the Ordnance Survey Act 1841, the survey has no effect on private boundaries or titles to land. The courts will, however, take note of Ordnance Survey practice[15] and if the boundary is clearly defined by reference thereto, it is thought that the presumption is excluded.

Clearly the presumption will also be rebutted by showing that the ditch was made while the lands on both sides of the disputed boundary were in single ownership.[16] It is entirely a question of construction of the conveyance and plan, and any other admissible evidence. In *Collis* v. *Amphlett*[17] an unsuccessful attempt was made to extend the presumption into a general doctrine that the owner of the hedge was presumed to own the land on the far side of the hedge to a "ditch width" of four feet. In spite of this decision, the contention is still met with on occasion, and in some parts of the country a customary ditch width may be admitted.

The presumption cannot be made where the two properties are separated by a ditch alone; its very basis is then done away with. If there is no bank, acts of ownership will have to be proved to support any claim. They are not in themselves conclusive for, as *Henniker* v. *Howard*[18] shows, acts of ownership done without the knowledge of the other party will not rebut any existing presumption. They might often be done for convenience, and not under any right. In *Henniker* v. *Howard*[18] the plaintiff and defendant were owners of adjoining lands, bounded by a bank with a hedge and ditch on the defendant's side. For nearly fifty years the defendant had trimmed the hedge, pollarded nearby trees and cleansed the ditch. There was no evidence that the plaintiff knew of these activities. It was held on the facts that these

---

15. See *Davey* v. *Harrow Corporation*, [1957] 2 All E.R. 305.
16. *Fisher* v. *Winch* [1939] 1 K.B. 666; [1939] 2 All E.R. 144. See also *Weston* v. *Laurence Weaver, Ltd.*, [1961] 1 All E.R. 478 where the presumption was considered incidentally.
17. [1918] 1 Ch. 232, reversed by the Court of Appeal, [1920] A.C. 271. There is an interesting review of the older case law at pp. 259–260 of the appellate report.
18. (1904), 90 L.T. 157. Acts of ownership include trimming a hedge, cleansing a ditch, and repairing a wooden fence or wall.

acts of ownership did not rebut the presumption that the hedge and ditch belonged to the plaintiff. If both parties can prove acts of ownership, this will be evidence from which joint ownership of the feature may be inferred.

In many cases, cleansing of the ditch leads to a crumbling away of its outer edge and a gradual encroachment onto adjoining land. Local customs frequently lay down distances from the centre of the hedge, and the width from there to the accepted boundary is known as freeboard or deerleap. Such strips are usually met with bounding an ancient park or forest, the derivation of the name clearly coming from the fact that the strips were adjacent to where deer were kept.[19]

It should be remarked that no presumption as to ownership can arise where there are two ditches, one on each side of a hedge, because then there is no foundation for it. Acts of ownership are obviously of no value if it is known on whose land the ditch is, but they may help to support a possessory claim, as in *Marshall* v. *Taylor*,[20] where a ditch was enclosed, cinders and paving stones were laid on part and a rose-bed and farm-houses were constructed on another part. If the presumption is inapplicable, and acts of ownership cannot be proved, the hedge is best regarded as being jointly owned. In that case, one co-owner could maintain an action for trespass against the other if the latter grubbed up the hedge, although no action would lie for merely clipping the hedge.[1]

When a fenced close adjoins a piece of waste land, there is, in the absence of evidence to the contrary, a presumption that the hedge or other fence belongs to the owner of the close. This would not, it seems, apply where there was a hedge and ditch.[2]

11 STOREY BOUNDARIES

(a) *Basements*

There are no presumptions relating to basements, including vaults and cellars. These can now be formed only with the consent of the

---

19. "It is the extent of a deer's leap and its purpose is to enable the Lord of the Manor to 'take the deer he happened to shoot as they leapt over his fence on to his neighbour's land'.": George C. Williamson, *Curious Survivals* (1932).
20. [1895] 1 Ch. 641.
1. *Voyce* v. *Voyce* (1820), Gow. 201. *Cf.*, *Guy* v. *West* (1808), 2 Sel. N.P. 1244.
2. *White* v. *Taylor*, [1968] 1 All E.R. 1015.

highway authority.[3] If a highway is dedicated with an existing cellar under it, the cellar will remain the property of the dedicator. Where, as is normal, the sub-soil of the road is vested in the adjoining owner, any basement constructed under the road (with the necessary consent) must be of a height that will not obstruct the public rights.[4] Land Registry practice is to show basement storeys if the position is made clear at the time of registration.[5]

(b) *Floors*

There is no presumption to determine the horizontal boundary between the strata of a building, although the conveyance would pass only the storey itself. The structures dividing flats and maisonettes horizontally are, in the opinion of this writer, party structures and thus subject to normal party rights. In Chapter 8 arguments are advanced in support of this view, which is consonant with such authority as there is.[6]

Clearly the conveyance of a lower floor of a flat or maisonette would not include the soil *usque ad inferos*, unless the parcels clause made this clear. Similarly, it is to be doubted whether the conveyance of a top storey would pass the roof space and so forth *usque ad coelum.*[7] The grant of part of a building divided horizontally or vertically will include the external walls enclosing the property conveyed or demised.[8] In view of the uncertainty surrounding this topic, the position should be made clear in the parcels clause, the important point being to define the matter in clear terms. Normally the beams and floorboards of a floor should belong to the owner of the upper

---

3. Highways Act 1959, s. 153, which prohibits the construction of a vault, arch or cellar "under the carriageway of a street" without consent. See also s. 154, *ibid.*, as regards openings into and repair of cellars and vaults in streets. If an improvement line has been prescribed under s. 72, *ibid.*, that would also be material.
4. The highway authority cannot themselves use the sub-soil for non-highway purposes in the absence of express authority: *Tunbridge Wells Corporation* v. *Baird*, [1896] A.C. 434.
5. L.R.R., 1925, r. 251.
6. See *post*, pp. 146–147.
7. As to the normal scope of the maxim see, *e.g.*, *Corbett* v. *Hill* (1870), L.R. 9 Eq. 671; *Devonshire* v. *Pattinson* (1887), 20 Q.B.D. 263, *per* Fry, L.J., at 273.
8. *Sturge* v. *Hackett*, [1962] 3 All E.R. 166.

flat while the ceiling consisting of plaster or plasterboard should belong to the owner of the lower flat.[9]

(c) *Projections*

A plan annexed to a conveyance normally shows the position at ground level. It may be that the foundations and eaves extend beyond the defined boundary line. This was the situation in *Truckell* v. *Stock*[10] where the premises were conveyed as "all that land, dwelling-house, office, garages, outbuildings and premises . . . delineated and coloured pink and red on the plan attached hereto". The foundations and eaves of the house projected beyond the coloured portion, but the Court of Appeal quite properly held that this did not exclude the projecting foundations and eaves.

At first sight this decision is in conflict with the earlier case of *Laybourn* v. *Gridley*.[11] Part of some premises overhung the adjoining property, and the freeholder leased both properties to different people. He subsequently conveyed the premises which were overhung by reference to a ground floor plan which described them as "hereditaments and premises, with the dimensions, abbutals and boundaries thereof . . more particularly delineated in the map or plan drawn on these premises and thereon coloured green". NORTH, J. held that the overhanging part of the adjoining premises passed by the conveyance, saying:

> "What is conveyed is the piece of land coloured green, with all the buildings thereon; that, in the absence of anything else to the contrary, passes everything above and below."

The conflict is more apparent than real because the parcels clause in the earlier case was quite unequivocal. In any event, the later decision accords more with commonsense and is to be preferred.

9. A precedent clause along these lines is to be found in (1958), 22 *Conveyancer* (N.S.) 701.
10. [1957] 1 All E.R. 74.
11. [1892] 2 Ch. 53, and apparently not cited in *Truckell* v. *Stock*, [1957] 1 All E.R. 74.

Chapter 4

DEFINING BOUNDARIES

"It is the duty of the conveyancer in framing a disposition upon sale not to take for granted that he is to follow the exact terms of the description of the existing title, but to make full inquiry into the facts in order that he may be able to describe correctly the subject to be disposed." *Per* LORD KINNEAR in *Gordon-Cumming* v. *Houldsworth*, [1910] A.C. 537, at 547.

INTRODUCTION

There are many methods of describing land which is to be conveyed or demised, and the paramount need is to identify the extent of the property with fully-defined boundaries. Precision in the parcels clause is essential.[1] The proper identification of the land is essential whether in an ordinary conveyance or in a Land Registry transfer. The parcels clause is all important and the greatest care should be taken in its drafting.

The land may be described by reference to its abuttals, by its dimensions, by a description of its nature or, very commonly, by giving a name or some denoting mark to the property. This is often done by referring to the street and the name or number of the house, and it is a useful practice to give the full postal address. In all cases the exact line of the boundary may still be in doubt. The boundaries then have to be determined by reference to the canons of construction, any admissible extrinsic evidence or, in proper cases, by legal presumptions relating to the different types of boundary feature encountered. In registered conveyancing, on an application for first registration the applicant must always furnish sufficient particulars to enable the land to be fully identified on the General Map.

Conveyancers frequently use plans in transferring the legal estate from vendor to purchaser, as well as in other documents such as grants

---

1. But note the effect of s. 62 of the Law of Property Act 1925.

of easements. This is a very convenient method of resolving the difficulty of framing a suitable verbal description, but the standard of draftsmanship as far as plans are concerned leaves much to be desired. Where a plan is used it should be accurate, dimensioned and of a suitable scale, and preferably based on the Ordnance Survey map. It should show the physical features existing on the ground. With an accurate and dimensioned plan, duly incorporated into the deed, there is strictly no need to set out dimensions in the written parcels, but it is normal to do so as a safeguard. Great clarity and accuracy can be achieved with a professionally drawn plan. In all cases the plan ought to be looked at as explaining the language of the deed.[2]

PLAN OR VERBAL DESCRIPTION?

Where there is a plan, the written parcels in the body of the deed usually state either that the property is more particularly described in the plan or that it is shown thereon "by way of identification only". The use of the latter phrase in general means that the plan is almost useless, and it seems that many practitioners use the qualification as an excuse for a slip-shod plan.

The inadequacy of many verbal descriptions is notorious. Although it is not possible to formulate a general rule that there must always be a plan, in all but the simplest cases it should be regarded as essential.[3] If it is preferred, one can rely solely upon a plan drawn on the conveyance and duly incorporated into the parcels clause, in which case the appropriate wording might be:

> "The Property is indicated by the colour red on the attached plan which shows the relevant measurements."

However, it is best to repeat the measurements in the body of the deed itself.

If the boundaries of the property being conveyed are to rest on a plan at all it should be drawn on the conveyance or expressly incorporated in the parcels clause. In traditional conveyancing this is best

---

2. *Taylor* v. *Parry* (1840), 1 M. & G. 604, at 616; *Lyle* v. *Richards* (1866), L.R. 1 H.L. 222, at 231.
3. See *Eastwood* v. *Ashton*, [1915] A.C. 900, especially *per* LORD SUMNER, at 916, quoted *post*, p. 67.

done by using some such phrase as "more particularly described in the plan annexed hereto". In *Eastwood* v. *Ashton*[4] LORD WRENBURY gave approval to this form of words of reference, saying "these words seem to me to mean that the previous description may be insufficient for exact delimitation, and that the plan is to cover all deficiencies, if any".[5] The court *may* refuse to have regard to a plan if it is merely annexed to the conveyance, without being incorporated by some appropriate words of reference in the parcels clause.[6] The admissibility of a plan was considered in *Leachman* v. *L. & K. Richardson, Ltd.*[7] In that case it was held that where the description of the parcels read in the light of the other admissible evidence leaves doubt as to what was to be included in the conveyance, the court is not necessarily precluded from referring to a plan which formed part of the conveyance when it was signed merely because the plan is not referred to in the conveyance. If one relies solely upon a plan, no other words of reference can have the same certain effect.

The Council of the Law Society has expressed the view that "the signing of plans annexed to documents was good conveyancing practice, and for such purposes a form of memorandum on the plan identifying the document to which the plan was annexed was desirable".[8]

In other words, unless the plan is drawn on the conveyance itself it should bear clear reference to it. The normal memorandum to be endorsed on the plan and signed by both parties is:

> "This is the plan referred to in the Conveyance made between A and B and dated ——."

WORDS OF REFERENCE

There are several phrases in common use by which an annexed plan is referred to in the parcels clause. In many cases plans are expressed to be "by way of identification only" but the use of this

---

4. [1915] A.C. 900.
5. [1915] A.C. 900, at 920.
6. *Re Otway* (1862), 13 I.Ch.R. 222; *Wise* v. *Leahy* (1875), I.R. 9 C.L. 384.
7. [1969] 3 All E.R. 20. See also *Neilson* v. *Poole*, [1969] 20 P. & C.R. 909.
8. *Law Society's Digest*, Opinion No. 157, referring to 11 *Encyclopaedia of Forms and Precedents* (3rd Edn.) 125 and 143. The Opinion refers to the desirability of plans annexed to contracts, conveyances and other documents, such as grants of easements, licences and so on. See also *Pearce* v. *Gardner*, [1897] 1 Q.B. 688.

common phrase should be eschewed. The basic rule is that the verbal description of the premises in the parcels clause of the conveyance will prevail over the plan, except, of course where it is made quite clear that the plan is to prevail. In *Webb* v. *Nightingale*[9] for example, it was decided that a boundary visibly marked out and shown to the purchaser would prevail where the plan was undimensioned and expressed to be for identification only.

The dangers of using the "identification only" formula in a modern context is well-illustrated by *Willson* v. *Greene*,[10] dealing with the not uncommon case of a large piece of land being split up and sold off for development, the boundary lines being drawn for the first time and not corresponding to any physical division. The decision of FOSTER, J. shows that the incorporation of an "identification only" plan in such circumstances is without effect. In *Willson* v. *Greene* the plaintiffs wished to buy one plot on which a house already stood and they entered into negotiations with X, a third party. At a site meeting the plaintiffs and X agreed that the land should be extended slightly so as to include part of a driveway and a path. X's agent then marked out the agreed boundary with pegs. As a result, the north-western boundary of the plot was no longer a single straight line but had a kink in it. The disputed land was triangular in shape, 16 feet long and 5 feet wide at its base. The contract plan showed a kink in the boundary but the plan incorporated in the conveyance did not. It was an "identification only" plan and the verbal description in the conveyance said no more on this point than that the "piece of land [had] . . . a depth on the north-west side of 230 feet or thereabouts . . .". There was no ambiguity as to the piece of land to which, in general terms, the verbal description and the plan referred, for it was described as having a bungalow erected thereon and as being known as Rock Poultry Farm. Although the property known till then as Rock Poultry Farm was the whole which was then being divided up, the plaintiffs' plot was the only part with a bungalow on it. But the verbal description could not refer to an existing piece of land known by name. Since it is only where there is an inconsistency that the plan is subordinated to the verbal description, the vague conveyance would not have carried into effect the contract between the

9. Unreported but noted in (1957), 107 L.J. 359.
10. [1971] 1 All E.R. 1098.

parties. The general principle is that a deed should be so construed as to give effect to all its parts.

Nonetheless, FOSTER, J. held that where the parcels are vague and the plan is for "identification only" the court can take surrounding circumstances into account. The surrounding circumstances included the boundary agreed and marked out on the land by the parties, so that the property to be conveyed was made a parcel of land identifiable on inspection of the ground. This was confirmed by *Webb* v. *Nightingale* where DENNING, L.J. said:

> "So [at the time of the contract] there was on the land a physical state of affairs which would enable people to see where this common boundary was. . . . It seems to me that the line of white stakes with the white peg at the south-west corner and the post and wire fence at the north-east corner, were physical features on the land showing what was being sold . . . On the land itself the metes and bounds of this property were sufficiently shown so that anyone looking at the land at the date of the conveyance could have seen perfectly well what was being sold".

FOSTER, J., having cited this passage, went on to hold that once the boundary was clearly marked out and accepted "the fact that the boundary was not so clearly marked at the date of the contract and conveyance does not, in my judgment, alter the position".

Similarly, in *Freeman and Taylor's Contract*[11] the phrase used about a contract plan was "for the purpose of delineation only" and each lot was marked with its number and the figures "30 ft.". KEKEWICH, J. took this endorsement to mean simply that the plan was not drawn to scale, and must be taken as correct. In the more recent case of *Wallington* v. *Townsend*[12] a similar point came before MORTON, J. who held that the plan must prevail where the phrase "more particularly delineated in" was used,[13] and so the latter phase has the same effect as "more particularly described".

The meaning and effect of "more particularly described" and of stating that the plan is for identification only was fully canvassed and discussed in *Eastwood* v. *Ashton*[14] which must now be considered at length. The point at issue in that case was whether a small strip of

---

11. (1907), 97 L.T. 39.
12. [1939] Ch. 588; [1939] 2 All E.R. 225.
13. See also *Re Daniel*, [1917] 2 Ch. 405; *Herrick* v. *Sixby* (1866), L.R. 1 P.C. 436, at 451.
14. [1915] A.C. 900.

land, providing a convenient access way, had been conveyed to the appellant by the conveyance. This described the property as being "more particularly described in the plan indorsed on these presents and are delineated and coloured red in such plan". The Court of Appeal held that the disputed strip was not comprised in the conveyance and that the purchaser was not entitled to complain on finding that the strip was in the adverse possession of strangers. The Court applied the principle laid down succinctly by PARKE, B., in *Llewellyn* v. *Earl of Jersey*:[15]

> "As soon as there is an adequate and sufficient definition, with convenient certainty, of what is intended to pass by a deed, any subsequent erroneous addition will not vitiate it, according to the maxim *falsa demonstratio non nocet.*"

The House of Lords reversed this decision, holding that the plan was part of it, and "the one accurate guide is this endorsed plan".[16] It could not be disregarded. The acreage of the property was described in the parcels as being "84 acres 3 roods and 4 perches *or thereabouts*" and was therefore not definitive. The italicised words have a weakening effect. The phrase "more particularly described" means exactly what it says: the plan controls the description as a whole.[17] It is misleading to give overlapping descriptions:

> "If, however, several different species of description are adopted, risk of uncertainty at once arises, for if one is full, accurate and adequate, any others are otiose if right, and misleading if wrong."[18]

PLAN FOR IDENTIFICATION ONLY

When a plan is said to be "for identification only" the assumption is that there is an adequate verbal description and this is often an erroneous assumption. A plan for identification only is meant to show in broad terms the extent and shape of the plot conveyed. LORD PARKER dealt with such plans in *Eastwood* v. *Ashton*,[19] saying that one is at liberty to make use of such a plan "at any rate for the

15. (1843), 11 M. & W. 183.
16. *Per* LORD PARKER OF WADDINGTON [1915] A.C. 900, at 908.
17. See also *Hopgood* v. *Brown*, [1955] 1 All E.R. 550. JENKINS, L.J. said there that the words "for identification only" prevent the plan from controlling the description. Reference may also be made to *Rudd* v. *Bowles*, [1912] 2 Ch. 60, where a right of way was implied from a plan.
18. *Per* LORD SUMNER, [1915] A.C. 900, at 916. *Cf.*, *Re Brocket*, *Dowes* v. *Miller*, [1908] 1 Ch. 185, *per* JOYCE, J., at 196.
19. [1915] A.C. 900.

purpose of ascertaining the position and situation of the lands so described".

Thus, the purpose of describing property in the written parcels as being described in an annexed plan "for purposes of identification only" is to ascertain the position and situation of the property and nothing more. There must be a full description of the property and its boundaries, preferably with dimensions.[20] Trouble can only be avoided if great care is taken in describing the property verbally. A description such as "all that property shown as coloured red in the annexed plan which is for purposes of identification only" is meaningless; it is no description at all.[1] It is as much in the vendor's interests as the purchaser's that the matter should be free from doubt, for despite Conditions of Sale there are grave dangers in misdescription. Where the phrasing of the parcels clause is ambiguous, and two conflicting constructions are possible, one of which would make the land conveyed agree with the quantity mentioned, that construction would prevail.[2]

The conveyancer has the choice of words of reference. If he uses "as more particularly described in the plan annexed hereto" the plan will control the description, and in the writer's opinion this is the best method. On the other hand, it may be that a carefully worded and full description is preferred, in which case "for identification only" may be used. This presupposes that a surveyor will be employed to draw an accurate plan: one drawn by the office boy is valueless.[3] Moreover, in the writer's view the "identification only" formula is only appropriate where the property is already known by its verbal description set out in the parcels and there can be no doubt as to its boundaries, or where the plot is clearly and unequivocally marked out on the land. In other cases, and especially where land is being split up for the first time and sold off, it is essential to have a properly surveyed plan and to allow the plan to control the verbal description.

---

20. See *Murly* v. *McDermott* (1838), 8 Ad. & El. 138, where a dimension was held to exclude a dividing wall.
1. See *Hopgood* v. *Brown* [1955] 1 All E.R. 550; *Webb* v. *Nightingale* (1957) unreported, and followed in *Willson* v. *Greene* [1971] 1 All E.R. 1098. See also *Sharwood Properties* (*Ealing*), *Ltd.* v. *Maclellan*, (1971), 219 *Estates Gazette*, 830.
2. *Herrick* v. *Sixby* (1866), L.R. 1 P.C. 436, at 451.
3. See *Taylor* v. *Parry* (1840), 1 M. & G. 604, where the plan was on such a small scale that no boundary could be accurately traced.

However, if accurate and dimensioned plans are used, there seems no point in weakening the plan's effect, particularly if the dimensions are repeated in the deed so that verbal description and plan are a coherent whole.

DIMENSIONS

The importance of dimensions is well shown by the case of *Boyd Gibbins, Ltd.* v. *Hockham*[4] where the plan measurements differed from the actual plot dimensions. The plaintiffs sought a declaration that the plot in question was bounded by the physical boundaries of the property, and did not extend to the figures and measurements shown in the conveyance. The defendant purchaser counterclaimed a declaration that he had been conveyed the plot by measurement and that he owned another 2 ft. 6 in. of land at its northern boundary, and damages for loss of use of the strip of land which had been incorporated into a footpath.

The plan attached to the conveyance was prepared from the layout plan of the estate, which was on a very small scale and gave no indication of the boundaries of the various plots. The parcels clause described the plot by number and as being "coloured pink on the plan annexed hereto and having a frontage of 35 ft. 6 in. or thereabouts to a new road . . . and a depth therefrom on the west side of 81 ft. or thereabouts together with the dwellinghouse and premises erected thereon." BUCKLEY, J., giving judgment for the defendant on his counterclaim said:

> "The parcel as set out in the agreement and conveyance was described by reference to the plan, and the plaintiffs would have it that the words 'coloured pink on the plan annexed hereto' gave a complete and certain description of the property intended to be conveyed, and that the dimensions which were then referred to were 'gilding the lily' and not an essential part of the property intended to be conveyed. That contention cannot be accepted. The description in the body of the agreement and the conveyance must be read as a whole. . . . There was no physical boundary which showed the dimensions of the plot when (the defendant) moved in, so the dimensions shown cannot be treated merely as a misdescription which could be ignored so far as necessary to make the document fit the physical facts."

---

4. (1966), 199 Estates Gazette 229.

This serves to emphasise the dual need for a plan of suitable scale and accuracy, with correct dimensions, prepared by a surveyor. Too much care cannot be exercised.

PURCHASER'S RIGHT TO A PLAN

"In all simple cases in which a plan would assist the description," said SWINFEN EADY, J. in *Re Sansom and Narbeth's Contract*,[5] "the purchaser has a right to have a plan on the conveyance. I am not, however, prepared to say that in every case a purchaser is entitled to have a description by plan."[6] This dictum is sometimes relied upon by a purchaser's solicitor as supporting a supposed rule that there must always be a plan; there is no such rule because the property can be sufficiently identified by description alone. However, although the purchaser is entitled to see that there is a sufficient and proper description of the property, the vendor is under an obligation to ensure accuracy, and if a plan is provided he can always object that a plan is unnecessary.[7]

In any event it is always best to provide a plan. By cl. 12 of the Law Society's Conditions of Sale (1973 Revision):

> "The purchaser shall accept such evidence of identity as may be gathered from the descriptions in the documents abstracted plus a statutory declaration made where required at the purchaser's expense that the property has been held and enjoyed for at least twelve years in accordance with the title shown but the vendor shall not be required to define exact boundaries, fences, ditches, hedges or walls or separately identify parts of the property held under different titles."

Except as mentioned in the clause, no further or other evidence is to be required as to the identity of the property described in the contract with the property to which title is shown by the abstract or registered title.[8]

---

5. [1910] 1 Ch. 741.
6. See also *Re Sparrow and James Contract*, [1910] 2 Ch. 60, at 62, *per* FARWELL, J.; *Law Society's Digest*, *Opinions Nos.* 127, 148 and 151; National Conditions of Sale (18th Edn.), cl. 12 (2).
7. See *Re Sharman and Meade's Contract*, [1936].
8. See cl. 13 as to misdescription.

THE PREPARATION OF PLANS

Ordnance Survey maps provide a valuable base for all conveyancing plans. It is usual in surveying practice to accept Ordnance Survey sheets as correct and simply to check round the boundaries and bring the plan up to date, *e.g.*, by adding additional buildings. Where a plan is going to be relied upon, it should always be checked against the current edition of the Ordnance Survey map, and this is a vital factor in applications for first registration.

Ordnance Survey sheets are Crown copyright and a licence to reproduce them should be obtained from: The Director-General, Ordnance Survey, Chessington, Surbiton, Surrey. However, the Law Society has made special arrangements with the Director-General for the benefit of practitioners who wish to copy Ordnance Survey maps. An annual licence authorising reproduction in part can be obtained on payment of a small annual fee.[9] Reproduction of the whole sheet is not permissible.

Where a property is described by reference to a plan, the plan forms part of the abstract of title and the vendor must furnish a copy of it at his own expense. Conveyancing plans are normally on a very small scale, and in the great majority of cases the plan is quite useless for scaling off dimensions. This is another reason for putting figured dimensions on the plan. A common scale for plans is 1/1250 (50 inch scale) and with skilled draftsmanship an accuracy of up to the nearest foot may be obtained, but this is really only suitable for an estate layout because a scale of 1/1250 represents one inch to approximately 104 ft. which is inadequate where small distances are important. The recommended scale is 1/500, and this permits sufficient detail to be shown. Specific dimensions should be given on the plan if possible, and the compass point should be shown although in the written parcels reference can be made to identifying letters for particular dimensions. Where there is any doubt about the boundaries at all, a competent professional survey of the site should be undertaken.

The plan should show clearly the land and the buildings and other structures at the date of the conveyance. If the house is not yet built,

---

9. For further details of this concessionary arrangement, see *Law Society's Gazette*, February 1957, p. 83. An acknowledgment of the source must be put on any plan based on an O.S. Map.

and a plan is relied on, the written parcels should contain the qualifying phrase "together with the dwellinghouse and garage to be erected thereon". At ground level the area within the boundaries is often coloured pink. Storeys projecting at ground level, *e.g.*, a cellar, should be shown projecting out and enclosed in a dotted line. The ownership of fences can be indicated by means of T marks on the appropriate side of the boundary as shown on the plan; party structures can be indicated by means of T marks on each side.[10]

Rights of way should be shown in some other colour—usually brown or green—and if possible the width of the way should be indicated and defined clearly, showing whether it is a footway only or not.[11] A conveyance of premises where part projects over a boundary, *e.g.*, a decorative cornice, will not include anything above or below the projection. If a right of access for repairs to an external wall is being reserved or granted, this should be shown by suitably coloured hatching. As already remarked, if the face of an external wall is shown as being the boundary things projecting thereover will be included.[12]

Because of the possibility of boundary disputes many practitioners find it convenient to add an additional precautionary inquiry to the standardised "enquiries before contract" made on behalf of the purchaser in both registered and unregistered conveyancing:

> "Has there been or is there any argument, dispute or disagreement whatsoever concerning the property or its appurtenances?"

INCONSISTENCIES IN DESCRIPTION

Occasionally one finds a discrepancy between the verbal description in the conveyance and the actual layout of the property. When that occurs a description related to physical objects is to be preferred to dimensions, for the surveyor's chain is not an infallible method of measurement. It is, however, usually possible to measure from some

---

10. Filed plans at the Land Registry do not normally show T marks, unless the documents lodged on first registration concern a statement relating to the ownership of specific walls, etc. A broken line is normally used on Land Registry plans as showing a boundary where no physical feature exists, and this is a convenient practice in all cases.
11. See *Keefe* v. *Amor*, [1965] 1 Q.B. 334; [1964] 2 All E.R. 517; *Bulstrode* v. *Lambert*, [1953] 2 All E.R. 728.
12. *Corbett* v. *Hill* (1870), L.R. 9 Eq. 671; *Truckell* v. *Stock*, [1957] 1 All E.R. 74.

fixed point such as a road junction and to note this fact on the plan. This is the method to be preferred.

An example of an inconsistency in description occurred in *Manning* v. *Fitzgerald*[13] where the property was described in the parcels by measurements and the words "with the houses now erected or to be erected thereon". It was proved that the foundations had been laid before the conveyance was executed, and it was held immaterial that the ground occupied by the house exceeded the measurements stated. This principle can be of particular importance where the purchaser contracts to buy a house on a new estate in the course of development. Most of the large building companies indicate the ownership of all fences on the estate plan by the usual T marks, and an extract of the estate plan is annexed to the assurance to the purchaser. However, there is frequently room for dispute because of the small scale on which such plans are drawn, and they are not sacrosanct.

Although there is no warranty that a plan in a conveyance is correct[14] if the plan is incorporated in the parcels clause it would be construed against the grantor on the principle of no derogation from grant.[15] Moreover, certain covenants for title are implied by s. 76 of the Law of Property Act 1925, if the vendor conveys "and is expressed to convey as beneficial owner" on sale, and it is thought that there may be qualified covenants as to the accuracy of the plan under that provision. Where a plan prevails over or replaces the verbal description in the parcels clause, an error in the plan might well have the same effect as a verbal misdescription.[16]

Wherever there is any doubt, the conveyancer should advise his client to have the plan checked on site for his own protection and also to prevent "arguments, disputes and disagreements" with neighbouring owners. The solicitor's duty in conveyancing is to make full

---

13. (1859), 29 L.J. Ex. 24. See also *Willson* v. *Greene*, [1971] 1 All E.R. 1098.
14. "I am not aware of any decision which shows that a plan on a conveyance amounts to a warranty that the plan is correct": *per* FARWELL, J. in *Re Sparrow and James's Contract*, [1910] 2 Ch. 60, at 62. The plan there was a copy of the Ordnance Survey sheet and on it was printed a statement that it was for reference only and its accuracy was not guaranteed. See on plans generally *Re Lindsay and Forder's Contract* (1895), 72 L.T. 832.
15. *Cowen* v. *Truefitt, Ltd.*, [1899] 2 Ch. 309: the plan must be treated as being one with the rest of the conveyance. See also *Re Otway* (1862), 13 Ir.Ch.R.
16. See *Bellotti* v. *Chequers Developments, Ltd.*, [1936] 1 All E.R. 89, *per* HILBERY, J.

inquiry so that he is able to describe correctly the subject-matter of the transaction.[17] In receiving a plan from a client, a solicitor is entitled to assume that it is correct because, subject to what is said above, its accuracy or otherwise is a matter for the surveyor. Nonetheless, here is a field which is ripe for co-operation between the two professions. As a precautionary measure, the solicitor can at least send to his purchaser client the plan taken from the abstract and, where appropriate, the result of the official search of the index map, parcels index, and filed plan. Checking and comparison have been known to bring to light boundary differences, which can then be corrected before contracts are exchanged.[18]

MISCELLANEOUS PROBLEMS

It may be that in spite of the conveyance, a proper plan, admissible evidence and any applicable presumption, there is no real indication of the ownership of walls and fences dividing properties in different ownership. Only limited help can be had from the way in which boundary features are constructed, and ownership is a question of fact. From a practical point of view an over-anxious client can be advised to let matters rest until trouble arises. Such trouble usually relates to a claim by one man that his neighbour is obliged to repair or maintain a fence. Investigation may show that ownership of the fence in question is completely unknown.

Where there is no evidence of ownership, no indication should be put on the conveyance plan. A problem of this sort can often be settled amicably by pointing out that whoever the fence may belong to, there is no general obligation to repair it. Therefore, it is convenient to treat the disputed fence as joint responsibility, and most neighbours are able to come to a sensible arrangement.

Those advising estate developers would do well to consider making all dividing fences "party structures" subject to s. 38 of the Law of Property Act 1925. In the absence of express provision in the deeds,

---

17. *Gordon-Cumming* v. *Houldsworth*, [1910] A.C. 537, the House of Lords holding, in the context of Scottish law, that the meaning of a descriptive name in a contract cannot be determined by a fixed rule of law without regard to the facts of the case. A purchaser cannot complain where the conveyance and plan, following the contract plan, includes less than he thought.
18. See 115 *Law Journal* 275.

there is no right of contribution in favour of one owner carrying out repairs as against the other owner.[19] However, there is much to be said—especially in leasehold practice—for making all dividing walls and fences party structures, and to provide that each lesssee will contribute equally towards the cost of repair. In leasehold conveyancing it is not good practice to make each lessee liable to repair one dividing fence, because there is neither privity of contract nor estate between adjoining lessees, and the repairing covenant would not be directly enforceable against the adjoining owner. That is a point of considerable practical importance in long leases.

---

19. *Re Jones*, [1893] 2 Ch. 461; *Kenrick* v. *Mountsteven* (1899), 48 W.R. 141. See further, Chapter 8, *post*, pp. 151–153.

Chapter 5

EVIDENCE OF BOUNDARIES

"Founded apparently on the propositions that all jurymen are deaf to reason, that all witnesses are presumptively liars, and that all documents are presumptively forgeries, (the law of evidence) has been added to, subtracted from and tinkered with for two centuries until it has become less of a structure than a pile of builders' debris." C. P. Harvey, *The Advocate's Devil*, p. 79.

THE NATURE OF EVIDENCE

The purpose of evidence is to establish facts in court; the English law of evidence is mainly exclusionary. It is concerned not so much with how facts may be proved, but with what facts may not be proved. By definition evidence includes:

> "all the legal means, exclusive of mere argument, which tend to prove or disprove any matter of fact, the truth of which is submitted to judicial investigation."[1]

The boundaries of land are a matter of evidence, and it is a question of fact whether or not a particular piece of land is or is not included in a grant.[2] As we have seen in Chapter 3, in the absence of a clear statement in the title deeds, (and any extrinsic evidence admissible to construe them), the court will be guided by evidentiary presumptions where the land in question is bounded by or defined by reference to certain physical features. These presumptions will then apply unless rebutted by contrary evidence.[3] The presumptions can have no application where the conveyance is clear and certain in its terms.

---

1. Taylor, *Law of Evidence*, vol. 1, (12th Edn.), p. 1.
2. *Lyle* v. *Richards* (1866), L.R. 1 H.L. 222; *Goodtitle d. Radford* v. *Southern* (1813), 1 M. & S. 299; *Kingsmill* v. *Millard* (1855), 11 Ex. 313, at 319.
3. *Duke of Beaufort* v. *Swansea Corporation* (1849), 3 Ex. 413.

The best evidence available in any boundary dispute is the title deeds of the properties. If the title deeds of the plaintiff and the defendant conflict, reference must be made to earlier deeds to throw light on the discrepancy. This applies *a fortiori* to registered land because Land Registry plans show only general boundaries.[4]

Basically, boundary disputes in most cases depend on the construction of the muniments of title, and the admissibility of extrinsic evidence to clear up ambiguities. Words which form an essential part of the description can never be rejected, but in many cases an apparently special description can be disregarded as *falsa demonstratio non nocet*, although there is no general rule as to which of two inconsistent descriptions is to prevail.[5]

> "Where a description of the parcels is partly true and partly false, if the true part describes the subject with sufficient legal certainty, the untrue part will be rejected as *falsa demonstratio* and will not vitiate the grant or devise. It does not matter in what order the true and untrue parts come."[6]

This was the situation in *Maxted* v. *Plymouth Corporation*[7] where, in an attempt to evade future liability for road charges, a conveyance plan had been drawn showing the boundary at the foot of the hedge, although the parcels referred to the Ordnance Survey Map which made it clear that the boundary was the centre line of the hedge. The boundary on the plan was rejected as *falsa demonstratio.*

It is for the court to decide between the conflicting descriptions, and only when that has been done can the *falsa demonstratio* rule be applied. In any event, the rule is subject to a qualification, which was put by PARKE, B. in this way:

> "Where there is a sufficient description set forth of the premises, by giving the particular name of a close or otherwise, we may reject a

---

4. *Ante*, Chapter 2, pp. 24–30. The statutory limitation of 15 years for commencement of title applies only as between vendor and purchaser: Law of Property Act 1969, s. 23.
5. *Eastwood* v. *Ashton*, [1915] A.C. 900, at 912, *per* LORD PARKER OF WADDINGTON.
6. *Per* LINDLEY, M.R. in *Cowen* v. *Truefitt, Ltd.*, [1899] 2 Ch. 309, at 311. There are numerous cases on the rule: see, *e.g.*, *Llewellyn* v. *Earl of Jersey* (1843), 11 M. & W. 183; *Manning* v. *Fitzgerald* (1859), 29 L.J. Ex. 24; *Hardwick* v. *Hardwick* (1873), L. R. 16 Eq. 168.
7. [1957], C.L.Y. 243; there is a more detailed report in (1957), *Times*, March 28th.

> false demonstration; but if the premises be described in general terms, and a particular description be added, the latter controls the former."[8]

Where the words of a grant or demise are clear and unambiguous, they are conclusive. No apology is needed for repeating here the well known dictum of COLERIDGE, J.:

> "Words in an instrument of grant, as elsewhere, are to be taken in the sense which the common usage of mankind has applied to them, in reference to the context in which they are found . . ."[9]

Extrinsic evidence is admissible only in limited circumstances.

ADMISSIBILITY OF EXTRINSIC EVIDENCE

> "I have never heard the general rule contradicted, that parol or extrinsic evidence cannot be admitted to contradict, vary or add to the terms of a deed."[10]

Parol evidence is admissible to clarify any ambiguity in the title deeds,[11] and to show what the parties knew at the time the deed was executed.[12] Extrinsic evidence is also admissible to show what the boundaries of the land as used before the grant were, as this tends to prove what it was intended to convey.[13] Moreover,

> "it may be laid down generally that all facts relating to the subject-matter and object of a deed, such as that the property comprised in it did or did not belong to the grantor, the mode of acquiring it, the local situation, limits and distribution of the property, are admissible to aid in ascertaining what is meant by the words used in the instrument."[14]

Apart from these instances, however, parol evidence is not admissible to add to, contradict, alter or vary the terms of a deed.

---

8. In *Doe d. Smith v. Galloway* (1833), 5 B. & Ad. 43. *Cf.*, *Taylor* v. *Parry* (1840), 1 M. & G. 604, at 623.
9. *Lord* v. *Commissioners of Sydney* (1859), 12 Moo. P.C.C. 473, at 497.
10. *Per* PARKE, J. in *Smith* v. *Doe d. Earl of Jersey* (1821), 2 Brod. & Bing. 473, at 541.
11. *Doe d. Gore* v. *Langton* (1831), 2 B. & Ad. 680; *Waterpark* v. *Fennell* (1857), 7 H.L. 650; *Lister* v. *Pickford* (1865), 34 Beav. 576; *Lyle* v. *Richards* (1866), 15 L.T. 1; *Goodtitle d. Radford* v. *Southern* (1813), 1 M. & S. 299.
12. *Murly* v. *Macdermott* (1838), 8 Ad. & El. 138; *Baird* v. *Fortune* (1861), 7 Jur. N.S. 926.
13. *Van Diemen's Land Co.* v. *Table Cape Marine Board*, [1906] A.C. 92, at 98, *per* LORD HALSBURY, L.C.
14. *Per* PARKE B. in *Doe d. Templeman* v. *Martin* (1833), 4 B. & Ad. 771. *Cf.*, *McMurray* v. *Spicer* (1868), L.R. 5 Eq. 527.

DISCOVERY OF DOCUMENTS

In a boundary dispute it is important to know the limits to the right of discovery, which in High Court proceedings is now governed by R.S.C., O. 24. In brief, either party is entitled to discovery of all deeds and documents in his opponent's possession which contain evidence of the joint title, or which tend to support the case of the party seeking discovery.[15] Documents material to the title of the opposing party must be disclosed.[16] However, a party need not produce any document which relates solely to his own title and which contains nothing tending to substantiate his opponent's case.[17] If the person against whom discovery is sought swears that the documents are not material, his oath is usually regarded as conclusive.[18]

There are limits to the right to discovery. Thus, a witness who is not a party to the proceedings cannot be compelled to produce his title deeds.[19] Privilege may also be claimed where a document relates solely to a party's own claim and contains nothing which would assist his opponent's case.[20] However, this privilege cannot be claimed where he has himself been responsible for confusing the boundaries.[1] In disputes between landlord and tenant, since it is the tenant's duty to keep the boundaries between his own lands and those of his landlord defined, the tenant cannot resist discovery and must produce his own title deeds to the lessor.[2] Secondary evidence of documents will be admissible where, *e.g.*, the other party refuses to produce a document after proper notice to do so.[3]

15. *Burrell* v. *Nicholson* (1833), 1 My. & K. 680, at 681; *Lind* v. *Isle of Wight Ferry Co.* (1860), 2 L.T. 503; *A.-G.* v. *Emerson* (1882), 10 Q.B.D. 191.
16. *Ind, Coope & Co.* v. *Emmerson* (1887), 12 App. Cas. 300; *A.-G.* v. *Storey* (1912), 107 L.T. 430.
17. *Morris* v. *Edwards* (1890), 15 App. Cas. 309; *Chowood, Ltd.* v. *Lyall*, [1929] 2 Ch. 406.
18. *Chowood, Ltd.* v. *Lyall* [1929] 2 Ch. 406.
19. *Pickering* v. *Noyes* (1823), 1 B. & C. 262. It would be different if the third party or his predecessor had given an acknowledgment for production.
20. *Bewicke* v. *Graham* (1881), 7 Q.B.D. 400; *Budden* v. *Wilkinson*, [1893] 2 Q.B. 432; *Brookes* v. *Prescott*, [1948] 2 K.B. 133; [1948] 1 All E.R. 907.
1. *Marquis of Bute* v. *Glamorganshire Canal Co.* (1845), 9 Jur. 1063.
2. *Southwell* v. *Thompson* (1837), 6 L.J. Ch. 196; *Brown* v. *Wales* (1872), 42 L.J. Ch. 45. Boundary disputes between lessor and lessee are considered in Chapter 9, *post*, p. 168.
3. *Dwyer* v. *Collins* (1852), 7 Exch. 639. He cannot then produce the original as part of his own case: *Doe d. Thompson* v. *Hodgson* (1840), 12 Ad. & El. 135; *Lewis* v. *Hartley* (1835), 7 C. & P. 405.

TYPES OF EVIDENCE

The general rules of evidence apply in boundary disputes as in other litigation. There are, however, particular types of evidence which are of special value in boundary disputes. It is proposed to consider this special evidence briefly here, and the different types are listed alphabetically.

1 ACTS OF OWNERSHIP

Where the title deeds are not clear as to the boundaries, evidence of acts of ownership will be admissible, although acts of ownership may be of limited value.[4] "The ground on which such acts are admissible," it has been said,[5] "is not the acquiescence of any party; they are admissible of themselves, *proprio vigore*, for they tend to prove that he who does them is the owner of the soil; though if they are done in the absence of all persons interested to dispute them, they are of less weight."

Perambulations by a lord of the manor have been held admissible to show the extent of the manorial boundaries.[6] In *Stanley* v. *White*[7] the ownership of a continuous belt of trees was in dispute. Acts of ownership by the plaintiff in respect of one part of the belt of trees were held admissible as tending to prove ownership of another part, since the belt had to be considered as a whole. Admissible acts of ownership include cultivation of the soil, the felling of timber, fishing in a river or stream, and turning off trespassers.[8] Acts of ownership are not conclusive, for they may have been done merely for convenience, *e.g.*, trimming a hedge. They may well be insufficient where the boundary feature in dispute is governed by some settled legal presumption.[9]

---

4. See generally *Stanley* v. *White* (1811), 14 East 332; *Tutill* v. *West Ham Local Board of Health* (1873), L.R. 8 C.P. 447; *Malcolmson* v. *O'Dea* (1863), 10 H.L. Cas. 593.
5. *Per* PARKE B. in *Jones* v. *Williams*, (1836), 2 M. & W. 326.
6. *Woolway* v. *Rowe* (1834), 1 Ad. & El. 114.
7. (1811), 14 East 332.
8. *Curzon* v. *Lomax* (1803), 5 Esp. 60; *University College, Oxford* v. *Oxford Corpn.* (1904), 20 T.L.R. 637.
9. See, *e.g.*, *Henniker* v. *Howard* (1904), 90 L.T. 157 (discussed in Chapter 3, *ante*, p. 58) where trimming a hedge and cleansing a ditch were held insufficient to displace the normal hedge and ditch presumption. See also *Earl Craven* v. *Pridmore* (1902), 18 T.L.R. 282.

Two contrasting cases involving acts of ownership may be noted. In *Simcox* v. *Yardley R.C.*[10] a road was laid out under an inclosure award, its width being stated as 30 ft. The defendant council, in whom the road was vested, claimed that they were entitled to the adjoining bank, hedge and ditch. It was held, however, that as the plaintiff had exercised acts of ownership over these features, and the width of the road was stated as being 30 ft. without them, he and not the defendants had made out title to them. Conversely, in *Leeke* v. *Portsmouth Corporation* (*No.* 2)[11] the plaintiff claimed a strip of land alongside the road as part of the manorial waste. He tendered evidence of acts of ownership over contiguous land without avail.

2 CONSTRUCTION OF BOUNDARY FEATURES

The construction of boundary features is not in itself any indication of ownership, but may be of help in settling a dispute between neighbours amicably. It is sometimes said that where a boundary wall is buttressed, the buttresses must be indicative of ownership, being placed on the side of the owner of the wall. There is no legal foundation for this assumption, although where the buttresses form part of the original wall, this may be *prima facie* evidence of ownership.

There is an equally common notion that where there is a wooden fence, the fence belongs to the man on whose side the posts and arris rails are. This idea is without legal foundation, as is the view that in erecting a fence one must present a "fair face" to the neighbouring owner, *i.e.*, so construct the fence that the palings are on his side. This view is based on the equally fallacious idea that a man may go onto his neighbour's property as of right in order to erect or maintain a fence or wall. There can, of course, be an easement to go on to another's land for the purpose of maintaining a wall.[12]

There are points in favour of either type of construction, and the ownership of any particular wall or fence will be a question of fact. It belongs, in general, to the person on whose land it is erected. If the rails are put on the outer side of the fence, it is then easily maintainable from its owner's side, and he has no need to seek his neighbour's permission to enter if he needs to effect repairs. If this method of

10. (1905), 69 J.P. 66.
11. (1913), 107 L.T. 260.
12. See *Ward* v. *Kirkland*, [1967] Ch. 194; [1966] 1 All E.R. 609.

construction is adopted, however, the palings would not enclose the strips of land between the uprights, and the neighbouring owner might acquire a possessory title thereto. It may be added that there is no rule, where there is a row of houses, that one fence or the other is the responsibility of one owner. Each case must be considered on its own facts, and as far as the writer is aware there is no local custom supporting this idea, which is prevalent amongst lay clients.

In cases like this, where the ownership of the fence or wall is uncertain or unknown, it is best to treat the disputed feature as a party structure maintainable at joint expense.[13]

3 DOCUMENTARY EVIDENCE

Apart from the title deeds and any plan annexed to them, other types of documentary evidence may be helpful in ascertaining boundaries. Section 4 of the Civil Evidence Act 1968 provides for the admissibility of statements contained in documentary records compiled in pursuance of a duty from information supplied, directly or indirectly, by a person with first-hand knowledge of the relevant facts.

(a) *Public documents*

The contents of public documents are admissible as evidence of the facts stated in them.[14] Under this exception to the hearsay rule all sorts of public registers, assessments and surveys are admissible. The manner of proving public non-judicial documents in court is prescribed by s. 1 of the Evidence Act 1845, and s. 14 of the Evidence Act 1851. To be a public document, it must have been made with the intention that it be retained for public inspection, by a public officer under an obligation to satisfy himself as to the truth of the facts recorded. The document must also be produced from proper custody. The first two requirements let out such things as private Crown surveys,[15] private Admiralty maps, and so on, although these may be admissible as evidence under another exception to the hearsay rule.[16]

---

13. See Chapter 8, *post*, pp. 151–153.
14. *Sturla* v. *Freccia* (1880), 5 App. Cas. 623. See also *Mercer* v. *Denne*, [1905] 2 Ch. 538, at 555. As to what is a public document, see *R.* v. *Sealby*, [1965] 1 All E.R. 701.
15. *Phillips* v. *Hudson* (1867), 2 Ch. App. 243.
16. *Mercer* v. *Denne*, [1905] 2 Ch. 538.

Verdicts, decrees, and judgments are thus admissible in evidence,[17] but not an arbitrator's award.[18] The following public documents have been admitted in evidence to prove boundaries:

(i) Admiralty charts and deposited plans;[19]
(ii) Domesday book and, in Ireland, the Down survey;[20]
(iii) Land tax and poor law assessments;[1]
(iv) Maps drawn by authority of a Royal Commmission;[2] surveys of Crown lands;[3] and surveyor's reports made by statutory authority.[4]

The Ordnance Survey maps, although public documents in one sense, are not generally admissible as evidence of private boundaries, because of the operation of s. 12 of the Ordnance Survey Act 1841. However, the Ordnance Survey maps may often be expressly adopted in private deeds and the boundaries therein defined by reference to them, in which case the Ordnance Survey maps are admissible.[5]

(b) *Ancient documents*

All ancient documents not less than twenty years old, produced from proper custody, are presumed to have been validly executed, and any alterations to them are presumed to have been made before execution.[6] They may be admitted as evidence of boundaries. What

17. *Evans* v. *Rees* (1839), 10 Ad. & El. 151—strictly as evidence of reputation; *Neill* v. *Duke of Devonshire* (1882), 8 App. Cas. 135.
18. *Ibid.*, but an award is admissible in a subsequent action between the same parties as evidence proper: *Breton* v. *Knight* (1837), cited in Roscoe's *Evidence at Nisi Prius*, (18th Edn.), p. 220. Boundary disputes may always be submitted to arbitration in accordance with the provisions of the Arbitration Act 1950.
19. *Birrell* v. *Dryer* (1884), 9 App. Cas. 345; *Mercer* v. *Denne*, [1905] 2 Ch. 538; *A.-G.* v. *Meyrick and Jones* (1915), 79 J.P. 515; *A.-G.* v. *Antrobus*, [1905] 2 Ch. 188.
20. *Alcock* v. *Cooke* (1829), 5 Bing. 340; *Duke of Beaufort* v. *Aird & Co.* (1904), 20 T.L.R. 602.
1. *Doe d. Smith* v. *Cartwright* (1824), 1 C. & P. 218; *Anstee* v. *Nelms* (1856), 1 H. & N. 225.
2. *New Romney Corporation* v. *New Romney Commissioners of Sewers*, [1892] 1 Q.B. 840.
3. *Doe d. William IV.* v. *Roberts* (1844), 12 M. & W. 520.
4. *Evans* v. *Merthyr Tydfil Urban Council*, [1899] 1 Ch. 241.
5. *Maxted* v. *Plymouth Corporation*, [1957] C.L.Y. 243.
6. See Evidence Act 1938, s. 4.

is proper custody depends on the facts of the case but, in the case of cancelled leases which have been held admissible under this head[7] it means from the custody of the lessor or lessee or those claiming under them.

(c) *Private maps and surveys*

Private maps and surveys are not generally admissible in evidence[8] but a plan annexed to a deed is part of the deed and is therefore receivable. The definition of documents in s. 10(1) of the Civil Evidence Act 1968, includes plans, and consequently they may be admissible under the Act.[9] Private maps may be admissible in evidence as statements of deceased persons, but then it would have to be established that the maker of the map had "competent means of knowledge of the facts".[10] Tithe commutation maps are not admissible as evidence of private boundaries.[11] Land Registry plans could only be used in evidence where the title to the land registered was in issue, in which case an office copy is admissible, but they are on such a small scale as to be virtually useless.[12]

(d) *Other documentary evidence*

Ecclesiastical terriers which set out in detail the temporal possessions of every parish church, are admissible in evidence if produced from proper custody. Terriers are drawn up under the provisions of canon law, and proper custody would be the episcopal or archidiaconal registry, the diocesan record office, or the charter chest of the parish church itself.[13] In order to be admissible the terrier must be signed by some competent official[14] and would not be evidence for the incumbent in any dispute concerning glebe lands unless signed by the incumbent and churchwardens.[15]

Books of general history and general atlases and maps may be given in evidence as facts within public knowledge, but not as ascertaining

7. *Plaxton* v. *Dare* (1829), 10 B. & C. 17.
8. *Anon.* (1718), 1 Stra. 95; *Wilkinson* v. *Allott* (1777), 3 Bro. Parl. Cas. 684; *Pollard* v. *Scott* (1790), Peake 26; *Wakeman* v. *West* (1836), 7 C. & P. 479; but see *Bishop of Meath* v. *Winchester* (1836), 3 Bing. N.C. 183.
9. See ss. 1–10 generally.
10. *Vyner* v. *Wirral R.D.C.* (1909), 73 J.P. 242.
11. *Wilberforce* v. *Hearfield* (1877), 5 Ch.D. 709.
12. Land Registration Act 1925, s. 113. The Land Registry maps would be of little use as evidence because of the general boundaries rule.
13. *Atkins* v. *Hatton* (1794), 2 Anst. 386.
14. *Ibid.* See also *Carr* v. *Mostyn* (1850), 5 Exch. 69.
15. See *Earl* v. *Lewis* (1801), 4 Esp. 1.

private rights.[16] The court will take judicial notice of the division of the country into counties,[17] but matters such as these are of little assistance in private disputes. Particulars of sale at an auction have been admitted as evidence of boundaries where the conveyance was ambiguous,[18] and a great many other documents may be admissible under other exceptions to the hearsay rule or under the Civil Evidence Act 1968.

4 EXPERT EVIDENCE

The general rule that a witness's opinion is not receivable in evidence has been altered by the Civil Evidence Act 1972, extending the application of the Civil Evidence Act 1968. The 1972 Act provides[19] that an expert's opinion on a matter on which he is qualified to give an opinion will be admissible in civil proceedings. This would of course, include ther expert evidence of a surveyor. Surveyor's marks on trees and other boundary features are, in the normal way, provable by secondary evidence.[20]

5 HEARSAY

The Civil Evidence Act 1968, s. 1, and the Civil Evidence Act 1972 extended the Evidence Act 1938, by making "first hand" oral or documentary hearsay generally admissible subject to rules of court, and so the admissibility of hearsay evidence in civil proceedings is now dealt with by statute. Section 9 of the 1968 Act preserves the admissibility of certain hearsay evidence formerly admissible at common law, *e.g.*, publications dealing with matters of a public nature. The general rule as to hearsay in civil proceedings may be said to be that it is admissible only by virtue of agreement or statutory provision.

Reputation generally is admissible in evidence generally where matters of public or general interest are concerned. It is inadmissible in cases of private boundary.[1] So, in *Brisco* v. *Lomax*[2] where the verdict of a jury was admitted, LITTLEDALE, J. remarked:

---

16. *Read* v. *Bishop of Lincoln*, [1892] A.C. 644; *White and Jackson* v. *Beard* (1840), 2 Curt. 480.
17. *Deybel's Case* (1832), 4 B. & Ald. 243.
18. *Ecroyd* v. *Coulthard*, [1897] 2 Ch. 554.
19. Section 3.
20. *Doe d. Coyle* v. *Cole* (1834), 6 C. & P. 359.
1. *Thomas* v. *Jenkins* (1837), 6 Ad. & El. 515. As to its admissibility for the purpose of proving pedigree, see Civil Evidence Act 1968, s. 9(4).
2. (1838), 8 Ad. & El. 198, at 210.

> "On a question of boundary, mere reputation is evidence. But I put this as a verdict, not as reputation. It is a trail by witnesses competent to speak to the facts. Now reputation being evidence, the verdict must be evidence . . . and this though the former proceeding was between different parties. It is not reputation; but it is as good evidence as reputation."

But reputation is very weak evidence at the best of times.[3] The *raison d'être* for admitting reputation of this sort, which may be oral or documentary, was put thus by the court in *Boardman* v. *Lessees of Ford and Reed*:[4]

> "That boundaries may be proved by hearsay testimony is a rule well settled, and the necessity or propriety of which is not now to be questioned. Some difference of opinion may exist as to the application of this rule, but there can be none as to its legal force. Landmarks are frequently formed of perishable materials, which pass away with the generation in which they are made. By the improvement of the country and from other causes, they are often destroyed. It is therefore important in many cases that hearsay or reputation should be received to establish ancient boundaries."

Since evidence of this sort is admissible only where the general or public interest is concerned, it would only be useful in cases of private boundaries where they are defined by reference to public boundaries, such as the bounds of a parish.[5] Evidence of reputation formerly admissible at common law is now admissible under the Civil Evidence Act 1968.

Declarations of Deceased People

A most important exception to the rule against hearsay is that which admits the declarations of persons deceased.[6] Three types of declaration may be admitted:

(i) Declarations by deceased persons against pecuniary or proprietary interest, at the time the declaration was made, from personal knowledge of the facts.

---

3. See *per* LORD ELLENBOROUGH, C.J. in *Weeks* v. *Sparke* (1813), 1 M. & S. 679, at 687.
4. (1832), 6 Peter's Rep. 328, at 341 (U.S.A.).
5. *Thomas* v. *Jenkins* (1837), 6 Ad. & El. 525.
6. *R.* v. *Bliss* (1837), 7 Ad. & El. 550; *R.* v. *Berger*, [1894] 1 Q.B. 823.

So in *Doe d. Molesworth* v. *Sleeman*[7] declarations of a deceased person were admitted as to the boundaries of a manor. However, a deceased tenant's statement as to the boundaries of the demised property would not be admissible because a tenant may not derogate from his landlord's title.[8]

(ii) Declarations made in the course of duty by persons deceased.

An oral or written statement by a deceased person recorded in the course of his duty is admissible if made about the time of the fact recorded, and without ulterior motive. Such declarations are now admissible under s. 4 of the Civil Evidence Act 1968. In *Mellor* v. *Walmsley*[9] entries made by a deceased land surveyor in a field book during the course of his professional duties on a drainage survey were admitted as evidence of boundary.[10]

(iii) Declarations of deceased persons concerning public or general rights and interests.

To be admissible, such a declaration must have been made before any dispute arose, and it must be about either a public right or a general right, *i.e.*, one affecting a particular class or group of people. So, in the case of statements by a deceased tenant of a manor, they must relate to the rights of all the tenants and not merely to one tenant's right.[11] In the leading case on the subject[12] LORD CAMPBELL, C.J., explained the limitations to this exception:

> "The term 'interest' here does not mean that which is interesting from gratifying curiosity, or a love of information or amusement, but that in which a class of the community have a pecuniary interest, or some interest by which their legal rights or liabilities are affected. The admissibility of the declarations of deceased persons in such cases is sanctioned, because these rights and liabilities are general."

In *Evans* v. *Merthyr Tydfil Urban Council*,[13] for example, such evid-

---

7. (1846), 9 Q.B. 298.
8. *Papendick* v. *Bridgwater* (1855), 5 E. & B. 166.
9. [1905] 2 Ch. 164.
10. See *White* v. *Taylor*, [1969] 1 Ch. 150; [1967] 3 All E.R. 349.
11. *Earl of Dunraven* v. *Llewellyn* (1850), 15 Q.B. 791.
12. *R.* v. *Bedfordshire (Inhabitants)* (1855), 4 E. & B. 535, at 541.
13. [1899] 1 Ch. 241.

ence was admissible where the point at issue was whether a piece of land was a common or subject to commonable rights.

Various classes of documents not otherwise admissible may be receivable under this broad exception to the rule against hearsay, and the person making the statement need not necessarily have lived in the locality, provided he had knowledge of the facts.[14]

A recent and relevant case on the foregoing is *White* v. *Taylor*,[15] where, in an action concerning individual rights of pasturage for sheep, the plaintiffs sought to adduce in evidence a copy of a draft made by a deceased valuer under ss. 33 and 55 of the Tithe Act 1836, as being a document containing relevant statements made in the course of duty or of general rights or as being a public document. The valuer had no first-hand knowledge with regard to the sheep rights. He had merely recorded what he discovered on enquiry from others. The relevant record was not a record of what he himself did. BUCKLEY, J. held that the draft was not admissible under any of the three heads. The learned judge observed that this exception from the hearsay rule is to be narrowly confined.

---

14. *Duke of Newcastle* v. *Broxtowe Hundred* (1832), 4 B. & Ad. 273.
15. [1967] 3 All E.R. 349.

Chapter 6

THE LAW OF FENCES

"A fence may consist of almost any kind of enclosure or division, but a hedge, ditch, bank or wall will be most commonly found to answer that term." Woolrych, *Party Walls and Fences*, p. 281.

NO GENERAL LIABILITY

At common law there is no obligation upon a property owner to erect and maintain fences around his land, or even to delineate the boundaries of his property in any way:[1]

> "He may, if he please, leave his property open, and separated from the land of the neighbouring owner, by nothing but the ideal invisible boundary which exists in contemplation of law."[2]

In practice some barrier is desirable, not merely to mark the boundary visibly, but also as a guard against intrusion. This point seems to be overlooked by those in favour of open plan development which, although it may have amenity value, disregards the need to keep out trespassers, and particularly dogs and cats. There is not even any general liability to fence land adjoining the highway, and there are modern statutory restrictions in some cases.[3]

---

1. *Star* v. *Rookesby* (1710), 1 Salk. 335; *Churchill* v. *Evans* (1809), 1 Taunt. 529; *Boyle* v. *Tamlyn* (1827), 6 B. & C. 329; *Hilton* v. *Ankesson* (1872), 27 L.T. 519; *Lawrence* v. *Jenkins* (1873), L.R. 8 Q.B. 274; *Jones* v. *Price*, [1965] 2 Q.B. 618; [1965] 2 All E.R. 625.
2. Hunt, *Boundaries & Fences*, (6th Edn.), p. 58.
3. The principal statutory restriction is to be found in s. 194 of the Law of Property Act 1925. It is unlawful to erect fences on common land, *i.e.*, in this context land subject to rights of common on 1st January, 1926 (s. 194(3)), unless the consent of the Secretary of State for the Environment is obtained. In considering whether to grant consent the Secretary of State must be satisfied that it is for the benefit of the neighbourhood: see the Commons Act 1876, s. 10. On the application of a local authority or person with a legal interest in the land the County Court has power to order the removal of any fence constructed without consent.

Liability to fence may arise by statute, by agreement, or by prescription, but all these cases are exceptional. The general rule remains that a man may fence or not as he wishes. He cannot be compelled to do so unless legally bound by covenant or otherwise. The only common law liability to fence relates to the somewhat exceptional case of excavations on land adjoining the highway, and the ordinary duty of care owed by an occupier to his visitors, which may demand fencing on occasion. Both of these matters have been touched by statute.

OCCUPIER'S RESPONSIBILITY

The Occupiers' Liability Act 1957, imposes on the occupier of premises a duty of care towards his lawful visitors. By s. 2 (2) of the Act, this common duty of care is defined as being:

> "a duty to take such care as in all the circumstances of the case is reasonably necessary to see that the visitor will be reasonably safe in using the premises for the purposes for which he is permitted by the occupier to be there."

The duty of care is not exclusive:

> "If the occupier does work on his own land, he is under the same duty as a contractor. The reason is because the duty arises, not out of the fact of occupation but out of the fact that he is doing work which he knows or ought to know may bring danger to others; and that gives rise to a duty of care."[4]

It follows that in certain circumstances an occupier may have to fence in order to meet his obligations, and make himself safe from claims for breach of duty.[5]

EXCAVATIONS ADJOINING THE HIGHWAY

There is no obligation cast by the general law on owners of land adjoining a highway to make, maintain and keep up fences enclosing the land from the highway.[6] However, it is well established that there is

---

4. *Per* DENNING, L.J., in *Riden* v. *A. C. Billings & Sons, Ltd.*, [1957] 1 Q.B. 46, at 56.
5. For further discussion, see the books on tort, and *post*, pp. 129–391.
6. *Potter* v. *Perry* (1859), 23 J.P. 644.

liability at common law to erect a fence where there is an excavation on land adjacent or near to a public highway.[7] This duty has now been supplemented by s. 144 of the Highways Act 1959, which imposes an obligation upon an owner of land adjoining a street adequately to fence anything on his land which is a source of danger to users of the street.[8] The common law duty still remains and arises in nuisance.[9] The duty is cast upon the occupier,[10] and it is immaterial if it existed before he took over, although it extends only to dangers which are artificially created.[11] In *Nicholson* v. *Southern Rail. Co. and Sutton and Cheam U.D.C.*[12] the plaintiff was injured in falling off the highway, which had been constructed above the level of adjoining land. He brought an action against the railway company as occupier, and the council as highway authority, alleging that a nuisance had been created. In dismissing the claim against the occupier, BRANSON, J. said:

> "It seems to me that this is putting a new and intolerable burden upon the occupiers of land adjoining highways. No doubt the common law is very strict to ensure that land adjoining a highway should never be used or allowed to get into such a condition as to make it a nuisance to the highway. It is not necessary to refer in detail to a number of the well-known cases which have been cited in support of that proposition. It is enough to refer to *Barnes* v. *Ward*.[13] Wherever one looks

---

7. *Barnes* v. *Ward* (1850), 9 C.B. 392; *Hounsell* v. *Smyth* (1860), 7 C.B.N.S 731; *Hadley* v. *Taylor* (1865), L.R. 1 C.P. 53; *Ross* v. *Keith* (1888), 16 R. (Ct. of Sess.) 86.
8. *Infra*. The highway authority may also be liable at common law. So, in *Whyler* v. *Bingham R.D.C.*, [1901] 1 K.B. 45, the council removed a fence which their predecessors had erected to protect the public from a dangerous ditch. A road user drove into the ditch and was killed, and the highway authority was liable for misfeasance. *Cf. R.* v. *Whitney* (1835), 7 C. & P. 208. Whether the land is or is not part of the highway is a question of fact, but if it is it is repairable with the highway. See now the Highways (Miscellaneous Provisions) Act 1961, s. 1, *Griffiths* v. *Liverpool Corporation*, [1966] 2 All E.R. 1015 and *Meggs* v. *Liverpool Corporation*, [1963] 1 All E.R. 1137 explaining the present liability of highway authorities for non-repair of the highway.
9. *Binks* v. *South Yorks. Railway Co.* (1863), 3 B. & S. 244.
10. But if the owner has undertaken responsibility for fencing, he is liable as between himself and the occupier: *Payne* v. *Rogers* (1794), 2 Hy. Bl. 350.
11. *Sedleigh-Denfield* v. *O'Callaghan*, [1940] A.C. 880; [1940] 3 All E.R. 349; *A.-G.* v. *Roe*, [1915] 1 Ch. 235; *Morrison* v. *London, Midland and Scottish Rail. Co.*, 1929 S.C. 1.
12. [1935] 1 K.B. 558.
13. (1850), 9 C.B. 392.

in order to see what is the obligation of an adjoining owner, one finds this, that his obligation is not to allow his land to be used in such a way as to constitute a nuisance to the highway, or to those using the highway."

That duty can sometimes be fulfilled only by erecting an adequate fence.

STATUTORY OBLIGATIONS TO FENCE

HIGHWAYS

The principal statutory obligation to fence is imposed by s. 144 (1) of the Highways Act 1959, which supplements the occupier's common law liability in nuisance in respect of excavations on his land. It is cast in the following terms:

> "If, in or on any land adjoining a street, there is an unfenced or inadequately fenced source of danger to persons using the street, the local authority may, by notice to the owner or occupier of that land, require him within such time as may be specified in the notice, to execute such works of repair, protection, removal or enclosure as will obviate the danger."

"Street" is defined by s. 295 as including any highway, road, lane, footpath, square, court, alley or passage, whether a thoroughfare or not, and includes part of a street. There is a right of appeal to the magistrates' court against a notice served by the local authority under this provision. The local authority has default powers to carry out the necessary works and recover the costs involved from the person in default. Such a notice is commonly served where a building is being demolished, but is appropriate where there is any "source of danger".

In *Myers* v. *Harrow Corporation*[14] a Divisional Court held that on its true construction s. 144 (1) is descriptive of a danger in or on land and to which a person using the highway may be subjected by something coming off the land, or which he may encounter if he inadvertently steps off the highway. Consequently, the occupier was not liable to carry out works where the source of danger was a difference

14. [1962] 2, Q.B. 442; [1962] 1 All E.R. 876.

in level between the pavement and the adjoining land, because there was no danger "*in or on*" his land.[15]

Section 67 (2) of the 1959 Act authorises a highway authority to "provide and maintain, in a highway maintainable at the public expense by them, being a highway which consists of or comprises a carriageway, such raised paving, pillars, walls, rails or fences as they think necessary for the purpose of safeguarding persons using the highway". They *must* pay compensation to any person who has sustained damage by reason of the execution by them of works under this provision, e.g., where the claimant's premises have been made inaccessible to the public as the result of fencing provided under s. 67 (2).[16]

Under s. 43 of the Public Health Act 1961, a local authority may provide and maintain in a private street such pillars, rails or fences as they think necessary for the purpose of safeguarding persons using the street. Compensation is payable to any person who sustains damage as a result. Disputes arising out of a claim for compensation under the Highways Act 1959, (or under s. 43 of the 1961 Act) are in general to be determined, if the parties agree, by arbitration, or in default of agreement by the county court: ss. 266 and 267 of the 1959 Act, the proceedings being by way of originating application. Certain disputes as to compensation are made determinable by the Lands Tribunal by s. 266, notably those deriving from the exercise of planning powers.

Compensation is payable where damage is sustained by the carrying out of street works even though the damage is caused by a merely temporary instruction. Thus, for example, in *Lingké* v. *Christchurch Corporation*,[17] the defendants in the exercise of statutory authority laid down a sewer in the street, and a heap of earth thrown up from the excavation obstructed the access to the plaintiff's house and shop and interfered with her business. She was held entitled to recover com-

---

15. See also s. 143 of the Highways Act 1959, as to danger from barbed wire fencing: *post*, p. 140.
16. This provision may be wider than at first sight appears. The compensation provisions in the Highways Act 1959, in relation to consequential loss are very odd. It may sometimes be possible to argue that damage was suffered as a result of fencing provided under s. 67 (2), and not to street works carried out under ss. 44 or 64 of the Highways Act 1959, for example, since these latter sections contain no provision for compensation.
17. [1912] 3 K.B. 595.

pensation under the appropriate statutory provisions, the Court of Appeal emphasising that a person is not disentitled to compensation merely because the state of affairs causing loss is temporary, provided it continues for more than a merely negligible time.

RAILWAYS

Section 68 of the Railways Clauses Consolidation Act 1845, imposed upon railway undertakers acquiring land compulsorily an obligation to erect and maintain fences in perpetuity. This obligation is expressed in the following terms:

> "... to erect and maintain sufficient posts, rails, hedges, ditches, mounds, or other fences, for separating the land taken for the use of the railway from the adjoining lands not taken, and protecting such lands from trespass, or the cattle of the owners or occupiers therefore from straying thereout, by reason of the railway".[18]

The duty now devolves upon the British Railways Board and the London Transport Board as successors to the old Railway companies.

Liability to fence does not come to an end merely because the railway line is enclosed. It lasts until the railway line itself is removed, and this can be of considerable practical importance in the case of property bounded by a disused railway line. The original undertakers could obtain release from this obligation to fence by paying compensation to owners and occupiers. Where such a release was made the fact will normally be stated in the conveyance of the land to the company. Inquiries about such matters should be addressed to the Estate and Rating Surveyor of the appropriate regional Board.[19] The payment of compensation to the owner of the land did not discharge the duty owed towards the occupier.[20]

---

18. See *R.* v. *Brown* (1867), 2. L.R.Q.B. 630; *Bessant* v. *Great Western Rail. Co.* (1860), 8 C.B.N.S. 368. The sort of fence to be erected depends on the existing use of the adjoining lands.
19. The addresses of the six Regional Boards are:—
    Eastern Railway Board, Liverpool Street Station, London, E.C.2.
    London Midland Railway Board, Euston House, Eversholt Street, London, N.W.1.
    North Eastern Railway Board, Railway Headquarters Offices, York.
    Scottish Railway Board, 200 West Regent Street, Glasgow C.2.
    Southern Railway Board, Waterloo Station, London, S.E.1.
    Western Railway Board, Paddington Station, London, W.2.
    The inquiry should be accompanied by a plan showing the parish and Ordnance Survey numbers of the land in question. A production fee may be payable.
20. *Corry* v. *Great Western Rail. Co.* (1881), 7 Q.B.D. 322.

The interpretation of s. 68 and the nature and extent of the Board's obligation can give rise to some difficulties. It is quite clear, however, that the land which is to be protected from trespassers is the land which is *not* taken for railway use, i.e., the land of adjoining owners and occupiers. The words "protecting *such lands* from trespass" necessarily refer back to the words "adjoining lands not taken". The obligation is owed to the owners and occupiers of adjoining lands and not to the public at large.[1]

The obligation to make and maintain fences under this provision is without limitation in point of time, although s. 68 made provision for the original companies to pay compensation in return for a release from their fencing obligations where the vendor agreed. Where no release was granted, the obligation lasts in perpetuity and is not extinguished merely because of the closure of the line. It continues until the railway line itself is removed.

The fencing obligation binds the Board to the same extent as it if were bound by prescription at common law.[2] It has been held to extend to the licensees of occupiers.[3] The duty is a two-fold one: firstly to protect adjoining lands from trespassers, whether human or animal; and secondly, to prevent the cattle of the adjoining owner or occupier from straying on to the line. It is thought, however, that this latter obligation is necessarily co-extensive with the former.

What sort of fence must the Board provide and maintain? The answer to this question is to be found by looking at the decided cases. The fence must be sufficient to resist the ordinary acts of cattle and to prevent them from straying on to the line from the adjoining land.[4] In *Bessant* v. *Great Western Rail. Co.*,[5] which is concerned with the standard of the obligation, Bessant pastured his sheep in a field adjoining the railway, using the quickset hedge forming the company's fence as one side of his fold. Some of the sheep escaped through a small hole in the hedge, got on to the line, and were killed. It was held that the company was liable, and that it was not a misdirection to tell the jury

---

1. *Buxton* v. *North-Eastern Rail. Co.* (1868), L.R. 3 Q.B.D. 549; *Parkinson* v. *Garstang and Knott End Rail. Co.*, [1910] 1 K.B. 615.
2. *Manchester, Sheffield and Lincs. Rail. Co.* v. *Wallis* (1854), 14 C.B. 213.
3. *Dawson* v. *Midland Railway Co.* (1872), L.R. 8 Exch. 8.
4. *Page* v. *Great Eastern Rail. Co.* (1871) 24 L.T. 585; *Bessant* v. *Great Western Rail. Co.* (1860) 8 C.B. N.S. 368.
5. (1860) 8 C.B. N.S. 368.

that under s. 68 the company were bound to keep their fences sufficiently strong to prevent sheep and cattle from straying out of the adjoining lands, the jury having found as a fact that the fence was insufficient.

However, there is one immediate difficulty, and this is to be found by considering the sketch and specifications of the British Railways standard form of fence. This is of post and wire construction, made from sound recovered railway sleepers impregnated with creosote. The straining posts are normally 7 ft. 2 ins. in height (increased to 8 ft. 6 ins. in unstable ground), and with either five or seven strands of wire. Probably, this type of construction is sufficient in most normal circumstances, but it is submitted that it is not necessarily sufficient in all cases.

This argument depends upon the meaning to be given to the word "cattle". At common law, the term "cattle" is synonymous with the old word "avers" and includes, horses, oxen, sheep, swine, asses, goats, domestic fowls, geese, ducks, and (probably) turkeys and peacocks. It follows that small animals such as lambs and piglets are included, as well as poultry. A fence of the standard construction would not necessarily be sufficient against "cattle" of this sort.

As the Railway Board's liability is co-extensive with the common law liability arising by prescription, it is submitted that the fence should be of sufficient standard to prevent poultry, and small animals, from wandering off or onto adjoining land. This is supported by *Child* v. *Hearn*,[6] which is a case on s. 68. The fence there was sufficient against oxen, horses and sheep; but there was enough space between the lowest rail of the fence and the ground for pigs to crawl through, and the pigs had in fact crawled under the fence and were killed on the line. It was held that the word "cattle" in s. 68 included pigs, and that the fence was, therefore, insufficient.

One modern case on s. 68, is *Cooper* v. *Railway Executive*,[7] where some cows were separated from their calves. During the night, the cows, anxious to rejoin their calves, broke down the railway fence which was in good repair and as strong as an ordinary farm fence, and three of them were killed by a train which was derailed on impact. The owners' claim for damages for breach of s. 68 was dismissed by DEVLIN, J., who awarded damages on the Railway Executive's

6. (1874) L.R. 9 Exch. 176.
7. [1953] 1 All E.R. 477. See also *Short* v. *British Railways Board*, [1974] 3 All E.R. 28

counterclaim for cattle trespass. Of course, the ratio here was simply that the quality of the fencing was sufficient to prevent cattle straying in normal circumstances, and that these particular cattle were acting unusually or else using exceptional force.

The point about the sufficiency or otherwise of the standard fence must, therefore, await judicial determination, but it is not without interest. Moreover, as another limb of the duty is to protect adjoining lands from trespass (*supra*), it would seem doubtful whether a fence of the standard pattern is proof against trespassers. At the same time, the statutory obligation must be interpreted reasonably, and the absence of litigation suggests that this problem is probably resolved by negotiation between the Railways Board and adjoining owners and occupiers.

If the land taken for railway purposes is adjacent to the highway, the duty is to fence the railway against cattle belonging to people lawfully using the road,[8] and not as against cattle straying on to the highway. There is no obligation to fence one part of railway property from another,[9] unless this is necessary for the protection of people lawfully using the property, *i.e.*, the ordinary duty owed by an occupier to his visitors. This is because the obligation imposed by s. 68 of the 1845 Act exists only between the railway company and the owners and occupiers of adjoining land. Of course, if cattle get on to the line through a defect in any fence which the railway company is bound to maintain, there will be liability for consequential damage.[10]

Additional liability attaches to the railway companies (and their successors) in connection with level crossings. Section 47 of the 1845 Act deals with public crossings in this way:

> "If the railway cross any turnpike road or public carriage road on a level, the company shall erect and at all times maintain good and sufficient gates across such road, on each side of the railway, where the same shall communicate therewith, and shall employ proper persons to open and shut such gates; and such gates shall be kept constantly closed across such road on both sides of the railway, except during the time when the (road traffic) passing along the same shall have to cross such railway."

---

8. *Manchester, Sheffield and Lincolnshire Rail. Co.* v, *Wallis* (1854), 14 C.B. 213; *Midland Rail. Co.* v. *Daykin* (1855), 17 C.B. 126.
9. *Roberts* v. *Great Western Rail. Co.* (1858), 4. C.B.N.S. 506; *Marfell* v. *South Wales Rail. Co.* (1860), 8 C.B.N.S. 525.
10. *Sharrod* v. *London Northern Western Rail. Co.* (1849), 4 Exch. 580.

To-day the gates at level crossings are more often than not operated automatically. The basic duty of care—owed to the public generally—remains the same. The British Railways Board are not insurers, but they are under a duty to take reasonable care in all the circumstances to see that the level crossing is safe. The general principles of negligence apply and, broadly speaking, all depends on the particular facts.[11]

MINES, QUARRIES AND TIPS

The Mines and Quarries Act 1954,[12] imposes a duty to fence on the owner of every abandoned mine, or mine that has not been worked for 12 months. The duty is to ensure that the surface entrance of every shaft or outlet is provided with a fence sufficient to prevent any person from accidentally falling down the shaft. There may also be liability in respect of injured animals. In *Groucott* v. *Williams*[13] for example, the defendant had mineral rights under the plaintiff's land and had sunk a mine shaft to work the concession. When he ceased to work the mine, he covered the shaft over insufficiently, and was held liable when the plaintiff's mare fell down the ill-fenced shaft and was killed.[14]

An unfenced shaft or outlet to a mine is a statutory nuisance for the purposes of Part III of the Public Health Act 1936, and may be dealt with summarily. In particular, there will be a statutory nuisance where a quarry (whether being worked or not) is not provided with an efficient and properly maintained barrier, and by reason of its accessibility from a highway or place of public resort it constitutes a danger to members of the public.[15]

The Mines and Quarries (Tips) Act 1969 makes provisions in relation to tips associated with mines and quarries to prevent disused

---

11. The duty imposed by s. 47 does not extend to crossings on private railways: *Matson* v. *Baird* (1878), 3 App. Cas. 1082. The more important cases are: *Gray* v. *North Eastern Rail. Co.* (1883), 48 L.T. 904; *Charman* v. *South Eastern Rail. Co.* (1888), 21 Q.B.D. 524; *Smith* v. *South Eastern Rail. Co.*, [1896] 1 Q.B. 178. See also *Law* v. *Railway Executive* (1949), 65 T.L.R. 251 where a subway replacing a level crossing was held governed by the same principles.
12. Section 151, replacing earlier statutory provisions.
13. (1863), 32 L.J.Q.B. 237.
14. See also *Hawken* v. *Shearer* (1887), 56 L.J.Q.B. 284.
15. See s. 92 of the Public Health Act 1936, as to the procedure, including the recovery of expenses from the person in default.

tips constituting a danger to members of the public. "Tip" is defined by s. 2 to mean, *inter alia*, an accumulation or deposit of refuse from a mine or quarry which is above ground. A distinction is drawn between "active tips" and "closed tips," but the provisions of the Act apply to both types. Section I requires that tips shall be made and kept secure, and gives power to make regulations to ensure that this is done.

ECCLESIASTICAL LANDS

(a) *Glebe or parsonage lands*

Glebe lands are those attached to an ecclesiastical benefice as part of its endowment. By virtue of the Ecclesiastical Dilapidations Measures 1923–1951, the incumbent for the time being is bound to repair and maintain the fences surrounding the glebe land of the parish. He may take estovers for that purpose but he may not otherwise cut down trees in the churchyard without the consent of the diocesan dilapidations board.[16] The main provision as to the repair of fences is set out in s. 4 (2) of the 1923 Measure.

(b) *Churchyards and Burial Grounds*

The Cemeteries Clauses Act 1847[17] imposes on cemetery companies a duty to enclose every part of their cemeteries by walls or other sufficient means of enclosure of prescribed materials and dimensions, and to keep these walls and fences in good repair. In the absence of special materials and dimensions, the duty is met by the erection of substantial walls or iron railings of at least 8 ft. in height.[18]

Local authorities are expressly relieved from this liability to fence where they provide a burial ground under the Public Health (Interments) Act 1879.[19] However, s. 16 of the latter Act imposes on them a positive duty to keep the cemetery and its buildings and fences in good order and condition. Cemetery authorities are otherwise subject to the normal duties of owners and occupiers.

---

16. See E. Garth Moore, *English Canon Law* (1966), p. 101. Where trees are felled with permission, and the wood is not used to repair the church, etc., the proceeds of sale must be devoted to that purpose.
17. Section 15.
18. See M. R. Russell Davies, *Burial and Cremation*, (2nd Edn.), p. 52.
19. By s. 10 of the Burial Act 1900.

The obligation continues in the case of disused burial grounds, and the parochial church council or other authority remains responsible for the upkeep of the boundary walls and fences.[20] By custom, the duty to maintain a particular churchyard wall or fence may fall upon the incumbent or a local landowner.

LIABILITY TO FENCE BY PRESCRIPTION AND GRANT

The obligation to fence may be created by prescription, and the law on the subject was stated with great clarity by ARCHIBALD, J. in *Lawrence* v. *Jenkins*:[1]

> "At common law the owners of adjoining closes are not bound to fence either against or for the benefit of each other; but, in the absence of fences, each owner is bound to prevent his cattle or other animals from trespassing on his neighbour's premises. By prescription, however, a landowner may be bound to maintain a fence on his land for the benefit of the occupier of the adjoining close. This obligation is described by Gale in his work on *Easements* as in the nature of a spurious easement affecting the land of the party who is bound to maintain the fence."

The relevant law relating to this "spurious easement" or "quasi-easement"[2] is usefully summarised in a more recent edition of Gale than that referred to by the learned judge:[3]

> "Anomalously, however, the courts have recognised what has been called a prescriptive obligation on the owners and occupiers of a piece of land to maintain a fence thereon for the benefit of the owners and occupiers of adjoining land. This obligation has been established by proof of long usage under which the quasi-servient owner or occupier has consistently repaired the fence when told to do so by the quasi-dominant owner or occupier, and therefore inferentially in performance of a binding obligation."

In *Lawrence* v. *Jenkins*[4] the facts were that a cow belonging to the

---

20. See the definition of disused burial ground in s. 4 of the Open Spaces Act 1887. *Cf.*, s. 18 of the Burial Act 1855 and the Parochial Church Councils (Powers) Measure 1921.
1. (1873), L.R. 8 Q.B. 274, at 278.
2. *Jones* v. *Price*, [1965] 2 Q.B. 618; [1965] 2 All E.R. 625.
3. Gale on *Easements*, (13th Edn.), pp. 33–34. The obligation is of great antiquity and formerly was enforceable by the writ *de curia claudenda*.
4. (1873), L.R. 8 Q.B. 274. See also *Anon.* (1675), 1 Vent. 274; *Star* v. *Rookesby* (1710), 1 Salk. 335; *Rooth* v. *Wilson* (1817), 1 B. & Ald. 59; *Boyle* v. *Tamlyn* (1827), 6 B. & C. 329; *Powell* v. *Salisbury* (1828), 2 Y. & J. 391; *Coaker* v. *Willcocks*, [1911] 2 K.B. 124.

plaintiff strayed on to the defendant's land through a gap in the hedge which had been caused by the defendant felling a tree. The cow ate the foliage of a yew tree on the defendant's land and died as a result. The defendant and his predecessors in title had repaired the fence for more than forty years, and for the previous nineteen years had repaired on notice from the plaintiff, who owned the adjoining land. It was found on these facts that there was a prescriptive obligation on the defendant to repair the fence, and accordingly the plaintiff was able to recover. It was pointed out that, at common law, the owners of adjoining closes are not bound to fence either against, or for the benefit of, each other. However, by prescription a landowner might be bound to maintain a fence for the benefit of the occupier of the adjoining close, as was established here on the basis of forty years' repairing as a matter of obligation. When such a prescriptive right exists, the obligation to maintain the fence is absolute. The servient owner is under a duty to maintain the fence without notice to repair it and, except in the case of damage by Act of God, he is liable for the consequence of the fence being in disrepair.[5]

It is doubtful whether this liability is a true easement because it involves the servient owner in a duty to take positive action and, in all probability, to incur expenditure.[6] However, Gale suggests that the right—or "quasi-easement"—would be enforceable against a subsequent purchaser without notice in the same way as an easement. What must be shown is that the fence has been maintained and repaired by the occupier[7] as a matter of obligation. It is not sufficient to show that the occupier of the "servient tenement" has repaired the fence in the interest of containing his own animals.[8] The fact that the repairs were done at the request of the occupier of the "dominant" tenement is

---

5. The plaintiff in *Lawrence* v. *Jenkins* (1873), L.R. 8 Q.B. 274 would, of course, have been able to resist a claim for cattle trespass at common law, and would now be able to resist a claim based on s. 4 of the Animals Act 1971, as to which see *infra*, pp. 119–121.
6. It is therefore unique, because other rights cannot be easements if they involve expenditure by the servient owner: *Regis Property Co., Ltd.* v. *Redman*, [1956] 2 Q.B. 612; [1956] 2 All E.R. 335, C.A.
7. *Cheetham* v. *Hampson* (1791), 4 Term Rep. 318. There is no obligation on the owner out of occupation.
8. *Jones* v. *Price*, [1965] 2 Q.B. 618, at 634–636. It *must* be shown that the fence was maintained as a matter of obligation towards the adjoining owner: *Egerton* v. *Harding*, [1974] 3 All E.R. 689.

highly significant,[9] although perhaps this is not the only method of proving the existence of the obligation.[10]

In *Boyle* v. *Tamlyn*,[11] which is a relevant and instructive case, BAYLEY, J. said that "the right to have a fence repaired by the adjoining proprietor is in the nature of a grant of a distinct easement affecting the land of the grantor". The true position is that an obligation to fence as a "spurious" or "quasi-easement" can arise by prescription or lost modern grant: it is a private right and obligation between adjoining landowners.[12]

The passage from Gale of which the foregoing quotation forms part received judicial approval in *Jones* v. *Price*[13] when *Lawrence* v. *Jenkins*[14] was considered and distinguished. The relevant law has been considered by the Court of Appeal very recently in *Egerton* v. *Harding*[15]. In both *Jones* v. *Price*[13] and *Egerton* v. *Harding*[15] the nature of this anomalous prescriptive right and the evidentiary difficulties surrounding it were fully explored, with extensive citation of both academic and judicial authorities. The problem was also considered by the Court of Appeal in *Crow* v. *Wood*,[16] and it is now clear that the "quasi-easement" of fencing may come into existence by immemorial user[17] or prescription, by last modern grant[18] or by express grant.[19] The three most recent cases will be considered in turn.

In *Jones* v. *Price*[20] a hedge formed the boundary between two Welsh farming properties. Through a gap in one length of it sheep belonging to one of the parties had trespassed on the property of the other. By way of defence to the plaintiff's claim for cattle trespass, the defendant

---

9. *Lawrence* v. *Jenkins* (1873), L.R. 8 Q.B. 274; and *per* WILLMER, L.J. in *Jones* v. *Price*, [1965] 2 Q.B. 618, at 645.
10. *Boyle* v. *Tamlyn* (1827), 6 B. & C. 329; *Barber* v. *Whiteley* (1865), 34 L.J.Q.B. 212; *Jones* v. *Price*, [1965] 2 Q.B. 618, at 636.
11. (1827), 6 B. & C. 329, at 339.
12. *Egerton* v. *Harding*, [1974] 3 All E.R. 689.
13. [1965] 2. Q.B. 618; [1965] 2 All E.R. 625.
14. (1873), L.R. 8 Q.B. 274.
15. *Supra.*
16. [1971] 1 Q.B. 77; [1970] 3 All E.R. 425.
17. *Lawrence* v. *Jenkins* (1873), L.R. 8 Q.B. 274; *Jones* v. *Price*, [1965] 2 Q.B. 618, pp. 634–636.
18. *Barber* v. *Whiteley*, (1865), 34 L.J.Q.B. 212; *Godfrey* v. *Godfrey* E.Y.B. 10 Ed. IV. 18; *Egerton* v. *Harding* [1974] 3 All E.R. 689.
19. *Crow* v. *Wood*, [1971] 1 Q.B. 77; [1970] 3 All E.R. 425; *Egerton* v. *Harding*, *supra.*
20. [1965] 2 Q.B. 618; [1965] 2 All E.R. 625.

alleged that there existed in favour of his property a prescriptive obligation to repair the part of the hedge in question. Evidence showed that repairs to the hedge had been carried out by the plaintiff and his predecessors in title, but there was no evidence that this had been done on demand by, or as a matter of obligation to, the defendant and his predecessors. The acts of repair extended back over half a century. If the plaintiff was under an obligation to fence, by prescription or otherwise, he would have no cause of action for cattle trespass.[1] On the facts the Court of Appeal held that no prescriptive obligation was established. No contractual obligation could be inferred. The headnote in a contemporary law report summarises the decision with exactitude:[2]

> "Although the law recognise[s] that a legal obligation on a servient tenement can exist for the benefit of an adjoining tenement that a boundary hedge on the servient tenement should be kept in repair by the occupier of the servient tenement, . . . no such prescriptive obligation could be established in the present case from the evidence of acts of repair, because these did not show that the repairs had been done as a matter of obligation on the part of the owner or occupier of the plaintiff's farm as servient tenement towards the owner or occupier of the defendant's farm as dominant tenement".[3]

Jones v. *Price* is of importance because of the discussion of the interesting question as to this "spurious easement" and the sort of evidence necessary to establish such a prescriptive right. As far as the latter is concerned, it seems essentially a question of fact, and little can be gleaned from the conflicting authorities. The obligation is not covered by the Prescription Act 1832.[4] The growth and uncertain nature of the obligation was well-described by DIPLOCK, L.J. in *Jones* v. *Price*. This right, he said:

> "is of very ancient origin and was originally enforceable by the writ *de curia claudenda*. It is by no means clear whether such an obligation can today be newly created so as to run with the land except by Act of Parliament. It can undoubtedly exist by immemorial usage. It is

1. Similarly, he would now be able to resist a claim based on statutory liability for straying livestock under s. 4 of the Animals Act 1971. See North, *The Modern Laws of Animals*, (1972), Chapter 4.
2. [1965] 2 All E.R. 625.
3. Prescriptive liability to "fence against the common" was admitted in *Coaker* v. *Willcocks*, [1911] 2 K.B. 124, although the extent of the liability was contested there. Now, the position is that once an immemorial usage of "fencing against the common" is established, the duty is to fence proved, provided always it can be shown that such a duty could have arisen from a lawful origin: *Egerton* v. *Harding*, [1974] 3 All E.R. 689.
4. *Peter* v. *Daniel* (1848), 5 C.B. 568, *per* WILLIAMS, J.

tempting to think that its real origin lies in local custom, but this origin was rejected in 1670 in *Polus* v. *Henstock*.[5] The rationalisation which has been current since then is that it can arise by prescription at common law, from which it must follow that in theory it is capable of being created by covenant or grant. In 1827 the Court of King's Bench was prepared to assume that it could be created by covenant (see *Boyle* v. *Tamlyn*);[6] but since it is a positive obligation this assumption cannot survive the decision of the Court of Appeal in *Austerberry* v. *Oldham Corporation*.[7] It was not in any event easy to reconcile with *Spencer's Case*.[8] In theory, therefore, it can lie only in grant. There is no precedent in the books for such a grant. I find it difficult to envisage its form. It would be interesting to consider whether the doctrine of lost modern grant is applicable to such an obligation, as well as the common law prescription. Most inclosures and their boundary hedges can be proved to have been created after 1189, so that if the obligation exists at all, it must be by virtue of a lost modern grant."[9]

In deciding what evidence is necessary to establish a prescriptive obligation to repair a fence or maintain a hedge, the older authorities are difficult to reconcile. The judgment of WILLMER, L.J. in *Jones* v. *Price*[10] is particularly helpful on this point, for he analysed carefully the two conflicting lines of authority. Thus, on the one hand in *Lawrence* v. *Jenkins*[11] there was evidence that the defendant and his predecessors in title had repaired a dividing fence for more than forty years, whenever repairs were called for. For the last nineteen years he had done this on request from the plaintiff and his predecessors. This was held sufficient to establish a prescriptive obligation to fence, and it has been suggested that it is sufficient to prove merely that the defendant has consistently carried out repairs for the required period in order to establish liability.[12]

5. (1670), 1 Vent. 97. But see *infra*, p. 108.
6. (1827), 6 B. & C. 329.
7. (1885), 29 Ch.D. 750.
8. (1583), 5 Co. Rep. 16a.
9. Further discussion of the status of this "spurious easement" is found in *Crow* v. *Wood*, [1971] 1 Q.B. 77; [1970] 3 All E.R. 425 and most recently in *Egerton* v. *Harding* [1974] 3 All E.R. 689.
10. [1965] 2 Q.B. 618.
11. (1873), L.R. 8 Q.B. 274.
12. Glanville Williams, *Liability for Animals*, 1939, pp. 203–226. A dictum of EDMUND DAVIES, L.J. where, relying on Williams, he said that whatever the legal basis of the duty to fence, the balance of authorities for centuries favoured the view that the obligation arose, when it existed, from proof that land was accustomed to be fenced and it was immaterial that the party had voluntarily fenced his premises for his own protection was expressly disapproved *per curiam* in *Egerton* v. *Harding* [1974] 3 All E.R. 689.

The court did not agree with this view in *Jones* v. *Price*:[14]

> "It seems to me that it is not open for us to accept this view unless we are prepared to say that *Hilton* v. *Ankesson*[13] was wrongly decided. That is a decision which has stood now for nearly one hundred years, and I am unaware that until this case it has ever been questioned in any subsequent case."[14]

It must be shown that the fence is maintained as a matter of obligation towards the adjoining owner.[15]

In *Hilton* the defendant and his predecessors had maintained a fence for fifty years or more, but this was held insufficient to found a prescriptive obligation. KELLY, C.B. thought that had the repairs been carried out on request, the matter might have gone to the jury.

This leads one to speculate that repairs must have been carried out on request in order to found a prescriptive claim. This is an attractive proposition, but was not upheld by the Court of Appeal in *Jones* v. *Price*, although counsel for the plaintiff urged the point. It may be a vital factor in one case, but it is not necessarily conclusive; each fact situation must be considered on its own merits in light of the surrounding circumstances. There is no general rule at all save that in order to establish a prescriptive right to have a fence maintained by an adjoining owner it must be shown that the repairs were carried out as a matter of duty.[16]

A prescriptive obligation to fence will be difficult to establish. By analogy, one may perhaps refer to acts of ownership such as trimming a hedge, cleaning out a ditch and so on, which may in some cases support a possessory claim under the Limitation Act 1939. In brief such acts are not conclusive because they might be done merely for convenience, and not under any right or obligation.

In *Crow* v. *Wood*[17] the Court of Appeal was provided with a further opportunity of determining the status of the "spurious" or "quasi-easement" of fencing and of confirming that the right to such an "easement" (or quasi-easement) can be acquired by grant. *Crow* v. *Wood*[17]

---

13. (1872), 27 L.T. 519.
14. [1965] 2 All E.R. 625, at 631, *per* WILLMER, L.J.
15. *Egerton* v. *Harding* [1974] 3 All E.R. 689; *Hilton* v. *Ankesson* (1872), 27 L.T. 519.
16. *Egerton* v. *Harding*, *supra*.
17. [1971] 1 Q.B. 77; [1970] 3 All E.R. 425. See (1971) 87 L.Q.R. 13.

emphasises that the right can be newly created, but like all the other reported cases hitherto, is concerned with an obligation to fence against animals. It is not, in fact, clear whether the obligation is limited in this way, and it is respectfully submitted that in future the right might well be extended by judicial interpretation to fencing for other purposes, *e.g.*, for amenity against trespassers.

The facts of *Crow* v. *Wood*[17] were that the plaintiff and the defendant had farms on Bilsdale West Moor in the North Riding of Yorkshire. For many years the defendant had had the right to graze forty sheep on the moor, and the plaintiff had the same right in respect of 130 sheep. In addition, the plaintiff kept cattle on an enclosed area of her farm. The moor and the farms had a common owner, the farms being sold off to individual farmers. Each conveyance conferred a right for each farmer to stray a number of sheep on the moor, and similar rights had been contained in the leases under which each farm was previously held. This was the basis of the rights of each party. Despite the trouble the plaintiff had taken to keep her cattle in and the sheep out, the defendant's grazing sheep had strayed from the moor onto the plaintiff's farm. For many years there had been a custom of the moor that each farmer fenced his farm to keep out the sheep and, when sued by the plaintiff for cattle trespass, the defendant pleaded that the plaintiff was bound to repair her walls so as to keep out the sheep. The Court of Appeal found unanimously for the defendant.

The Court considered that it was not necessary to decide whether the "easement of fencing" is or is not a true easement. The Court of Appeal held that it it is a right in the nature of an easement, capable of being granted by law so as to run with the land and be binding on successors in title. The obligation was thus extended from the area of prescription into that of implied grant. The right is one which is within s. 62 (1) of the Law of Property Act 1925 and is a right which passes on a conveyance of the land as being an easement, right or advantage, appertaining or reputed to appertain to the land. In reaching this conclusion the Court applied its own decision in *Wright* v. *Macadam*[18] and, it is submitted, it follows that the right can also be the subject of express grant.[19]

---

18. [1949] 2 K.B. 744; [1949] 2 All E.R. 565. It is prudent to curtail the effect of s. 62 (1) by conditions of sale.
19. Lord Denning, M.R. pointed out that the custom of the moor was very important. It established that the advantage of being able to make another farmer fence was something which appertained to each plot.

The Court of Appeal summarised the position in this way:

> "A right to have your neighbour keep up the fences is a right in the nature of an easement which is capable of being granted by law so as to run with the land and to be binding on successors. It is a right which lies in grant and is of such a nature that it can pass under s. 62 of the Law of Property Act 1925".[20]

The most recent decision in this area is that of the Court of Appeal in *Egerton* v. *Harding*,[1] which establishes that once an immemorial usage of fencing against a common as a matter of obligation is established, the duty to fence is proved, provided that it can be shown that such a duty could have arisen from a lawful origin. In *Egerton* v. *Harding* the defendant's farm and the plaintiff's cottage adjoined Binswood Common in Hampshire. Both parties had grazing rights over the common. The plaintiff did not exercise her rights, but the defendant had grazed cattle on the common since 1968. In August, 1971, some of the cattle strayed off the common and into the plaintiff's garden through a blackthorn hedge which was no longer stock-proof. The plaintiff sued for damages for cattle trespass at common law; the defendant claimed that she was under a duty to fence her land against the common.

The trial judge found that by custom a liability existed in owners of land adjoining the common to fence against cattle lawfully on the common and that it was for the defendant to prove the existence of such a duty, which he had done. He also found that there was no evidence of enclosure, grant or presumption of lost modern grant, and dismissed the plaintiff's claim. The plaintiff appealed and attacked the trial judge's positive finding of custom. The Court of Appeal dismissed the appeal, holding that the judge, having found as a fact immemorial usage, could not be faulted for attributing it to custom. In fact, their lordships said, it was not necessary to go so far: once immemorial usage was established, a lawful origin of usage was to be presumed, provided a lawful origin was possible.

Scarman, L.J., giving the judgment of the Court, pointed out that an obligation to fence as a "spurious" easement could arise by prescription or lost modern grant. It was a private right and obligation between neighbouring landowners. His lordship emphasised that the easement, whether spurious or genuine, owed nothing to custom, from which it

---

20. [1971] 1 Q.B. 77, at 84–85.
1. [1974] 3 All E.R. 689.

was totally distinct. Custom, which is local law, displaces within its own locality the common law, whereas an easement is a private right enforceable by the general law. In the present case, the defendant could not establish a right in the nature of an easement because there was no evidence of any enclosure of the plaintiff's cottage, nor any evidence directly implicating its occupiers of prescriptive right or lost modern grant.

There was evidence, his lordship said that for a number of years the occupiers of the cottage had maintained the hedge in a stock-proof condition but there was no indication as to whether this was done voluntarily or as a matter of obligation towards the common. This evidence was insufficient because, so the Court held, it has to be shown that the fence was maintained as a matter of obligation towards the adjoining owner.[2] Their lordships agreed with the trial judge that the defendant had failed to establish that the cottage was subject to an easement of fencing against the common. The matter did not end there: the Court of Appeal turned to the judge's finding of custom and considered the plaintiff's argument that a duty to fence could not be derived from custom, based on dicta in both *Jones* v. *Price*[3] and *Crow* v. *Wood.*[4] The Court of Appeal concluded that these *obiter* statements were historically unsound.[5] Moreover, in the Court's opinion, once an immemorial usage of fencing was established, the duty to fence was proved, provided that it could be shown that such a duty could have had a lawful origin.[6] The evidence was sufficient to enable the trial judge to reach the conclusion which he had reached, and accordingly the Court of Appeal dismissed the plaintiff's appeal and upheld the defendant's argument.

---

2. *Jones* v. *Price*, [1965] 2 Q.B. 618, at 635, *per* WILLMER, L.J., applying *Hilton* v. *Ankesson* (1972), 27 L.T. 519 and disapproving a dictum of EDMUND DAVIES, L.J. in *Crow* v. *Wood*, [1971] 1 Q.B. 77, at 87, where, relying on passages in Glanville Williams's, *Liability for Animals*, pp. 203, 208, he said that it was immaterial that a party had voluntarily fenced for his own protection.
3. [1965] 2 Q.B. 618; [1965] 2 All E.R. 625.
4. [1971] 1 Q.B. 77; [1970] 3 All E.R. 425.
5. *Polus* v. *Henstock* (1670), 1 Vent. 97, which was cited in the earlier cases, was authority only that an easement or right akin to an easement which was limited to a particular boundary could not arise by custom. It did not decide that within a manor there could be no custom to fence against the waste of the manor.
6. *L.N.W.R.* v. *Commissioners of Fobbing Levels Sewers Commissioners* (1896), L.T. 629, *per* WILLS, J. at 632.

Where a prescriptive or analogous obligation to fence—or to maintain a fence—is proved, the quasi-servient owner will be liable if his neighbour's cattle escape and suffer damage.[7] He will also be liable if injury is caused to anyone because of the defective state of the fence.[8]

DUTY ARISING BY AGREEMENT

Liability to fence may arise by covenant or agreement.[9] A contractual obligation to maintain a boundary fence does not run with the land; it binds only the parties to the contract.[10] The cases of freehold and leasehold land must be considered separately.

FREEHOLD LAND

A covenant in a freehold conveyance to erect and maintain a fence, or to share the expense of erection and maintenance, is not enforceable against the successors in title of the covenantor. The burden of a positive covenant does not run with the land either at law or in equity,[11] although the benefit will run. Only the original covenantor is bound by a positive covenant. He remains liable on the covenant by privity of contract, and in practice on a subsequent sale will take an indemnity from the purchaser who will usually comply with the obligation. The value of a covenant to fence is considerable, but there is no way of ensuring *direct* enforcement as against subsequent purchasers. Even if the covenant contains positive and negative obligations, only the restrictive part will run with the land.[12]

This is the central problem in the enforceability of fencing covenants, and while the prudent convenantor will probably take an indemnity

---

7. *Lawrence* v. *Jenkins* (1863), L.R. 8 Q.B. 274; *Crow* v. *Wood*, [1971] 1 Q.B. 77; [1970] 3 All E.R. 425.
8. *Barber* v. *Whiteley* (1865), 34 L.J.Q.B. 212; *Holgate* v. *Bleazard*, [1917] 1 K.B. 443; *Park* v. *J. Jobson & Son*, [1945] 1 All E.R. 222; *Sutcliffe* v. *Holmes*, [1947] K.B. 147; [1946] 2 All E.R. 599.
9. *Hilton* v. *Ankesson* (1872), 27 L.T. 519; *Firth* v. *Bowling Iron Co.* (1878), 3 C.P.D. 254; *Doe d. Mence* v. *Hadley* (1849), 14 L.T.O.S. 102; *Nussey* v. *Provincial Bill Posting Co. & Eddison.*, [1909] 1 Ch. 734; *Jones* v. *Price* [1965] 2 Q.B. 618; [1965] 2 All E.R. 625.
10. *Jones* v. *Price*, [1965] 2 Q.B. 618, at 633, 639, and 644–647; *Austerberry* v. *Oldham Corporation* (1885), 29 Ch.D. 750; *Hilton* v. *Ankesson* (1827), 27 L.T. 519.
11. *Austerberry* v. *Oldham Corporation* (1885), 29 Ch.D. 750; *S.E. Rail. Co.* v. *Associated Portland Cement Co., Ltd.*, [1910] 1 Ch. 12.
12. *Tulk* v. *Moxhay* (1848), 2 Phil. 774 is itself an example of this.

from a purchaser, this is no real answer to this gap in the law. With an unbroken chain of indemnities enforcement may still be possible, even after a lapse of time, but the costs are out of proportion to the point involved. Moreover, as the Committee on Positive Covenants affecting Land observe in their report, even where there is a chain of indemnity covenants, "in practice this device sooner or later becomes ineffective, either in consequence of the death or disappearance of the original covenantor, or because a break occurs in the chain of indemnities".[13]

There may be an implied agreement to maintain a fence[14] and this question came up as a subsidiary point in *Jones* v. *Price*[15] The Court of Appeal there affirmed that even if an agreement between the predecessors in title of the parties could be inferred, the contractual obligation so created would not run with the land.[16] WILLMER, L.J. put it this way:[17]

> "There is nothing, for instance, to prevent adjoining occupiers from making an agreement between themselves that one or other shall keep the boundary fence in repair; but such an agreement binds on the parties to it. For a covenant to perform positive acts, such as would be involved in the maintenance of a fence, is not one the burden of which runs with the land so as to bind the successors in title of the covenantor."

The only limitation to the enforceability of a covenant between the parties to a conveyance is that the action must be brought within twelve years from the date of the breach.[18]

Three methods of making a fencing covenant enforceable against the owner for the time being may be mentioned, but none of them are completely satisfactory. The first method is to make the cost of repairing the fence a charge on the land. This was apparently the basis of the decision in *Morland* v. *Cook*,[19] where there was a covenant in a partition deed providing for the maintenance of a sea wall. If a

13. Cmnd. 2719 of 1965, para. 8.
14. *Barber* v. *Whiteley* (1865) 34 L.J.Q.B. 212; *Haigh* v. *West*, [1893] 2 Q.B. 19.
15. [1965] 2 All E.R. 625.
16. *Austerberry* v. *Oldham Corporation* (1885), 29 Ch. D. 750.
17. [1965] 2 All E.R. 625, at 630. Sometimes one finds a covenant not to permit the growth of trees or a hedge beyond a specified height. This is a positive covenant requiring the cutting of the trees or hedge, and would not be binding on successors, even with notice: *Haywood* v. *Brunswick Permanent Benefit Building Society* (1881), 8 Q.B.D. 403.
18. Limitation Act 1939, s. 4.
19. (1868), L.R. 6 Eq. 252.

charge is imposed on the land, it may then be assigned with the land benefited by the covenant, but the procedure is somewhat clumsy.[20] The essence of the idea is that the covenant to pay money towards the cost of repairs for the benefit of several people may then run with the land as a charge.

The second method involves directly creating a rentcharge out of the land burdened with the covenant, reserving a right of re-entry for breach of the covenant, the positive obligation to fence being attached to the rentcharge. The legal interest thus created would be sanctioned by the statutory remedies[1] but the right of re-entry must apparently be exercised within the perpetuity period (except in the case of a conveyance of Crown land by the Crown Estate Commissioners in the case of rentcharges created prior to July 15th, 1964).[2] The subjection of re-entry to the perpetuity rule has been abolished for rentcharges created after July 15th, 1964.[3] The perpetuity rule does not apply to any powers or remedies for recovering a rentcharge.[4] In those parts of England, such as Manchester, where the fee simple is sold in return for the payment of a perpetual rent, supported by a right of re-entry for non-payment, this would appear to be a useful method, and it has been adopted in some modern building estates.[5] However it should be pointed out that s. 191 of the Law of Property Act 1925 provides that the person subject to the rentcharge can redeem it at any time if it is for a fixed amount.

The third method awaits judicial clarification, and depends upon the device of enlargement. It involves the purchaser granting a lease of at least 300 years at a rent of no money value and without a right of re-entry. A covenant to repair a fence could be imposed in the lease. The covenantor/lessor could then enlarge the leasehold into a fee simple, under s. 153 of the Law of Property Act 1925. Section 153 (8) provides:

> "The estate in fee simple so acquired by enlargement shall be subject to all the same trusts, powers, executory limitations over, rights, and

20. See Scammel, "Positive Covenants in Conveyances" (1955) 18 *Conveyancer* (N.S.) 561 ff.
1. See ss. 1 (2) (b) (c) and 121 of the Law of Property Act 1925.
2. *Re Hollis Hospital Trustees and Hague's Contract*, [1899] 2 Ch. 540; *Re Da Costa*, [1912] 1 Ch. 337; s. 3 (8) of the Crown Estates Act 1961.
3. Perpetuities and Accumulations Act 1964, s.11.
4. Law of Property Act 1925, ss. 121 (6) and 4 (3).
5. See generally (1950), 14 *Conveyancer* (N.S.) 354.

> equities, *and to all the same covenants and provisions relating to user and enjoyment, and to all the same obligations of every kind, as the term would have been subject to had it not been so enlarged.*" (Italics supplied.)

Any covenant inserted in the original lease would, therefore, be enforceable against successive holders of the freehold. However, this method has never been challenged judicially and since there is no right of re-entry it is doubtful whether there are any effective means of enforcing the positive covenant. There is a complete absence of authority as to what damages would be recoverable, since the enlargement means that there is no reversion which can sustain damage. It may be that the covenant continues in force without limitation on damages, but on general principles it seems likely that no damages would be awarded.[6] Until the matter is before the courts, this is one method suggested.

One other possible method of enforcing a covenant to fence may be mentioned, and this has attracted support in some quarters.[7] In *Halsall* v. *Brizell*[8] there was a positive covenant made by a separate deed, whereby purchasers of land on an estate agreed to contribute towards the cost of repairing the roads. UPJOHN, J., as he then was, held that,

> "the defendants here cannot, if they desire to use their house, as they do, take advantage of the trusts concerning the user of the roads contained in the deed and the other benefits created by it without undertaking the obligations thereunder."[9]

In other words, a person exercising a right is bound to observe any conditions attached to it. At first sight this would appear to be contrary to the rule in *Austerberry* v. *Oldham Corporation*,[10] but in fact

6. The measure of damages is the injury to the reversion in most cases. No injunction would be granted to restrain breaches by a tenant of a covenant to repair fences: *Rayner* v. *Stone* (1762), 2 Eden 128.
7. Notably in Parker, *Modern Conveyancing Precedents*, 123n., 125n. See also Scammel, "Positive Covenants in Conveyances", (1955) 18 *Conveyancer* (N.S.) 561 on the problem in general. Preston and Newsom, *Restrictive Covenants Affecting Freehold Land*, (5th Edn.), Chapter 3. *Cf.*, *Aspden* v. *Seddon* (1876), 1 Ex. D. 496, at 504, and a precedent for the sale of freehold flat in (1956), 20 *Convey* (N.S.) 651, which relies on the principle *qui sentit commodum sentive debet et onus*, which was the basis of *Aspden* v. *Seddon*. See also *Re Ellenborough Park*, [1956] Ch. 131.
8. [1957] Ch. 169.
9. [1957] Ch. 169, at 183.
10. (1885), 29 Ch. D. 750.

the deed appears to have created easements in favour of the purchasers. If they wished to take advantage of the easements, they had to contribute towards the burden involved. If this decision is to be taken at its face value, a positive obligation to share the expense of maintaining a fence or wall could be enforced provided some right was granted to the adjoining owner, *e.g.*, a right of support, on the ground that if such a clause grants one party a benefit, of which he and his successors take advantage, he and they must also assume any concomitant burden. This is a very attractive argument, but the decision has not found general acceptance,[11] probably because of the uncertainty. However, there is the decision of the Court of Appeal in *E. R. Ives Investments, Ltd.* v. *High*[11] where LORD DENNING, M.R. dealt with the question of mutual benefit and burden in this way:

> "When adjoining owners of land make an agreement to secure continuing rights and benefits for each of them in or over the land of the other, neither of them can take the benefit of the agreement and throw over the burden of it. This applies not only to the original parties, but also to their successors. The successor who takes the continuing benefit must take it subject to the continuing burden".

It is thought, therefore, that the doctrine of *Halsall* v. *Brizell*[12] is a method of circumvention.

LEASEHOLD LAND

In general there is no difficulty at all in enforcing a positive covenant in a lease as between lessor and lessee, although there is no tried method of making such covenants enforceable as between neighbours. The tenant's obligation to preserve the boundaries of the demised property[13] does not impose any obligation to fence by itself, but covenants to erect or maintain fences or to contribute towards the cost of repairs are commonly inserted in leases.[14] The effect of ss. 141–142 of the Law of Property Act 1925, is that the benefit of tenant's covenants and the burden of those by the landlord will run with the reversion. The burden and benefit of covenants which

11. [1967] 1 All E.R. 504, at 507. See also *Hopgood* v. *Brown*, [1955] 1 All E.R. 550, *May* v. *Belleville*, [1905] 2 Ch. 605.
12. [1957] Ch. 169; [1957] 1 All E.R. 371.
13. *A.-G.* v. *Fullerton* (1813), 2 Ves. & B. 263; *Brown* v. *Wales* (1872), L.R. 15 Eq. 142.
14. *Park* v. *J. Jobson & Son* [1945], 1 All E.R. 222 illustrates the position.

"touch and concern" the land will run at common law under the rule in *Spencer's Case*[15] where it was said:

> "When the covenant extends to a thing *in esse*, parcel of the demise, the thing to be done by force of the covenant is *quodammodo* annexed and appurtenant to the thing demised, and shall go with the land and bind the assignee, although he be not bound by express words."

The distinction between a thing *in esse* and one *in posse* is of no importance since 1926, by virtue of the operation of s. 79 of the Law of Property Act 1925, which applies to covenants made on or after January 1st, 1926. In the case of pre-1926 covenants to erect a fence (as opposed to those to repair an existing fence), the burden of the former covenant will not run with the land unless it includes the tenant and his assigns.[16]

A positive covenant will not normally be enforced by injunction or specific performance.[17] But there is nothing to prevent the parties suing for breach if damage is caused. The tenant is under strong pressure to keep any existing fences in repair in any event, since as occupier he will be liable for any damage caused by defective fencing, unless the landlord has covenanted to repair.[18]

A yearly tenant or tenant at will is not liable for permissive waste, but this does not relieve him from his obligation as occupier to keep the fences in good repair.[19] It has been held that it would be waste to grub up or destroy a growing hedge, and the tenant would be liable. It is not waste to cut quickset hedges, but "rather good husbandry, because they will grow the better".[20] If the tenant fails to keep the fences in good repair and order, the lessor can maintain an action against him for injury done to the reversion because the tenant has a duty

---

15. (1583), 5 Co. Rep. 16a.
16. *Spencer's Case* (1583), 5 Co. Rep. 16a; the distinction between covenants *in esse* and *in posse* has been adversely criticised, *e.g.*, *Minshull* v. *Oakes* (1858), 2 H. & N. 793, but remains important in the case of pre-1926 covenants. For a general discussion see Cheshire, *Modern Law of Real Property* (11th Edn.), p. 442ff.
17. *Rayner* v. *Stone* (1762), 2 Eden 128; *Wheatley* v. *Westminster Brymo Coal Co.* (1869), L.R. 9 Eq. 538; but see *Carpenters' Estates, Ltd.* v. *Davies*, [1940] C.L. 160.
18. *Cheetham* v. *Hampson* (1791), 4 Term. Rep. 318; *Mint* v. *Good*, [1951] 1 K.B. 517.
19. *Whitfield* v. *Weedon* (1772), 2 Chit. 685; *Cheetham* v. *Hampson* (1791), 4 Term Rep. 318.
20. *Gage & Smith's Case* (1613), Godb. 209.

to repair the fences and to preserve the boundaries of the demised land.[1] The tenant is entitled to fell timber for the purpose of repairing fences, this being part of his right to estovers.[2] Timber is oak, ash or elm of more than twenty years' growth[3] and other trees in some parts of the country.[4]

SETTLED LAND

A tenant for life is not subject to any special rules regarding fencing, but unless the settlement makes him unimpeachable for waste he is liable for voluntary waste, *i.e.*, active damage. This would include damage to fences. He is not liable for permissive waste unless the settlement imposes on him an obligation to keep the property and its appurtenances in repair.[5] Breaches of any positive obligation of this kind may be restrained by injunction, and any person interested under the settlement may sue. Repairs to fences are ordinary outgoings and must be paid for out of income, subject to the right to take estovers.

The erection of new fences is work of a capital nature, and as such constitutes an improvement which may be paid for out of capital. It falls into the first of the three authorized categories of improvement.[6] "Improvements [mean] something which is more than an ordinary repair which a tenant for life does or an occupier of a dwelling-house or property habitually does from time to time in order to keep the place tidy, watertight and the rest."[7] The tenant for life is not required to repay any money expended under this head. The work must be done

---

1. *A.-G.* v. *Fullerton* (1813), 2 Ves. & B. 263; *Whitfield* v. *Weedon* (1772), 2 Chit. 685.
2. *Courtenay* v. *Fisher* (1826), 4 Bing. 3; *Simmons* v. *Norton* (1831), 7 Bing. 640, at 649.
3. *Aubrey* v. *Fisher* (1809), 10 East 446, at 455; *Whitty* v. *Lord Dillon* (1860), 2 F. & F. 67; *Honywood* v. *Honywood* (1874), L.R. 18 Eq. 306, *per* JESSEL, M.R., at 309.
4. Beech in Buckinghamshire: *Dashwood* v. *Magniac*, [1891] 3 Ch. 306; birch in Yorkshire: *Cumberland's Case* (1610), Moore 812; willow in Hampshire: *Layfield* v. *Cowper* (1694), 1 Wood 330.
5. *Woodhouse* v. *Walker* (1880), 5 Q.B.D. 404; *Re Cartwright* (1889), 41 Ch.D. 532; *Re Parry & Hopkins*, [1900] 1 Ch. 160.
6. Settled Land Act 1925, 3rd Sched., Part I.
7. *Per* FARWELL, J. in *Re Lindsay's Settlement (No. 2)*, [1941] Ch. 119; [1941] 1 All E.R. 143. But note that the Agricultural Holdings Act 1948, ss. 88(1) 94(1), allows the payments of repairs out of capital money in the case of settled agricultural land: see *Re Sutherland Settlement Trusts*, [1953] Ch. 792; [1953] 2 All E.R. 27.

to the satisfaction of a surveyor or engineer employed independently of the tenant for life.[8] The power to pay for improvements out of capital is not available to trustees under a trust for sale.[9] Apart from these minor matters, a tenant for life is in the same position as any other owner or occupier as far as fencing goes.

ACCESS FOR REPAIR OF FENCES

Where an owner does erect a fence along his boundary he does not thereby acquire any right of entry on to the neighbouring property for the purposes of maintenance and repair. The right to enter and repair may be acquired by express grant, and where a plan attached to a contract indicates that a wall is on the boundary line, an express power of entry for repair and allied purposes should be granted. This is especially important in the case of new housing developments where space is at a premium, and there is no possibility of the right arising by implication of law.

The right to maintain a boundary wall or fence is capable of subsisting as an easement. It may therefore arise by prescription or, in appropriate cases, by virtue of the general words of s. 62 of the Law of Property Act 1925. A relevant and instructive case is *Ward* v. *Kirkland*[10] where, for many years before 1928 a cottage, a plot of land and a farmhouse and lands were in the ownership of the incumbent of a benefice. The yard of the farm immediately adjoined one wall of the cottage. The rector, with the consent of the Ecclesiastical Commissioners, conveyed the cottage and a plot of land to the plaintiff's predecessors in title, together with the right to use the adjoining yard for unloading coal. This transaction took place in 1928. The defendant occupied the farmhouse and lands as tenant of the rector in 1942. Twelve years later, in 1954, the cottage and plot of land were conveyed to the plaintiff. Repairs to the wall of the cottage adjoining the farm-yard were carried out from time to time from the yard, which provided the only possible access to the wall. Prior to 1958 there was no evidence of permission of the freeholder for entry onto the farm-yard for the purpose of repairing the wall. From 1942 to 1954 work to the wall was done with the defendant's permission as tenant. Between 1954 and 1958 the plaintiff did not

8. Settled Land Act 1925, s. 84.
9. *Re Wynn, Public Trustee* v. *Newborough*, [1955] 2 All E.R. 865.
10. [1967] Ch. 194; [1966] 1 All E.R. 609.

ask for such permission, and after the defendant purchased the farm in 1958 he refused the plaintiff permission to enter for the purposes of repair.

UNGOED-THOMAS, J. held that the plaintiff was entitled to go on to the land for the purpose of maintaining the wall; the right to enter and repair was capable of being a valid easement. The learned judge also held that although the right was not created by implication in the present case (since it was not a continuous and apparent easement within the principle of *Wheeldon* v. *Burrows*,[11] since the advantage had in fact been enjoyed, whether by permission or not) it was transformed by s. 62 of the Law of Property Act 1925 into an easement on the occasion of the conveyance in 1928.

The vendor can of course restrict the application of the general words of s. 62 by inserting an appropriate clause in the conveyance but this is not common in practice.[12]

COVENANTS AGAINST FENCING

Negative or restrictive covenants against fencing *i.e.*, those not to fence, are very common, particularly on the modern open-plan estates of speculative developers. In theory there is no difficulty about enforcing such covenants. In *Doherty* v. *Allman*[13] LORD CAIRNS, L.C. pointed out that where a defendant commits a breach of a negative covenant with his eyes open and after notice the court will grant a mandatory injunction against him. However, there is and must be some limitation to this practice. If the plaintiff suffers no real damage and the granting of a mandatory injunction would inflict damage on the defendant out of all proportion to the relief which the plaintiff ought to obtain, the court will probably refuse to grant the order. Thus, in *Shepherd Homes, Ltd.* v. *Sandham*,[14] the company had bought and developed a housing estate in Glamorganshire. The estate was designed on an open plan with no fences in front of the building line and the plots were largely sold off leasehold. Each lease (and conveyance) contained a covenant not to "erect or plant or grow . . . any fence or

11. (1879), 12 Ch.D. 31.
12. For an example of such a clause see *Re Peck and London School Board*, [1893] 2 Ch. 315.
13. (1878), 3 App. Cas. 709.
14. [1971] Ch. 340; [1970] 3 All E.R. 402.

hedge in advance of the said building line". The defendant erected a fence in advance of the building line in order to prevent repeated incursions by Welsh mountain sheep and some horses, which were causing considerable damage to his garden.

MEGARRY, J. refused to grant an interlocutory injunction partly on the grounds of delay, but in his judgment emphasised that in cases of this sort the judge must produce a "fair result", and this involved the exercise of judicial discretion. It may be noted, however, that the usefulness of this phrase was later doubted by the Court of Appeal.[15]

---

15. In *Charrington* v. *Simons & Co. Ltd.*, [1971] 2 All E.R. 588, C.A., *per* RUSSELL, L.J. at p. 592, also doubting the correctness of the decision in *Woollerton and Wilson, Ltd.* v. *Richard Costain, Ltd.*, [1970] 1 All E.R. 483.

Chapter 7

LIABILITY IN TORT

Sic utere tuo ut alienum non laedas.

The principle underlying this ancient maxim is the foundation of much of the modern law of torts, and a landowner whose fencing is inadequate or defective may find a claim against him in tort. This liability may be considered in several ways, but is principally concerned with responsibility for animals and dangerous objects on land.

ANIMALS[1]

The law relating to liability for animals is now largely contained in the Animals Act 1971, which came into force on October 1st, 1971,[2] although there may also be liability for harm done by animals under the more general heads of liability in tort. The Act, it has been said, "is overlaid upon a basis of common law liability"[3] and one important common law concept which is specifically included by reference is the obligation to fence.[4]

Liability for animals and the associated problems of fencing may be considered under a number of heads:

1 STRAYING LIVESTOCK

The common law action of cattle trespass has been abolished[5] but it has been replaced by a statutory liability for straying livestock.[6] It is

1. For a useful analysis of the law see P. M. North, *The Modern Law of Animals* (1972). The classic monograph on the former law is Professor Glanville Williams's, *Liability for Animals*.
2. Animals Act 1971, s. 13 (3).
3. North, *op. cit.*, p. 20.
4. Animals Act 1971, s. 5 (6).
5. Animals Act 1971, s. 1 (1) (c).
6. *Ibid*, s. 4.

provided by s. 4 that the owner of trespassing livestock is strictly liable for any damage done when it strays on to someone else's land and causes damage there. Although the liability is strict it is necessary for there to be proof of damage ("damage is done") *or* in the alternative there must be expenses incurred by the owner or occupier of land either in keeping the livestock until it can be restored to its owner or under the statutory right of detention.[7] The liability is in respect of "livestock" which is defined for the purposes of s. 4, as: "cattle, horses, asses, mules, hinnies, sheep, pigs, goats and poultry, and also deer not in the wild state".[8] "Poultry" is defined as: "the domestic varieties of the following, that is to say, fowls, turkeys, geese, ducks, guinea-fowls, pigeons, peacocks and quails".[9]

This definition of "livestock" is slightly wider than the old common law *avers*. Dogs, cats and bees are not included:

> "Generally speaking the owner of an animal is responsible if it trespasses: but the common law in its common sense admits of exception to this general rule, and among the exceptions is the dog . . . and there is no distinction between a dog and a cat."[10]

This is still the position so far as s. 4 liability is concerned, but it is interesting to note that there would now appear to be liability for straying pigeons which cause damage.[11]

The converse of the statutory liability for straying livestock is to be seen in the fact that, since there is no common law obligation on a landowner to maintain fences around his land, if one man's livestock stray on to neighbouring property and are injured there because of the livestock owner's failure to fence, he will have no claim against his neighbour.

If the owner of the land upon which the livestock stray is under a duty to fence—however that duty arose—he cannot complain if the trespass is due to his failure to maintain an effective fence.[12] A statutory defence is available to the owner of the livestock[13]: he can plead that the

---

7. Animals Act 1971, s. 7.
8. *Ibid*, s. 11.
9. *Ibid*, s. 11.
10. *Per* Bankes, L.J. in *Buckle* v. *Holmes*, [1926] 2 K.B. 125.
11. P. M. North, *The Modern Law of Animals*, p. 93. See *per* Johnson, J. in *Brady* v. *Warren*, [1900] 2 I.R. 632, at p. 645.
12. *Boyle* v. *Tamlyn* (1827), 6 B. & C. 329.
13. The Animals Act 1971, s. 5. The effects of failure to fence are considered more fully below, p. 127.

damage is due wholly or partly to the plaintiff's own fault. However, the damage is *not* to be treated as due to the fault of the plaintiff merely because be *could* have prevented it by fencing;[14] to provide otherwise would be tantamount to saying that every landowner must fence. The position is different, however, where there is a *duty* to fence "by a person having an interest in the land", for then no liability attaches to the owner of the straying livestock.[15]

Stock-proof fences

At this point it is convenient to consider the question of "stock-proof fences" because a common covenant is that a purchaser or lessee "will erect and forever thereafter maintain a good and sufficient stock-proof fence". There is no direct authority as to what is meant by "stock-proof"[16] although it has been said that the duty to fence "is only to keep reasonable fences to prevent the escape of ordinary (livestock) in ordinary circumstances".[17] The usual fence erected is one of vertical posts and horizontal strands of barbed wire of a type sufficient to be proof against cattle, sheep and stock of that sort. In the writer's view the covenantor is bound by such a covenant to erect a fence which is proof against all forms of livestock, including poultry. In the former edition of this book, two arguments were adduced to support this proposition. Firstly, there could be liability in cattle trespass for poultry, and marauding poultry could (and can) do just as much damage as a wandering cow. Secondly, the dictionary definition of stock included "all the animals on the farm", and since almost all farms include poultry among the livestock, although poultry are not strictly animals, the obvious intention of the covenant is to guard against intrusion by any livestock. Thus, quite apart from the Animals Act 1971, the covenantor was, at common law, liable to erect a fence which was proof against poultry as well as animals if he was to meet his obligation.[18]

---

14. Animals Act 1971, s. 5 (6). It is remarkable that there is no indication in the sub-section as to whom the fencing obligation must be owed, and since this is a matter of considerable importance in a book devoted to boundaries and fences, the problem is considered below, p. 127.
15. This duty can clearly arise by prescription, lost modern grant or custom as well as by agreement.
16. Called in some parts of the country (e.g., Cumberland), a *turnable fence*.
17. Williams, *Liability for Animals*, p. 214. The word "livestock" has been substituted in the quotation for the word "cattle" in the original.
18. The common law term *avers* included oxen, cows, sheep, goats, horses, asses hens, geese and ducks.

A fortiori since the advent of the Animals Act 1971 for, as we have seen, there is a statutory definition of "livestock" which includes not only four-footed beasts but also "poultry" as defined—and even domestic pigeons.[19] It is thought that many so-called "stock-proof fences" erected pursuant to covenants up and down the country are, in fact, nothing of the sort, subject to what is said below about locality. The draftsman can, of course, amend the wording of a proposed covenant so as to *exclude* poultry (or any species thereof) if this represents the intention of the parties. Alternatively, the covenant can read, *e.g.*, "a good and sufficient fence proof against cattle, poultry and other livestock" or "a good and sufficient fence proof against livestock as defined in s. 11 of the Animals Act 1971".

The duty is to erect and maintain such fences proof against livestock in ordinary circumstances. As was said in one case, using a pig as illustration, the obligation is to erect "such a fence that a pig not of a peculiarly wandering disposition, nor under any excessive temptation, will not get through it".[20] It is probable that the obligation is to provide only such fences as are usual in the area. Thus, in *Coaker* v. *Willocks*[1] the Court of Appeal held that the defendant, who admitted that he was under a prescriptive obligation to fence against commonable animals on Dartmoor, was only bound to fence sufficiently to keep out the ordinary sheep of the district and not Scottish sheep "of a peculiarly wandering and saltative disposition, straying and jumping in a way which distinguishes them from sheep which have hitherto been turned on to the unenclosed land, wandering as other sheep do not and jumping as other sheep cannot".[2] The defendant's fences were like those generally erected in the area, and sufficient in height and strength to keep out ordinary moorland sheep. They were not strong enough to keep out the plaintiff's Scottish sheep, which by all accounts possessed remarkable agility.[3]

---

19. Animals Act 1971, s. 11.
20. *Child* v. *Hearn* (1874), L.R. 9 Exch. 176, at p. 182.
1. [1911] 2 K.B. 124.
2. *Per* DARLING, J., [1911] 1 K.B. 649, at p. 654.
3. See also *Spry* v. *Mortimore*, [1946] L.J.C.C.R. 83; *Cooper* v. *Railway Executive (Southern Region)*, [1953] 1 All E.R. 477; *Bessant* v. *Great Western Rail. Co.* (1860), 8. C.B.N.S. 368; *Page* v. *Great Eastern Rail. Co.* (1871), 24 L.T. 585; and see *Wiseman* v. *Booker* (1878), 3. C.P.D. 184, at 188.

2 ANIMALS AND THE HIGHWAY[4]

Section 8 of the Animals Act 1971 abolishes the general rule in *Searle* v. *Wallbank*;[5] the side-note to s. 8 reads "Duty to take care to prevent damage from animals straying on to the highway". Section 8 (1) provides, in effect, that there is the ordinary duty of care to prevent damage from animals straying on to the highway. The liability depends upon the common law of negligence. Thus, there would be no liability, it is thought, where it was reasonable to graze animals on the land (or to keep a dog in an unfenced or ungated garden) because the road was little used by traffic, and motorists might be expected to be aware of the presence of animals.

It may be noted, at this juncture, that the fact that livestock was lawfully on a highway before it strayed is a defence to an action under s. 4. The principle of this defence was explained by BLACKBURN, J. in *Fletcher* v. *Rylands*.[6] Those who have property adjacent to the highway must accept some inevitable risk, and this defence was recognised in a number of cases at common law, such as *Tillett* v. *Ward*[7] and *Gayler and Pope, Ltd.* v. *Davies & Son, Ltd.*[8] There need be no contiguity between the land and the highway: the defence applies to any land. The reason for this was explained by the Law Commission which said that it could be supported "on the ground that if cattle do find their way from the highway to the plaintiff's land it is not unreasonable to assume as a matter of fact that the land is affected by the risks of the highway".[9] Thus, animals on highways may give rise both to a cause of action and a defence.

The general rule of negligence liability as laid down in s. 8 (1) of the 1971 Act is subject to a number of exceptions which are expressed in s. 8 (2). The animal's owner is not to be regarded as being in breach of his duty of care "by reason only" of his having placed the animals by right on (a) common land or a town or village green; or, (b) "land situated in an area where fencing is not customary".

For s. 8 (2) to operate, the land must be "unfenced land", but the first

---

4. See P. M. North, *The Modern Law of Animals*, Chapter 5.
5. [1947] A.C. 341; [1974] 1 All E.R. 12.
6. (1866), L.R. I Ex. 265, at p. 268. The statutory defence is in s. 5 (5) of the Animals Act 1971.
7. (1882) 10 Q.B.D. 17.
8. [1924] 2. K.B. 75.
9. Law Commission Report No. 13, para. 67, note 97.

exception requires little comment. Common land has the same meaning as in the Commons Registration Act 1965, and "town or village green" is defined by reference to the same Act.[10] Commoners generally have no rights in the soil to enable them to fence and s. 194 of the Law of Property Act 1925 requires the consent of the Secretary of State for the Environment before common land can be fenced.[11]

The vague wording of the second exception, *viz.*, "land situated in an area where fencing is not customary" is, however, to be deplored. When is "land in an area where fencing is not *customary*"? Presumably this does not necessarily require proof of custom in the legal sense, but is a question of common usage in the area,[12] which can be "anything from a couple of farms to Cumberland or South-East England".[13]

"Fencing" is defined[14] as including "the construction of any obstacle designed to prevent animals from straying" and is thus wider than the common law definition of "fence". It is submitted that it extends to cattle-grids and to all those ditches which are designed to retain animals. If a person erects any obstacle designed to prevent animals from straying it comes within the statutory definition of "fencing".

Although s. 8 does not create any fencing liability as such, it is clear that in populous areas or in the case of land near to heavily-used roads, the duty of care can only be met by adequate fencing. "Highway" is not defined in the Act, but its common law meaning is "a thoroughfare open to all subjects of the Queen to pass along on their lawful occasions".[15]

It should, perhaps, be noted that—somewhat remarkably in this day and age—there is no legal liability placed on the Department of the Environment (as successors to the Ministry of Transport) to fence in motorways against wandering animals. In practice, the Department always erects stock-proof fences along motorways as part of the accommodation works carried out when land is compulsorily acquired, but in

10. Animals Act 1971, s. 11, referring to the Commons Registration Act 1965, s. 22 (1).
11. A person having a right to graze cattle on common land can license another to have cattle there so as to give the protection of s. 8 (2): *Davies* v. *Davies*, [1974] 3 All E.R. 817.
12. *Cf. Coaker* v. *Willocks*, [1911] 2 K.B. 124. North, *op. cit.*, says that "The custom is that of the area and not of the particular land in question": p. 159.
13. 313 H.L. Deb. c. 460, quoted in North, *op. cit.*, p. 159.
14. Animals Act 1971, s. 11.
15. Garner, *Rights of Way*, (2nd Edn.), p. 9. Pratt and Mackenzie, *Law of Highways*, (21st Edn.), p. 3, defines highway as meaning "all portions of land over which every subject of the Crown may lawfully pass".

law the Department's position is no different from that of any other person.

Under s. 35 of the Highways Act 1959 it is an offence to allow any horses, cattle, sheep, goats or swine to stray in the highway or lie at the side of the road. The penalties under the section—which re-enacts earlier provisions—are provided for the protection of the public and do not render the owner of the animals liable to an action at law.[16] The provision does not apply where the highway crosses common, waste or unenclosed ground, but it has been held that the proviso relating to unenclosed ground applies only to pieces of land of some considerable size.[17] It is further provided that "nothing in this section shall prejudice or affect any right of pasture on the side of a highway",[18] but an owner exercising this right must keep his animals from straying, except temporarily, or lying on the actual road.[19] The maximum fine for an offence under s. 135 is a derisory 25 p for each beast (with a maximum of £1.50p) plus the reasonable cost of removing the strays.

3 STRICT LIABILITY

Section 1 of the Animals Act 1971 swept away the former common law rules relating to animals *ferae naturae*, *scienter* and cattle trespass and the special provisions of s. 1 of the Dogs Act 1906, as amended, dealing with a dog owner's liability for injury to cattle or poultry.

Strict liability for damage done by dangerous animals is created by s. 2, sub-section (1) of which states:

> "Where any damage is caused by an animal which belongs to a *dangerous species*, any person who is a *keeper* of the animal is liable for the *damage*, except as otherwise provided by this Act." (Italics supplied.)

"Dangerous species" is defined[20] as one,

> "(a) which is not commonly domesticated in the British Islands; and, (b) whose fully-grown animals normally have such characteristics that they are likely, unless restrained, to cause severe damage or that any damage they may cause is likely to be severe".

---

16. *Heath's Garage, Ltd.* v. *Hodges*, [1916] 2 K.B. 370.
17. *Bothamley* v. *Danby* (1871), 24 L.T. 656; *Golding* v. *Stocking* (1869), L.R. 4 Q.B. 516; *Plumbley* v. *Lock* (1902), 67 J.P. 237.
18. Section 35 (5).
19. *Freestone* v. *Caswell* (1869), L.R.4. Q.B. 519; *Bothamley* v. *Danby* (1871), 24 L.T. 656.
20. Animals Act 1971, s. 6 (2).

This represents a simplification of the former law, placing emphasis on the degree of risk which the particular species represents in this country.

Since the liability is strict, a keeper of animals of a "dangerous species" must keep sufficient fences at his peril.

So far as animals belonging to a harmless species are concerned, there is strict liability if the particular animal has abnormal or dangerous characteristics of which its keeper is aware.[21] To bring this liability into operation the keeper must know of the animal's characteristics which are dangerous in that they either make it likely to inflict damage of the kind which in fact results or make it likely that any damage of the kind it may cause will be severe. The necessary knowledge may be acquired through the keeper's servant or a member of his household under the age of sixteen years.[1] Defences to actions brought under ss. 2 to 4 of the 1971 Act are set out in s. 5:

(a) The damage is due wholly or partly to the plaintiff's own fault.
(b) Voluntary assumption of risk.
(c) There is no liability to an injured trespasser provided that the animal either was not kept to protect persons or property or if it was so kept "that keeping it there for that purpose was not unreasonable".
(d) Where a dog injures livestock, its keeper is not liable if the stock was trespassing and the dog either belongs to the occupier or its presence on the land was authorised by him.
(e) It is a defence, as noted, in the case of straying livestock, that it strayed from the highway and its presence there was a lawful use of the highway.[2]

Apart from the liability created by the Animals Act 1971, it must be remembered that there may also be liability for animals under the

---

21. Animals Act 1971, s. 2 (2).
1. *Ibid.*, s. 2 (2) (c).
2. Drovers on the highway are under the ordinary duty to use reasonable care: *Wright* v. *Callwood*, [1950] 2 K.B. 515, at p. 526. The foregoing represents merely an outline account of some parts of the Animals Act 1971, and for detailed discussion reference should be made to P. M. North, *Modern Law of Animals*.

ordinary rules of negligence[3] or nuisance[4] or trespass[5] or occupier's liability[6] or *Rylands* v. *Fletcher*.[7]

4 FAILURE TO FENCE AND LIABILITY FOR ANIMALS

The effects of failure to fence are relevant to liability affecting animals in a number of ways.[8] Where there is an obligation to fence, it is enforceable by way of an action on the case for damages,[9] and a mandatory injunction could be sought to compel the servient owner to erect or maintain a fence.[10] Defective or non-existent fences may provide a defence to a statutory action for straying livestock brought under s. 4 of the Animals Act 1971, s. 5 (6) of which affects that part of the law of fences which is relevant to this statutory action.

Section 5 (6) provides:

> "In determining whether any liability for damage under section 4 of this Act is excluded by subsection (1) of this section[11] the damage shall not be treated as due to the fault of the person suffering it by reason only that he could have prevented it by fencing; but a person is not liable under that section where it is proved that the straying of the livestock on the land would not have occurred but for a breach by any other person, being a person having an interest in the land, of a duty to fence".

It is remarkable that s. 5 (6), dealing with such an important matter of principle, says nothing about to whom the duty of fence must be owed in order for the defence to be applicable. What is clear is that the defence provided by s. 5 (6) is operative only where it is proved that the straying would not have occurred but for a breach of a fencing obligation. Where

---

3. See *per* LORD ATKIN in *Fardon* v. *Harcourt-Rivington* (1932), 48 T.L.R. 215, at p. 217. See also Chapter 6, "Liability at Common law", in P. M. North, *Modern Law of Animals*, which discusses the question of liability for harm done by animals outside the ambit of the Animals Act 1971.
4. *Pitcher* v. *Martin*, [1937] 3 All E.R. 918; *Peech* v. *Best*, [1931] 1 K.B. 1.
5. *Baker* v. *Webberly* (1631), Het. 171; *R.* v. *Pratt* (1855), 4 E. & B. 860, at pp. 864–865.
6. See P. M. North, *Occupiers' Liability*, pp. 91–92.
7. (1866), L.R. 1 Exch. 265; affirmed (1868), L.R. 3 H.L. 330; *Brady* v. *Warren*, [1900] 2 I.R. 632, at 651.
8. See P. M. North, *Modern Law of Animals*, Chapter 4.
9. Formerly by the writ *de curia claudenda*. The action is not between adjoining freeholders, but between adjoining possessors of land: *Cheetham* v. *Hampson* (1791), 4 Term Rep. 318.
10. See *Redland Bricks, Ltd.* v. *Morris*, [1970] A.C. 652; [1969] 2 All E.R. 576 as to the principles involved in the award of a mandatory injunction.
11. Section 5 (1) provides: "A person is not liable under sections 2 to 4 of this Act for any damage which is due wholly to the fault of the person suffering it".

the plaintiff owes an obligation to fence to someone other than the defendant, *e.g.*, a fencing obligation owed by a tenant to his landlord under covenant, it is thought that if there was a breach of this duty, the defence would be made out because of the plain words of the statute.[12] Whether this was the intention of Parliament is another matter, although the same principle appears to underly the decision of the Court of Appeal in *Crow* v. *Wood*.[13] In other words, if the plaintiff is in breach of any fencing obligation, the s. 5 (6) defence would appear to be available.

There are various other permutations of this situation which are relevant to the whole question of animal liability.[14]

DANGEROUS THINGS

1 STRICT LIABILITY

> "The person who, for his own purposes, brings on his lands and collects and keeps there anything likely to do mischief if it escapes, must keep it in at his peril, and if he does not do so, is *prima facie* answerable for all the damage which is the natural consequence of its escape . . ."[15]

In these words BLACKBURN, J. formulated the rule of strict liability known as the rule in *Rylands* v. *Fletcher*[16] whereby the law imposes strict liability if a man's activities on his own land deleteriously affect another's land. It is the duty of an occupier to prevent the escape from his land of dangerous things, because there will be liability if they escape, independently of nuisance or negligence.[17] So in the old case of *Tenant* v. *Goldwin*[18] there was liability where a man let his

---

12. *Holgate* v. *Bleazard*, [1917] 1 K.B. 443 and *Park* v. *J. Jobson & Son*, [1945] 1 All E.R. 222, would, therefore, be decided differently today in the context of the statutory liability.
13. [1971] 1 Q.B. 77; [1970] 3 All E.R. 425. See especially *per* LORD DENNING, M.R., at p. 85. A similar assumption appears to underly *Egerton* v. *Harding*, [1974] 3 All E.R. 689.
14. Reference should be made to P. M. North, *op. cit.*, pp. 35 ff., where the problems are fully explored in the statutory context.
15. *Per* BLACKBURN, J. in *Fletcher* v. *Rylands* (1866), L.R. 1. Ex. 265, at p. 279; affirmed by the House of Lords *sub. nom. Rylands* v. *Fletcher* (1868), L.R. 3 H.L. 330. See *Read* v. *J. Lyons & Co., Ltd.*, [1946] 2 All E.R. 471 as to the "escape" element, which is essential.
16. (1866) L.R. 1 Ex. 265, at p. 279.
17. There must be non-natural use of land, as well as a dangerous accumulation of something for the defendant's own purposes. Quantities of water, gas, fuel, sewage, electricity, explosives, etc., have all been held to be "things likely to do mischief if they escape". See also *A.-G.* v. *Corke*, [1933] 1 Ch. 89, where some caravan dwellers were held to be within the rule!
18. (1710), 1 Salk. 360.

boundary wall fall into disrepair, and as a result sewage escaped on to neighbouring property and caused damage there. Defences to an action in strict liability will be the plaintiff's own default, act of a third party, common purpose, statutory authority, or *force majeure*.

2 NEGLIGENCE AND NUISANCE

Inherently dangerous articles and substances may also give rise to liability in negligence. The law imposes on those who control such objects a duty to take precautions and to save the persons and property of third parties from being damaged.[19] There is a duty to guard against foreseeable injury to another's legally protected interests by taking the precautions which the (hypothetical) reasonable man would take. There may thus be liability for the escape of something from one's land in negligence or nuisance, and "non-natural use" of land does not have to be proved.[20]

3 THE OCCUPIERS' LIABILITY ACT 1957

It has already been noted that occupiers of property are under a special duty of care to their lawful visitors and their property. This liability will now be examined. To such people they owe a "common duty of care" which is statutorily defined[1] as being:

> "a duty to take such care *as in all the circumstances of the case* is reasonable to see that the visitor will be reasonably safe in using the premises for the purposes for which he is permitted by the occupier to be there." (Italics supplied).[2]

Special care must be taken in the case of a child:

> "an occupier must be prepared for children to be less careful than adults."[3]

---

19. *Parry* v. *Smith* (1879), 4 C.P.D. 325; *Dominion Natural Gas Co.* v. *Collins*, [1909] A.C. 640; *Blacker* v. *Lake & Elliot, Ltd.* (1912), 106 L.T. 533; *Anglo-Celtic Shipping Co.* v. *Elliot* (1926), 42 T.L.R. 297; *M'Alister (or Donoghue)* v. *Stevenson*, [1932] A.C. 562.
20. *Castle* v. *St Augustine's Links, Ltd.* (1922), 38 T.L.R. 615; *Bolton* v. *Stone*, [1951] A.C. 850; *A.-G.* v. *P.Y.A. Quarries, Ltd.*, [1957] 2 Q.B. 169—dust and splinters from a quarry. See also *Farrer* v. *Nelson* (1885), 15 Q.B.D. 258—a large number of game birds. There must be some period of continuity for a nuisance action to succeed: *Metropolitan Properties, Ltd.* v. *Jones*, [1939] 2 All E.R. 202.
1. Occupiers' Liability Act 1957, s. 2 (2).
2. See generally P. M. North, *Occupiers' Liability*.
3. Occupiers' Liability Act 1957, s. 2 (3) (a); *Cooke* v. *Midland Great Western Railway of Ireland*, [1909] A.C. 229.

Although the Act does not impose liability to fence as such, in many cases an occupier will be able to escape *prima facie* liability only by showing that he has fenced. In some circumstances the display of a warning notice may be sufficient, but in others it is thought the duty can be discharged only by fencing, *e.g.*, in the case of a permanent open excavation:

> "In determining whether the occupier of premises has discharged the common duty of care to the visitor, regard is to be had to all the circumstances . . ."[4]

Recently, protection has been given to trespassers. This arises from the introduction by the House of Lords, in *British Railways Board* v. *Herrington*,[5] of a test of "common humanity" to determine the precautions which an occupier is required to take for the safety of trespassers in general and trespassing children in particular. In *British Railways Board* v. *Herrington*,[5] LORD DIPLOCK provided some practical guidelines on the effect of warning notices. It would seem that where a child is too young to read such a notice, common humanity may demand that the occupier fences:

> "If the duty is owed to small children too young to understand a warning notice the duty may require the provision of an obstacle to their approach to the danger sufficiently difficult to surmount as to make it clear to the youngest unaccompanied child likely to approach the danger, that beyond the obstacle is forbidden territory".[6]

Further guidance was given by the Court of Appeal in *Pannett* v. *P. McGuinness & Co., Ltd.*,[7] which concerned a five year old child injured by a fire on a demolition site. EDMUND DAVIES, L.J. emphasised that to warn off trespassing children in such a manner as to bring home to them that they have no right to enter premises is not, of itself and without more, in all circumstances sufficient to exculpate the occupier against liability if a trespassing child comes to harm by entering those premises.

The most recent case is *Southern Portland Cement, Ltd.* v. *Cooper*,[8] where the Privy Council emphasied that the duty of an occupier to

---

4. Occupiers' Liability Act 1957, s. 2 (4).
5. [1972] A.C. 877; [1972] 1 All E.R. 749.
6. [1972] 1 All E.R. 749, at p. 794.
7. [1972] 2 Q.B. 599; [1972] 3 All E.R. 137.
8. [1974] 1 All E.R. 87.

to potential trespassers is to do what a humane man with the occupier's financial and other limitations would do in the particular circumstances in order to prevent injury:

> "The rights and interests of the occupier must have full consideration. No unreasonable burden must be put on him. With regard to dangers which have arisen on his land without his knowledge he can have no obligation to make enquiries or inspection. With regard to dangers of which he has knowledge but which he did not create he cannot be required to incur what for him would be large expense".[9]

This is a robust statement of the law, but these cases do make clear that in a great many cases an adequate and secure fence is the only answer.[10] Glass or spikes or barbed wire along a wall or fence are a permissible deterrent, although regard must be had to the height of the wall or fence and its proximity to the highway.[11]

TREES ON BOUNDARIES

Trees and shrubs growing on or near boundaries can cause difficulties in a variety of ways.

1 OWNERSHIP

Nice problems can arise where a tree stands on the boundary of adjoining properties because the ownership of such features is not firmly settled. The propositions set out here can be deduced from the decided cases, but essentially each problem must turn on its own facts. Although acts of ownership may help to settle a dispute, they are not decisive. A tree belongs to the owner in whose land it was planted, even if its trunk, roots and branches extend into the adjoining property. So in *Masters* v. *Pollie*[12], in an action for trespass, it was held that since the body

9. *Per curiam* [1974] 1 All E.R. 87, at p. 97.
10. The older cases on traps or allurements for children are still helpful, *e.g.*, *Glasgow Corporation* v. *Taylor*, [1922] 1 A.C. 44; *Williams* v. *Cardiff Corporation*, [1950] 1 K.B. 514; [1950] 1 All E.R. 250.
11. See *post*, pp. 138–141.
12. (1620), 2 Roll Rep. 141; *Waterman* v. *Soper* (1698), 1 Ld. Raym. 737; *Holder* v. *Coates* (1827), Mood. & M. 112. In, *Hetherington* v. *Galt* (1905), 7 F. 706, a Scottish case, LORD DARKIN held that trees whose trunks are wholly on the land of one man, with roots extending a good way across the boundary, are not jointly owned. See also Theobald, *Law of Land* (2nd Edn.) p. 239.

of the tree was on the plaintiff's land, and it had been there planted, it belonged to him.

Where it cannot be shown who planted the tree, ownership may be inferred from the circumstances, and it is here that acts of ownership are especially relevant, *e.g.*, regular lopping or topping of a tree. The ownership of a particular boundary tree is a question of fact in each case. If it cannot be proved one way or the other, it is submitted that the position of the trunk will be decisive. In cases of doubt, and where the tree stands more or less equally on both sides of the boundary, it should be treated as jointly owned.[13]

2 OVERHANGING TREES

The law relating to encroaching tree roots and branches was comprehensively reviewed by the Court of Appeal in 1957 in *Davey* v. *Harrow Corporation.*[14] It was there reaffirmed that an owner of land on which a tree grows is liable if its roots or branches encroach on adjoining land and cause damage, and it is immaterial for this purpose whether the tree is planted or self-sown. The appropriate remedy is an action for nuisance, although no action for nuisance will lie unless actual damage is caused by the encroaching branches or roots.[15] So in *Butler* v. *Standard Telephone & Cables, Ltd.*[16] poplars reached a height of 40 ft. in nine years, and their roots caused damage to the foundations of an adjoining house, making underpinning necessary. The defendants were held liable for the damage so caused. Poplars are a particularly dangerous sort of tree to plant anywhere near a boundary or adjacent building. They have a very extensive root growth and in spite of their usefulness as a screen, they should be avoided.

The remedy of injunction is also available to restrain a landowner from continuing to permit injury being caused by overhanging branches or undergrowing roots. Thus, in *McCombe* v. *Read*,[17] HARMAN, J. granted an injunction restraining a continuing nuisance from encroaching roots, and awarded damages for the settlement

13. *Waterman* v. *Soper* (1698), 1 Ld. Raym. 737 *per* HOLT, C.J.
14. [1958] 1 Q.B. 60; [1957] 2 All E.R. 305; *Morgan* v. *Khyatt*, [1964] 1 W.L.R. 475.
15. *Smith* v. *Giddy*, [1904] 2 K.B. 448.
16. [1940] 1 K.B. 399; [1940] 1 All E.R. 121.
17. [1955] 2 Q.B. 429; [1955] 2 All E.R. 458.

caused to the plaintiff's house by the root growth. In the majority of cases an ordinary action for nuisance will be sufficient except where, as in *McCombe* v. *Read*, failure to remedy the cause of the nuisance might cause considerable further injury.[18] Since trees grow from year to year, no prescriptive right to allow them to overhang or encroach can be claimed.

Poisonous trees require special mention. In *Crowhurst* v. *Amersham Burial Board*[19] the defendants planted a yew tree on the cemetery boundary. The plaintiff's horse was poisoned by eating the leaves from the branches overhanging his land. The defendants were liable. This is, perhaps, best considered as an aspect of the rule in *Rylands* v. *Fletcher*[20] and not as nuisance *simpliciter*:

> "for though the consequence is natural, it is not good husbandry to plant poisonous trees, which may overhang another's field in which domestic animals are kept, and is therefore not a natural use of land."[1]

However, there will be no liability if the plaintiff's beasts are trespassing on adjoining property and eat poisonous leaves from a tree growing there, assuming that the defendant is under no liability to fence.[2] Similarly, since a tenant takes the demised property as he finds it, if the branches of a poisonous tree growing on adjoining property retained by the landlord poison the tenant's cattle, he will be without remedy.[3]

There is no duty imposed upon a landowner to lop or top a well-grown tree growing on his premises, even if it is near the highway, unless there is something that would signify danger to a prudent householder.[4] However, apart from an action in nuisance or remedy by injunction, an adjoining owner troubled by overhanging branches or undergrowing roots may exercise self-help and cut off the offending

---

18. See *Middleton* v. *Humphries* (1913), 47 Ir. L.T. 160.
19. (1878), 4 Exch. D. 5, explaining *Wilson* v. *Newberry* (1871), L.R. 7 Q.B. 31.
20. (1868), L.R. 3 H.L. 330.
1. Underhill, *Law of Torts*, (16th Edn.), p. 237.
2. *Ponting* v. *Nokes*, [1894] 2 Q.B. 281. There would be no liability if the poisonous leaves appeared on the joining property inexplicably, unless there was negligence: *Wilson* v. *Newberry* (1871), L.R. 7 A.B. 31. See also *Mackie* v. *Dunbartonshire C.C.* (1927), 91 J.P. 158 as to liability in negligence for trees.
3. *Cheater* v. *Cater*, [1918] 1 K.B. 247; *Erskine* v. *Adeane* (1873), 8 Ch. App. 756.
4. *Noble* v. *Harrison*, [1926] 2 K.B. 332; *Caminer* v. *Northern and London Investment Trust, Ltd.*, [1951] A.C. 88; [1950] 2 All E.R. 486.

shoots, even where no damage has been caused. The leading case on abatement is *Lemmon* v. *Webb*[5] where the House of Lords, affirming the Court of Appeal, held that the defendant was justified in cutting off projecting branches, without going on to the plaintiff's land, and not having given notice of intention.[6] Notice is only necessary where abatement involves entry, and even here is unnecessary where the occupier is responsible for the creation or continuance of a nuisance (*i.e.*, damage is being caused) or in an emergency.[7]

Self-help is, however, fraught with danger. Care must be taken to cut off only the branches actually overhanging the property of the abator and those only to the boundary.[8]

3 FRUIT OF BOUNDARY TREES

The fruit and branches of a tree belong to its owner even after they have been severed by the adjoining owner in abating a nuisance. The cuttings, etc., should be offered back to their owner.[9] A neighbour has no right to branches or fruit which fall accidentally on to his land from trees on adjoining property. He is liable in conversion if he appropriates them. Thus if in abating a nuisance one lops boughs with fruit on them, and retains the fruit, there will be liability for the value of the fruit.[10]

It is not clear whether the owner of a tree may enter on adjoining land to recover fallen branches and fruit. The point was left undecided in *Mills* v. *Brooker*[11] but dicta in older cases and such other authority as there is suggests that the owner may enter to retake his property.[12] It may well be, as implied in one case, that entry for re-caption is not

---

5. [1894] 3 Ch. 1; [1895] A.C. 1. *Pickering* v. *Rudd* (1815), 4 Camp. 219.
6. The same principle applies to roots, even though the tree is destroyed as a result of their being cut off: see *per* LINDLEY, L.J. [1894] 3 Ch. 1, at 14. But the abator cannot destroy the tree directly by felling or poisoning it.
7. *Jones* v. *Williams* (1843), 11 M. & W. 176. It should be mentioned that by s. 10 of the Land Powers (Defence) Act 1958, certain Ministers have power to order trees and hedges interfering with airfields to be pruned or lopped. As to the powers of highway authorities see *post*, pp. 137–138.
8. *Pickering* v. *Rudd* (1815), 1 Start. 56; *Houghton* v. *Butler* (1791), Term Rep. 364; *Roberts* v. *Rose* (1865), 4 H. & C. 103.
9. *Forsdick* v. *Collins* (1815), 1 Starkie 173; *Houghton* v. *Butler* (1791), Term Rep. 364.
10. *Mills* v. *Brooker*, [1919] 1 K.B. 555, at 558.
11. [1919] 1 K.B. 555.
12. Y.B. Ass. 8 Edw. 4.; *Mitten* v. *Faudrye* (1626), Poph. 161; *Smith* v. *Kenrick* (1848), 7 C.B. 515.

justified unless a prior request has been made.[13] In view of this uncertainty the proper course is to ask permission to enter. If this is refused, and the demand for the return of the produce is denied, there will be evidence of conversion, although in most cases it will not be worth litigation. It is also uncertain whether a man can lop his tree so that its branches fall on to neighbouring land.[14]

4 TREES OVER OR ADJOINING THE HIGHWAY

In general the same principles apply to trees over the highway as to those overhanging adjoining property. A recent case is *British Road Services, Ltd.* v. *Slater.*[15] There a lorry belonging to the plaintiffs was carrying packing cases stacked some 16 ft. above the ground. The upmost case collided with the branch of an oak tree growing beside or on the verge of the road, and was knocked into the highway. In trying to avoid it, another lorry belonging to the plaintiffs went off the road and was extensively damaged. The plaintiffs sued the defendant occupiers on the ground that they had caused or continued a nuisance[16]. LORD PARKER, C.J. found that the branch was a nuisance taking into account the fact that lorries using the highway carried high loads. It was only a nuisance,

> "by the fortuitous circumstances that these two heavy lorries happened to meet in the dark at the point where the bough was over the road."[1]

On the facts the learned judge held the defendants not liable for continuing the nuisance on the principle laid down in *Sedleigh-Denfield* v. *O'Callaghan*,[2] but he suggested *obiter* that in some circumstances the prudent occupier ought to have trees lopped and topped regularly, *i.e.*, where his premises front on to a main arterial road.[3]

---

13. *Anthony* v. *Haney* (1832), 8 Bing. 186, at 192; 20 Viner's *Abridgment* (1793 Edn.), Trespass, 1 a; Trees E. 1.
14. See *Dike and Dunston's Case* (1586), Gdb. 52.
15. [1964] 1 All E.R. 816.
16. It is a nuisance to allow trees or bushes to grow over the highway: see *per* KAY, L.J. in *Lemmon* v. *Webb*, [1894] 3 Ch. 1, at 24.
1. [1964] 1 All E.R. 816, at 820.
2. [1940] 3 All E.R. 349.
3. *Caminer* v. *Northern and London Investment Trust, Ltd.*, [1951] A.C. 88; [1950] 2 All E.R. 486. Lopping is to cut the lateral branchs of a tree: *Unwin* v. *Hanson*, [1891] 2 Q.B. 115. See also *Quinn* v. *Scott*, [1965] 2 All E.R. 588, where failure to cut an unhealthy, top-heavy tree, part of which fell across the highway in the path of vehicles, amounted to breach of the duty of care owed by an owner of land adjoining the highway to prevent danger to highway users. The defendants were held liable in negligence; knowledge of the tree's condition was imputed to them although their forester had not reported this condition to them. See further *Cunliffe* v. *Banks*, [1945] 1 All E.R. 459 where negligence was not established.

Trees are frequently found growing in the verges of highways, and s. 82 of the Highways Act 1959, enables a highway authority to plant trees and shrubs in the verges, but they must not be set,

> "or allowed to remain in such a situation as to hinder the reasonable use of the highway by any person entitled to the use thereof, or so as to be a nuisance or injurious to the owner or occupier of premises adjacent to the highway."

Where trees are planted under this provision the authority will be liable for damage caused by roots and branches or the falling of the tree itself. They are liable to pay compensation for damage caused by trees they plant.

Trees planted in the highway before its dedication and those which spring up subsequently without human intervention belong to the owner of the soil, *i.e.*, normally the adjoining owner.[4] It seems, however, that he can maintain an action for trespass and nuisance against a highway authority if he is troubled by encroaching roots and overhanging branches from trees set in the verge. *Stillwell* v. *New Windsor Corporation*[5] indicates that the highway authority has a *right* to cut down or lop trees on roads which are "ancient highways"[6] in the interests of public safety. And it seems that they have a sufficient interest in the trees to make them liable in trespass or nuisance where appropriate, for if such trees become a danger to the public it is suggested that the highway authority is under a *duty* to deal with them.[7] The adjoining owner may himself remedy the nuisance, but he cannot break open the surface of the road to destroy penetrating roots.[8] Trees growing adjacent to the highway and not in the limits of the road itself are the responsibility of the proprietor concerned.[9] Where a road is vested in the highway authority, they have sufficient possession of the verges to enable them to remove obstructions and dangers and they are under a duty to do so. This does not necessarily relieve

4. *Goodtitle d. Chester* v. *Alker* (1757), 1 Ken. 427.
5. [1932] 2 Ch. 155.
6. An ancient highway is one which was a public right of way prior to 31st August, 1835, the day on which the Highway Act 1835 received the Royal Assent.
7. As to the authority's liability see further an article by Professor J. F. Garner in (1956), J.P.L. 487 and two articles cited there in (1948), 112 J.P.N. 22 and 198 where there is a comprehensive review of the authorities.
8. *Hyde Corporation* v. *Oldham, etc., Tramway* (1900), 16 T.L.R. 492.
9. Where a road is vested in the Secretary of State for the Environment the position is exactly the same as in the case of any other highway authority.

the adjoining owner from liability, because the property in the tree remains in him.[10]

Local authorities have very wide powers of dealing with overhanging trees and vegetation on property near to the highway. The owner of land may thereby be compelled to behave reasonably. The main provisions may be summarised briefly. Section 10 of the Highways (Miscellaneous Provisions) Act 1961, enables the local authority to serve notice on the owner or occupier of land requiring him to cut or fell any hedge, tree or shrub, in a condition which is likely to cause danger to road users. This notice may be served where it appears to the authority that any such vegetation is diseased, damaged, dead or insecurely rooted and by reason of its condition is likely to cause danger by falling on to the road or footpath. There is a right of appeal to the magistrates. The notice becomes operative 14 days from the date of service, and the authority have the usual default powers.

Similar power is contained in s. 134 of the Highways Act 1959, which provides that the authority may by 14 days' notice require an owner or occupier to lop or cut any hedge, tree or shrub overhanging a highway or any other road or footpath used by the public, which obstructs or interferes with the view of motorists or pedestrians. Default power is given to the authority, and there is a similar right of appeal to the magistrates' court. In Cornwall, Devon, Dorset, Somerset or Wiltshire the highway authority may cut back any hedge or other vegetation on a bank which is obstructing the highway, with the consent of the owner or occupier.

Power to compel the pruning, cutting or lopping of trees, hedges or other vegetation which is causing damage to a carriageway[11] is contained in s. 120 of the 1959 Act. The marginal note to the section reads "Damage to highway consequent on exclusion of sun or wind." The highway authority may make a complaint to the justices, and an order may be made for the carrying out of the necessary works between October 1st and March 31st in any year. The penalty for non compliance with a magistrates' order within 10 days is a fine not

10. See *per* LORD PARKER, C.J. in *British Road Services* v. *Slater*, [1964] 1 All E.R. 816, at 818–819.

11. Carriageway is defined by s. 258 as being a way constituting or comprised in a highway (other than a cycle track) over which the public have a vehicular right of way.

exceeding £2, and the highway authority has default powers. The section also gives power to prune by agreement.

Finally, s. 123 of the Highways Act 1959, restricts the planting of trees in a made-up carriageway, or within 15 ft. from its centre. There is a special exemption in the case of dual carriageways and roundabouts, as s. 65 (2) gives local authorities power to plant trees, shrubs or other vegetation on them "either for ornament or in the interests of safety." Likewise, s. 82 gives power to highway and local authorities to plant trees, shrubs and other vegetation in highways maintainable at the public expense. A person contravening the provisions of s. 123 may be required to remove the offending foliage within 21 days of notice being served by the highway authority. The penalty for contravention is a fine not exceeding 50p, and a daily fine of like amount for a continuing offence.

DANGEROUS FENCES

There may be liability in negligence or nuisance or both where a fence is in a dangerous or dilapidated condition. In appropriate circumstances there would also be liability under the Occupiers' Liability Act 1957, even in the case of a wall or fence which was not subject to any positive obligation to repair. The injury complained of must be reasonably foreseeable for there to be liability in negligence.[12] An illustration of such liability is to be found in *Firth* v. *Bowling Iron Co.*,[13] where the lessee of a colliery covenanted to fence his works for the benefit of the lessor and the adjoining tenants. He erected wire fences, which fell into decay, and pieces of the rusting wire fell on the adjoining property. One of the adjoining occupier's cows was killed by eating the pieces of rusting wire. The covenantee was held liable because he was aware of the nature of the fence and the damage caused was its natural consequence.

It has been said that "a rotten fence close to a highway is an obvious nuisance"[14] and there are a number of cases where a passerby has recovered damages for injuries suffered owing to defective fencing.

---

12. See the unreported case of *Morton* v. *Wheeler* (1956), *Times*, 31st January, where someone fell against spikes on a window sill and was fatally injured.
13. (1878), 3 C.P.D. 254. See also *Lax* v. *Darlington Corporation* (1879), 5 Ex. D. 28.
14. *Jewson* v. *Gatti* (1886), 2 T.L.R. 441.

Thus, in *Harrold* v. *Watney*[15] the plaintiff, aged four, while passing along a road climbed up on the defendant's fence to watch some children playing on the other side. The fence was so defective as to constitute a nuisance and fell upon the plaintiff and injured him. The Court of Appeal upheld his claim for damages. The boy was merely indulging his natural instincts and doing something which the defendant ought to have contemplated as likely to be done, and thus there was liability.[16] Conversely, in *Liddle* v. *Yorkshire (North Riding) County Council*[17] a child was injured when climbing over a heap of soil to a new wall, from which he fell backwards. The defendant council had carried out the works in connection with a road improvement scheme. The Court of Appeal found that there was no evidence to show the child to be an invitee or a licensee—he had been warned off on several occasions. In sitting on the wall he was a trespasser, and thus without redress. The defendants had not created a trap or injured him intentionally; but the position would probably be different to-day.

It has already been remarked that an occupier is entitled to take reasonable precautions to guard against intrusion by trespassers. He may, for example, set broken glass or spikes in cement along the top of his wall. Such action can be fraught with danger if the wall is low and near to the highway. So in *Fenna* v. *Clare & Co.*[18] spikes were set on a low wall in front of a shop window. A child who fell on them recovered damages from the owner, it being held that where the evidence shows that an injury might have been caused to a person passing along the highway by a public nuisance existing thereon, the jury is entitled to infer that the injury was the result of the nuisance.[19]

However, it is thought that spikes or broken glass are *prima facie* not a nuisance if set vertically in a wall of reasonable height, even abutting a highway. The position is different if they are set to project horizontally or if the wall is so low that users of the highway, or lawful

15. [1898] 2 Q.B. 320.
16. *Robertson* v. *Glasgow Corporation* 1950 S.C. 502. See also *Barker* v. *Herbert*, [1911] 2 K.B. 633.
17. [1934] 2 K.B. 101. But see now *British Railways Board* v. *Herrington*, [1972] A.C. 877, *ante*, p. 130.
18. [1895] 1 Q.B. 199.
19. But see *Gibson* v. *Plumstead Burial Board* (1897), 13 T.L.R. 273 where a horse fell on a spiked fence 4 ft. 6 ins. in height and was injured. The defendant was not liable, the court holding that a fence of that height, even though consisting of spikes, was not a nuisance on the highway.

visitors to the property, falling against them are likely to be impaled, as in *Fenna* v. *Clare.*[20]

It has long been recognised that barbed wire fences along a road may be a nuisance, *i.e.*, they are likely to cause injury to road users. For example, in *Stewart* v. *Wright*[1] the plaintiff was walking along the highway when a gust of wind caught his coat and blew it on to a barbed wire fence. He was successful in his claim for damages. The position is now governed by statute. By s. 143 of the Highways Act 1959, where land adjoining a highway is fenced with barbed wire, or with a fence containing barbed wire, and the wire is a nuisance to the highway, the highway authority has power to serve a notice on the occupier requiring its removal with a period of not less than one month nor mor than six months.[2] Barbed wire is defined by s. 143 (4) as: "wire with spikes or jagged projections". Barbed wire is deemed to be a nuisance to the highway, "if it is likely to be injurious to persons or animals using the highway."[3]

If the local authority is the occupier of land adjoining a highway, and there is a barbed wire fence, any ratepayer may make a complaint. The local authority have default powers where a magistrates' court has made an order requiring the occupier to abate the nuisance and he fails to do so within a reasonable time, and they may then recover their reasonable expenses. In most cases, service of the notice by the local authority is sufficient to produce speedy action.

Fences in a defective or dangerous condition which adjoin the highway may be dealt with by the local authority under ss. 24 and 25 of the Public Health Act 1961. Section 24 of the 1961 Act amends s. 58 of the Public Health Act 1936, and empowers the magistrates, on complaint by the local authority, to make an order requiring works to be carried out where any building or structure or part thereof is in such a condition as to be dangerous to a person in the street, in the premises themselves, or in adjoining premises. Failure to comply with the order within a reasonable time as specified is an offence punishable with a fine not exceeding £10. The local authority may then carry out the works at the owner's expense. Section 25 contains

---

20. [1895] 1 Q.B. 199.
1. (1893), 9 T.L.R. 280; and see *Fenna* v. *Clare* [1895] 1 Q.B. 199; *Meara* v. *Daly* (1914), 48 Ir. L.T. 223.
2. The notice must be in writing: 1959 Act, s. 200(1).
3. For a discussion of the cases on the subject see 56 J.P. 163 and 76 J.P. 230.

an emergency procedure applicable where immediate action is necessary. The local authority may take any necessary action to abate the nuisance, if possible giving due notice of their intention to the owner or occupier, and recover the expenses involved from the person in default.[4]

ELECTRIFIED FENCES

Electric fences are a common feature of the countryside, and their existence may give rise to claims in negligence or nuisance if persons or animals come into contact with them and are injured. There appear to be no regularly reported cases on the topic, but there is a fairly recent County Court decision. This is *Geldard* v. *Weeks*[5] where the plaintiff sued for nuisance and negligence in respect of personal injuries he had sustained. He was riding his horse along a bridleway, which was six feet in width, bounded on the north side by a grass verge some four feet wide, edged by a non-live electric fence. On its south side was a grass bank seven feet wide, rising to a height of three feet above the bridleway itself, and bounded by a live electric fence. The plaintiff's horse came into contact with the north fence and careered across the bridleway, mounted the bank and came into contact with the live fence. It bolted further and, forty yards on, threw and injured the plaintiff.

The learned judge found for the defendant, saying:

> "I have found that the plaintiff has not satisfied me that the north fence was the cause of the horse being originally startled or, if it was (say if a short piece of wire protruded from a join), that the fence was a nuisance. Assuming that after the original fright the horse came into contact with the south fence, which was live, can I hold that it was a nuisance to persons lawfully using the highway? The [south] fence was on top of a fairly steep bank three feet above the track and seven feet from the nearest part of the trodden way. I cannot see that the ordinary reasonable farmer could foresee that a live fence in that position could be a danger or nuisance to persons using the bridleway. No rider in the ordinary way would guide his horse or permit it to walk up the bank and the evidence was clear (as in fact I saw) that the trodden way was clearly defined. Nor do I think that such a farmer would anticipate

4. These provisions replace those in s. 145 of the Highways Act 1959.
5. (1967), October 24th, Haywards Heath County Court, HIS HONOUR JUDGE HAROLD BROWN, discussed by A. Samuels in (1968) *Solicitors' Journal* 494. I am grateful to Mr Samuels for allowing me to incorporate the substance of his article here.

> that in such rural surroundings far from traffic a horse would become so startled that it would charge across the path and mount the bank".

This decision does not lay down any general principle of negligence or nuisance for electric fences but shows the judicial approach. It is thought that where an ordinary electric fence is installed by a competent contractor and is competently managed,[6] no action in nuisance would normally lie because such fences are common, their nature is well-known and the current through the fence is very low.

---

6. See *Green* v. *Fibreglass*, [1958] 2 Q.B. 245; [1958] 2 All E.R. 521; *Cook* v. *Broderip* (1968), 112 Sol. Jo. 193.

Chapter 8

PARTY WALLS

A party wall is "any wall which parts or divides adjoining lands, whether built upon or not, held by different owners." Rudall, *Party Walls* (3rd Edn.), p. 1.

DEFINITION

The name "party wall" is not a term of art, and as Rudall's definition makes clear it is not necessarily a wall separating buildings.[1] At common law the term might be used in four different senses, as FRY, J. pointed out in *Watson* v. *Gray*.[2] The first of these—a wall of which two adjoining owners were tenants in common—is now obsolete, since s. 38 of the Law of Property Act 1925 provides that party structures are to be treated as being vertically severed. Each owner has such rights of user and support over the whole wall as they would have enjoyed had they been tenants in common under the old law. This was in fact the most usual method of holding party walls before 1926, and in the absence of evidence to the contrary this form was presumed.[3] So in *Wiltshire* v. *Sidford*[4] BAYLEY, J. said:

> "Where the builder of two houses grants off one, it is more reasonable to presume that he grants the whole wall in undivided moieties, than that he should leave either party the power of cutting the wall in half. That would be the case if the houses were built by one and the same person. If two persons built at the same time, the probability is that they

---

1. A party wall may, for example, separate open yards. In the Building Regulations 1972, the neutral term "separating wall" is used for a wall separating two buildings. A recent practical definition is found in *The Architect's Journal Legal Handbook* (1972), p. 73; "Walls which are divided down the long axis on plan into two strips, each strip belonging to the owner of the land on which it stands".
2. (1880), 14 Ch.D. 192, at 194, where a declaration in a conveyance that the wall was a party wall was held to create a tenancy in common.
3. *Wiltshire* v. *Sidford* (1827), 1 Man. & Ry. 404; *Cubitt* v. *Porter* (1828), 8 B. & C. 257; *Mason* v. *Fulham Corporation*, [1910] 1 K.B. 631, at 637.
4. (1827), 1 Man. & Ry. 404.

> would take a conveyance of an undivided moiety of the ground on which the wall was to be erected, in order that the property might afterwards be kept in the same state."

This assumption still holds good as preliminary to the application of s. 38 of the 1925 Act.

TYPES OF WALL

There are now three categories of party wall.[5] First, and most commonly, where the wall is divided vertically, the whole wall being subject to reciprocal easements.[6] Secondly, where the wall is divided vertically into strips, one belonging to each adjoining owner.[7] Finally, where the wall belongs entirely to one adjoining proprietor, subject to the other's rights to have it maintained as a dividing wall.[8] Each of these three cases requires special consideration.

1 WALLS SUBJECT TO RECIPROCAL EASEMENTS

Under the old law most party walls were held by tenancy in common, each owner being entitled to support from the wall (where appropriate), together with mutual rights to prevent destruction of the wall. The Law of Property Act 1925, has substituted a division of the wall with reciprocal easements. It can still be assumed, unless there is contrary evidence, that the wall was formerly held by tenancy in common, before the 1925 Act can be applied.

Section 38 of the 1925 Act dealt with the position in the following terms:

> "Where, immediately before the commencement of this Act, a party wall or other party structure is held in undivided shares, the ownership thereof shall be deemed to be severed vertically as between the respective owners, and the owner of each part shall have such rights to support and user over the rest of the structure as may be requisite for conferring rights corresponding to those subsisting at the commencement of this Act."[9]

---

5. In London the position is governed by the London Building Acts, and certain special rules and definitions apply. See *post*, pp. 155–164.
6. *Watson* v. *Gray* (1880), 14 Ch.D. 192, at 195.
7. *Matts* v. *Hawkins* (1813), 5 Taunt. 20.
8. *Watson* v. *Gray* (1880), 14 Ch.D. 292.
9. See also s. 39 and Schedule I, Part IV, *ibid.*

By s. 38 (2) the court has power to make a declaration as to the rights in a party structure, where there is a dispute, on the application of any interested party.

In the result most party walls come within this category, and where both parties use the wall this form will still be presumed, because common user of a wall is *prima facie* evidence of it being common property.[10] The adjoining owners have similar rights or reciprocal easements against each other.[11] If the wall varies in thickness throughout its height, the centre line would presumably follow variations in the thickness, although no doubt ignoring buttresses on one side as *de minimis*.

Primarily the rights imported by s. 38 are those of support and user only. Each party may use the wall for support and so on, and in the absence of negligence there will be no liability for inconvenience arising from such use.[11] One owner could not, however, put an excessive load on the wall thereby endangering its stability.[12] There would be liability if damage was caused to the adjoining property by underpinning.[13] In *Jones* v. *Pritchard*[14] it was decided that where there is a party wall between two houses subject to cross-rights there will be implied between the two owners such reciprocal easements as are necessary to give effect to the common intent. However, if each owner exercises his rights without negligence, he will not be liable for any damage caused by subsidence or otherwise. Pulling down and then rebuilding a party wall to a greater height will not constitute trespass.[15] It is, however, doubtful whether the rights of user and support conferred by s. 38 of the Law of Property Act 1925, allow more than this, because there must be continued enjoyment of the reciprocal easements.[16]

---

10. *Cubitt* v. *Porter* (1828), 8 B. & C. 257. There are various structures which have to be joint property in this sense, *e.g.*, gutters, gullies, fallpipes, etc., and they cannot be severed along a median line.
11. *Richards* v. *Rose* (1853), 9 Exch. 218; *Howarth* v. *Armstrong* (1897), 77 L.T. 62.
12. *Sheffield Improved Industrial and Provident Society* v. *Jarvis* (1871), W.N. 208.
13. *Bradbee* v. *Christ's Hospital* (1842), 11 L.J.C.P. 209.
14. [1908] 1 Ch. 630, on conveyance on sale.
15. *Cubitt* v. *Porter* (1828), 8 B. & C. 257.
16. See *Stedman* v. *Smith* (1857), 26 L.J.Q.B. 314, where the erection of a roof over a wall, preventing the adjoining owner exercising his rights, amounted to trespass.

Party structures

Section 38 quite clearly refers to "a party wall or other party structure", and it is submitted that its provisions must apply to all party structures and not merely to party walls as is often assumed. It is true that the section goes on to speak of the severance being vertical, but this would not appear to prevent the rules applying to ceilings and floors between flats and maisonettes. A horizontal structure can be taken to be severed along its median plane:

> "If the walls are vertical, the line of severance will be vertical in the ordinary sense; but if the division (*e.g.*, a ceiling or floor) is itself horizontal, the line of severance must be taken through the ceiling and floor as if that were itself vertical."[17]

This is borne out by *Phelps* v. *City of London Corporation*[18] where the point came up incidentally in relation to a ceiling. It was unfortunately left open in the more recent case of *Sturge* v. *Hackett*,[19] which concerned the extent of a demise of a flat, DIPLOCK, L.J. saying that on the inside face of the external wall, the flat

> "must have extended to at least the underside of the floor joists to which (the) ceiling was attached. It is unnecessary to decide whether it extended half-way through the thickness of the floor joists or to the the top side of them . . ."

Difficulty can be avoided by expressly providing in a lease or conveyance where the line of severance is to run, and the floors and ceilings could be made party structures.[20] There is no logical reason to suppose that s. 38 applies to walls alone, and it is suggested that the fact that the spaces between floor and ceiling joists are normally hollow is quite immaterial.

---

17. Wolstenholme & Cherry, *Conveyancing Statutes*, 12th Edn., vol. 1, p. 628; W. A. Leach, *Party Structure Rights in London*, p. 8; W. A. Leach, *Practical Points on Leases* (1961), p. 19. See also 14 *Conveyancer* (N.S.) (1950), p. 381.
18. [1916] 2 Ch. 255. It should be noted that party structure is defined in s. 4 of the London Building Acts (Amendment) Act 1939, so as to include a floor or other partition.
19. [1962] 3 All E.R. 166, at 172.
20. A precedent declaration as to horizontal severance is set out in 22 Conv. (N.S.) 701, the line of severance being the underside of the floor joists. It may be considered fairer and better to make the whole structure joint property, in which case the whole of it belongs to both owners, because it is difficult to repair or rebuild one half without dealing with the other.

The difficulty in fact appears to be more literary than legal, for it seems to be generally assumed in the case of party property that the two (or more) owners are jointly liable for the repair and maintenance of the whole structure. In fact, in the absence of agreement or prescriptive or customary obligation to that effect, there is no positive obligation placed on either party to repair. Some structures such as guttering and rainwater fallpipes must be joint (or "party") property and should be maintainable at the equally shared expense of the owners. Clearly such structures cannot be severed for the purposes of s. 38 of the Law of Property Act 1925, but walls and floors can be. The point is that the word "party" can have several meanings, and so it is essential to state the legal position in the clearest possible terms so that there is no room for argument.

2 WALLS DIVIDED VERTICALLY

Where a boundary wall is erected partly on the land of two adjoining owners along the boundary line, its ownership follows the land, even though the wall is built at joint expense.[1] It is not subject to joint ownership and each neighbour owns the half on his side. It is a question of fact whether the wall is built exactly on the boundary, but any minor discrepancy will be ignored as *de minimis*.[2] The rights of the parties in such a case will be as agreed, either expressly or impliedly. This may sometimes give rise to a right of contribution towards the cost of repair under local custom.[3] In all cases where a party wall is in divided ownership, there is a mutual right of support and neither owner can pull down his portion of the wall so as to disturb the rights of the other.[4] There is nothing to prevent one neighbour demolishing his half of the wall, without negligence, if this does not prejudice any easements enjoyed by the other owner,[5] but he cannot do so, *e.g.*, if any existing right of support would be disturbed.

Interference with any existing easement would make the demolishing owner liable, and it is immaterial that he has employed an inde-

1. *Matts* v. *Hawkins*, (1813), 5 Taunt. 20; *Mayfair Property Co.* v. *Johnston*, [1894] 1 Ch. 508. *Cf.*, *Waddington* v. *Naylor* (1889), 60 L.T. 480.
2. *Reading* v. *Barnard* (1827), Moo. & M. 71 and see *Jones* v. *Read* (1876), 10 I.R.C.L. 315, at 320.
3. 3 *Halsbury's Laws*, 3rd Edn., 381.
4. *Wiltshire* v. *Sidford* (1827), 1 Man. & Ry. K.B. 404.
5. *Mayfair Property Co.* v. *Johnston*, [1894] 1 Ch. 508; *Kempston* v. *Butler* (1861), 12 I.R.C.L. 516.

pendent contractor to execute the works of demolition, although the contractor may also be liable.[6] This form of ownership imposes no positive obligation to repair, and neither owner need take any active steps to prevent the wall falling into a ruinous condition, unless some express, implied or customary agreement can be shown.[7]

3 WALLS IN SINGLE OWNERSHIP

If a wall is built entirely on one man's land, it is his to do with as he pleases. A wall will be a party wall so far as it is used as such and no further.[8] The adjoining owner may acquire rights in respect of the wall by agreement or prescription but unless such rights can be proved to exist the wall will not be a party wall in the proper sense. It follows that if a wall belonged originally to one owner he may demolish it if he pleases, subject to any express or acquired right of support that may exist.[9] Although a man may erect a boundary wall hard up against the boundary, there is no right to place the footings on adjoining land, without the consent of the neighbouring owner.[10] There is similarly no inherent right of access for purposes of repair.

An easement of support may be acquired prescriptively under the Prescription Act 1832, by user as of right for twenty or forty years.[11] A leading textbook summarises the common situation well:[12]

> "Where adjoining buildings support one another it is therefore difficult for their owners to preserve their liberty to demolish them for more than 20 years. Probably their only course is to issue a writ claiming a declaration that no easement as yet subsists, so preventing user as of right."

---

6. *Bower* v. *Peate* (1876), 1 Q.B.D. 321; *White* v. *Peto* (1888), 58 L.T. 710. It would be no defence to show that the wall was unstable: *Hoare* v. *McAlpine*, [1923] 1 Ch. 167.
7. *Southwark and Vauxhall Water Co.* v. *Wandsworth Board of Works*, [1898] 2 Ch. 603, at 612.
8. *Weston* v. *Arnold* (1873), 8 Ch. App. 1084; *Drury* v. *Army and Navy Stores Auxiliary Co-operative Supply, Ltd.*, [1896] 2 Q.B. 271; *London and Gloucestershire Dairy Co.* v. *Morley*, [1911] 2 K.B. 257.
9. *Wiltshire* v. *Sidford* (1827), 1 Man. & Ry. K.B. 404.
10. *Thornton* v. *Hunter* (1898), unreported except in *Building News*, 4th February, 1898. A right to do so may be given by statute, *e.g.*, s. 45 of the London Building Acts (Amendment) Act 1939.
11. *Dalton* v. *Angus & Co.* (1881), 6 App. Cas. 740; *Bond* v. *Nottingham Corporation*, [1940] Ch. 429.
12. Megarry & Wade, *Law of Real Property*, (3rd Edn.), p. 873.

RIGHTS AND DUTIES OF OWNERS

1 SUPPORT

Apart from statute a man cannot claim a right of support for his property unless he has acquired that right by grant, reservation, or prescription. At common law there is no obligation cast on the owner of a house to keep it repaired in a substantial manner. The only duty is to prevent it becoming a nuisance.[13] Damage to property resulting from a neighbour's negligence would, of course, be actionable. Where houses are erected contiguous to each other by the same owner, mutual support is necessarily required. This is acquired by presumed grant or reservation when the owner sells one of the houses, by virtue of the general words of s. 62 of the Law of Property Act 1925.[14]

Unless there is proof that there exists some right of or duty to support, no liability can attach to an adjoining owner if he demolishes his property. Thus, in *Smith* v. *Thackerah*[15] the plaintiff was entitled to a natural right of lateral support for his land, but not to support for a wall which was built on it. The defendant dug a well in his own property, and later filled it in inadequately. Subsidence occurred and the neighbour's wall tumbled down. He was held to have no cause of action. Had there been no wall on the land, there would have been no appreciable damage. It would have been an unwarranted extension of the law to hold the defendant liable for using his own land in a reasonable fashion: *damnum sine injuria.*

One reason for the common law presumption that a party wall was held by tenancy in common was that where each owner held part of the wall separately, he could pull down his half, unless there was an agreement to the contrary.[16] This is still good law, and if such a case arises to-day no action will lie against the demolishing owner,

---

13. *Chauntler* v. *Robinson* (1849), 4 Ex. 163.
14. See *Ward* v. *Kirkland*, [1966] 1 All E.R. 609 discussed in Chapter 6, *ante*, p. 116.
15. (1866), L.R. 1 C.P. 564.
16. *Bradbee* v. *Christ's Hospital* (1842), 11 L.J.C.P. 209. It was desirable (but not essential) to give notice of intention: *Massey* v. *Goyder* (1829), 4 C. & P. 161; *Chadwick* v. *Trower* (1839), 6 Bing. N.C. 1.

provided that he does the work without negligence. This is so even if the other half of the wall falls down unless a right of support had been acquired. There is no right to have a wall shored up in the absence of an easement of support or some statutory provision.[17] If there is negligence action will lie even where there is no easement of support, *e.g.*, where one owner damages his neighbour's part of the wall in carrying out improvements to his own property.[18] Walls subject to s. 38 of the Law of Property Act 1925, will enjoy a right of support, and this comprises the greater number of party walls. In the other two cases, an easement of support may be acquired. A local authority demolishing property under statutory power is bound to provide alternative support where an easement of support exists.[19]

Threatened withdrawal of support would be restrained by injunction in appropriate cases, but in general no action for nuisance can be maintained until actual damage has been caused.[1] The servient owner is not obliged to maintain a structure for the benefit of the dominant owner,[2] and in effecting repairs to a party wall is bound only to act in a reasonable manner, so as not to cause unnecessary damage.[3] Where a third party damages a wall governed by s. 38 of the 1925 Act, each owner can recover for the damage to that half of the wall which is vested in him.[4]

One of the most illuminating cases on withdrawal of support, and the damages recoverable in respect thereof, is *Upjohn* v. *Seymour Estates, Ltd.*[5] There two properties were separated by a party wall, which was governed by s. 38 of the Law of Property Act 1925. The defendants began to demolish their building, and their part of the wall collapsed, exposing two apertures in the plaintiff's premises. Dirt and debris fell through these holes, damaging the plaintiff's stock. GODDARD, J., as he then was, found that the defendants had not trespassed on the party wall, but held that the adjoining premises enjoyed

---

17. *Kempston* v. *Butler* (1861), 12 I.C.L. 516. A relevant statutory provision is Public Health Act 1961, s. 29.
18. *St. Anne's Well Brewery Co.* v. *Roberts* (1928), 140 L.T. 1.
19. *Bond* v. *Nottingham Corporation*, [1939] 2 All E.R. 610; *Birch* v. *Wigan Corporation*, [1953] 1 Q.B. 136; [1952] 2 All E.R. 893.
1. *Smith* v. *Giddy*, [1904] 2 K.B. 448.
2. *Sack* v. *Jones*, [1925] Ch. 325; *Dalton* v. *Angus* (1881), 6 App. Cas. 740.
3. *Thompson* v. *Hill* (1870), L.R. 5 C.P. 564; *Bower* v. *Peate* (1876), 1 Q.B.D. 321.
4. *Apostal* v. *Simons*, [1936] 1 All E.R. 207.
5. [1938] 1 All E.R. 614.

an easement of support, which had been disturbed. The measure of damages was all the loss which could be proved to have resulted from the wrongful withdrawal of support, including damage to the stock and the disturbance of business caused by the collapse.

2 REPAIR[6]

The statutory rights conferred by s. 38 of the Law of Property Act 1925, do not extend to a positive obligation to keep the wall in repair. This follows from *Leigh* v. *Dickson*[7] where it was held that one tenant in common of a party wall who spent money on repairs could not compel his co-tenant to contribute.[8] In the absence of agreement, therefore there is no responsibility for repair. It was similarly held in *Sack* v. *Jones*,[9] confirming earlier authorities, that in the case of walls divided vertically (Class (2) above), there is no repairing liability. The neighbouring owner may, however, enter and carry out the necessary works himself.[10]

One writer[11] distinguishes *Leigh* v. *Dickson*[12] on the grounds that it refers only to ordinary repairs, and goes on:

> "It is apprehended that where a party wall held in common by owners of adjoining houses which it divides and which depend on it for support, becomes ruinous, so that its repair is absolutely necessary, and one part owner spends money in repairing and rebuilding it, a court of equity would decree contribution on the ground that the expenditure made was in the nature of a salvage payment."

He cites the American case of *Campbell* v. *Mesier*[13] in support of this view. There contribution was decreed in such circumstances in

---

6. For a comprehensive discussion see J. B. Nance (1950), 14 *Conveyancer* (N.S.) 380.
7. (1883), 12 Q.B.D. 194; on appeal (1884), 15 Q.B.D. 60.
8. As to acquiescence while expenditure is incurred on one's land see 14 *Halsbury's Laws*, 2nd Edn., 639 and *Ward* v. *Kirkland*, [1966] 1 All E.R. 609.
9. [1925] Ch. 235. See also *McPherson* v. *London Passenger Transport Board* (1946), 175 L.T. 279.
10. The fact that there is no obligation to repair does not permit an owner to do some positive act of misfeasance, *e.g.*, putting a rockery against a wall and thereby causing damp: *Broder* v. *Saillard* (1876), 2 Ch.D. 692.
11. Rudall, *Party Walls* (3rd Edn., 1922), p. 13.
12. (1883), 12 Q.B.D. 194; on appeal (1884), 15 Q.B.D. 60.
13. (1820), 4 John Ch. Rep. 334.

respect of an old party wall between two buildings. At the best this is merely persuasive authority, and,

> "there is no doubt that, strictly speaking, salvage is not a recognised head of claim in the common law as it is at sea."[14]

The better opinion is that neither party has any right of contribution against the other unless there is an agreement to that effect.[15] However, if a party wall is in a ruinous condition, and a third party was injured as a result, it is thought that the owner(s) would be liable in tort, under the Occupiers' Liability Act 1957 or in negligence or nuisance.[16]

Two practical solutions suggest themselves in a case like this. Firstly, the neighbouring proprietors can agree to have the wall repaired at joint expense. Failing amicable settlement, the second alternative is for one neighbour to report the matter to the local authority, and seek action under the relevant statutory powers.[17] Any formal agreement between neighbours should declare the wall to be a party structure for the purposes of s. 38 of the Law of Property Act 1925, and provide for a definite proportion of the cost to be borne by each party.[18]

Very often disputes between neighbours over party walls stem from the fact that the solicitors who have dealt with the titles of the two properties concerned have failed to apply their minds to the technical points involved. It is worth bearing in mind that the "status" of a dividing wall must in general depend on the "title" of its site. This

---

14. *Per* BUCKNILL, L.J. in *Sorrell* v. *Paget*, [1950] 1 K.B. 252; [1949] 2 All E.R. 609; See also *Macclesfield Corporation* v. *Great Central Rail Co.*, [1911] 2 K.B. 528; *Falcke* v. *Scottish Imperial Insurance Co.* (1889), 34 Ch.D. 234, at 246, *per* BOWEN, L.J and *per* FRY, L.J., at 254. It would be different if the expenditure was incurred in anticipation of an interest in someone else's land: *Inwards* v. *Baker*, [1965] 2 Q.B. 29; [1965] 1 All E.R. 446.
15. *Re Jones*, [1893] 2 Ch. 461 *Kenrick* v. *Mountsteven* (1899), 48 W.R. 141. 3 *Halsbury's Laws*, 3rd Edn., 381, note (s) inclines in favour of *Campbell* v. *Mesier* (1820), 4 John Ch. Rep. 334, and so supports Rudall's view.
16. Chapter 7, *ante*, pp. 129–131.
17. For example, ss. 24 and 25 of the Public Health Act 1961, discussed, *ante*, p. 141.
18. A positive obligation to contribute towards the cost of repairing anything used in common is probably enforceable on the principle laid down in *Halsall* v. *Brizell*, [1957] Ch. 169, discussed *ante*, pp. 112–113. See also *Aspden* v. *Seddon* (1876), 1 Ex. D. 496.

is but another illustration of the difficulties involved in defining boundaries precisely. It is little wonder that these disputes crop up and those asked to advise are filled with perplexity.

When consideration is given to a particular dividing wall, and provision for it is contained in the deeds, it is usual to declare the wall to be a party wall and to state that "the same shall be maintainable accordingly". As we have seen, in the absence of express provision or prescriptive obligation neither party is bound to execute repairs or replacement, but in the writer's view the effect of stating that a wall "shall be maintainable (or, stronger still, repairable) accordingly" is to imply a covenant by each party to repair his half, where it is subject to s. 38 of the Law of Property Act 1925. This would certainly be so in the case of a clause in the following form[1]

> "The walls and/or fences dividing the property hereby conveyed from (the adjoining properties on both sides thereof) are party walls and/or fences and shall henceforth be repaired and maintained as such."

Such a covenant is a positive one, and while its benefit can be assigned, the burden does not pass with the land. If there is an unbroken chain of indemnities from purchaser to vendor, and if all the parties can be traced, enforcement would be possible but costly. If the writer's view is correct, and the principle of *Halsall* v. *Brizell*[2] applies, it would seem that under such a covenant one owner could repair a delapidated wall and recover half the cost from the other. However, as this is a matter of some doubt it is best to insert an express covenant to repair.[3]

Where there is a covenant to maintain and repair as a party wall, the demolition of one tenement would not alter the position. Suppose, for example, that the site of a dwellinghouse and extant outbuildings are sold subject to a covenant in the original conveyance and provisions relating to a party wall which is still standing. The right for both adjoining owners to use the party wall will still subsist—the demolition of one of the houses will not have affected this—and even if one adjoining owner does not use the wall this would not relieve him, at any rate in theory, of his liability to contribute to the expenses.

---

1. Leicester Law Society's Conditions of Sale, clause 12 (b) (ii).
2. [1957] Ch. 169; [1957] 1 All E.R. 371.
3. See Emmett on *Title*, (14th Edn.), vol. 1, pp. 444, 505, 507.

3 WEATHERPROOFING

The decision of the Court of Appeal in *Phipps* v. *Pears*[4] has caused some misgivings in this general field. There one of two contiguous houses had been demolished in 1930 and rebuilt with a dividing wall touching the adjacent and existing wall. This new wall was not weatherproof. The other house was pulled down some thirty years later, and as a result the newer wall was exposed to the operation of the elements and its state deteriorated. The court held that the present owner had no redress, for English law does not recognise the existence of an easement of weatherproofing, which was what was being claimed. LORD DENNING, M.R., pointed out that if such an easement did exist it was a negative one, and the law was chary of creating new easements of this type. If an adjoining owner wished to protect himself, he must take a covenant from the neighbour that the latter would not pull down his house. The "right" which was being claimed was in the same category as a pleasant view, and could not pass under s. 62 of the Law of Property Act 1925, for the court, applying *Wright* v. *Macadam*[5] held that it was not within the expression "easements, rights and advantages whatsoever appertaining or reputed to appertain" to the property.

Phipps v. *Pears* decided that there can be no easement of protection or shelter in respect of a house. In spite of this decision, it is submitted that a lower flat or maisonette can enjoy such a right from its upper counterpart and from the roof of the building.[6]

It has been thought that *Phipps* v. *Pears*[4] will cause difficulty in the troublesome field of freehold flats and maisonettes. On the conveyance of a freehold flat or maisonette, the conveyance may well provide for the grant of mutual easements of support between upper and lower owners, and for the reservation of easements of shelter and protection between lower and upper owners. *Phipps* v. *Pears* would suggest that the reservation creates no easement, and so the upper owner's successors in title will not be bound by it. This, it is thought, would be a harsh doctrine and probably it can be avoided by the use of suitably drawn covenants, provided the right is clearly and sufficiently defined by the

---

4. [1965] 1 Q.B. 76; [1964] 2 All E.R. 35, C.A. See also *Wheeldon* v. *Burrows* (1879), 12 Ch.D. 31; *Thompson* v. *Hill* (1870), L.R. 5 C.P. 564.
5. [1949] 2 All E.R. 565.
6. Wurtzburg and Mills, *Building Society Law*, (13th Edn.) 1970, pp. 159 and 162.

conveyance. Otherwise the enforceability of such a reservation would depend on the doctrine of *Halsall* v. *Brizell.*[7]

A local authority demolishing a house under statutory powers are under the same obligations as its owner.[8] This problem is largely circumvented, and the possible effects of *Phipps* v. *Pears* mitigated by the provisions of s. 29 of the Public Health Act 1961, which gives local authorities extensive powers in relation to the demolition of houses of a cubic content of more than 1,750 feet. This is an external measurement. The local authority may, by notice served on the person undertaking the demolition of the whole or part of a building (generally within a period of six weeks from the beginning of the demolition), require him *inter alia*, to weatherproof and shore up any surfaces of an adjacent building which are exposed by the demolition.

This applies not only to party walls, but to all contiguous walls. However, s. 29 (10) provides that the recipient of such a notice may appeal against it, when it requires shoring up, on the grounds that there is no existing right of support, and that the adjoining owner ought to pay or contribute towards the expenses of shoring up. Similarly, where the notice requires weatherproofing, he may claim contribution from the adjoining owner, and the court may make such order as to the apportionment of expenses as it thinks fit on hearing the appeal.

It should be noted that s. 29 is purely an enabling section giving the local authority the right to require the carrying out of accommodation works. The "dominant" owner cannot insist that the notice be served, and no rights as such are conferred upon him against the local authority or the demolishing owner. However, as a matter of practice most local authorities will exercise these powers on request in appropriate cases. Where they themselves are undertaking a demolition they invariably carry out the necessary works.

PARTY STRUCTURES IN LONDON

Party structures in inner London are subject to special rules contained in Part VI of the London Building Acts (Amendment) Act 1939, as amended, although in general the Act does not apply to Crown

7. [1957] Ch. 169; [1957] 1 All E.R. 371, discussed at pp. 112–113, *ante*. See R.E. Megarry in 80 L.Q.R. 321.
8. *Bond* v. *Nottingham Corporation*, [1940] Ch. 429.

property or that of the Inns of Court.[9] The area of operation of the 1939 Act is the City of London and the Boroughs of Camden, Greenwich, Hackney, Hammersmith, Islington, Kensington and Chelsea, Lambeth, Lewisham, Southwark, Tower Hamlets, Wandsworth, and Westminster. The common law rules discussed earlier are excluded to the extent of these statutory provisions. However, it is expressly provided that the provisions do not affect the legal title to the structure or to any easements or rights in connection with them.[10] Local legislation may also affect the position in other parts of the country.[11] Some reference to the special position in London must be made, but no detailed analysis of the statutory provisions will be attempted.[12]

1 DEFINITIONS

Special definitions apply to party structures in London.

Party wall has a special meaning ascribed to it for the purposes of Part VI of the 1939 Act:[13]

> (i) a wall which forms part of a building and stands on lands of different owners to a greater extent than the projection of any artificially formed support on which the wall rests; and,
>
> (ii) so much of a wall not being a wall referred to in the foregoing paragraph (i) as separates buildings belonging to different owners."

For the general purposes of the London Building Acts 1930–1939 a party wall is one,[14]

> "forming part of a building so far as used or constructed or adapted to be used for separating adjoining buildings belonging to different owners or occupied or constructed or adapted to be occupied by different persons, together with the remainder (if any) of the wall vertically above such before-mentioned portion of the wall."

---

9. 1939 Act, ss. 151 and 152; London Government Act 1963, s. 43.
10. 1939 Act, s. 54.
11. Notably in Bristol where the position is governed by the Bristol Improvement Act 1847, ss. 24–32, as amended by ss. 91–93 of the Bristol Corporation Act 1926.
12. See W. A. Leach, *Party Structure Rights in London*, (1961).
13. 1939 Act, s. 44.
14. London Building Acts (Amendment) Act 1939 s. 4.

A *party structure* includes a party wall as defined,[14]

> "and also a floor partition or other structure separating buildings or parts of buildings approached solely by separate staircases or separate entrances from without. The floor partitions in flats are normally excluded, unless the flat has a separate outside entrance."

A *party fence wall* is,[14]

> "a wall (not being part of a building) which stands on lands of different owners and is used or constructed to be used for separating such adjoining lands but does not include a wall constructed on the land of one owner, the artificially formed support of which projects into the land of another owner."

The statutory provisions do not affect the legal title to a party structure, and so even where work is being carried out under the 1939 Act the provisions of s. 38 of the Law of Property Act 1925 will apply if appropriate.[15] All easements and rights in connection with party walls are expressly preserved.[16] It is the right to execute works to a party wall which is governed by the provisions of the Act, which in general requires proper notice to be given.[17]

Throughout the Act references are made to the "owner" and the "building owner", and these terms are defined in s. 5 of the London Building Act 1930. *The owner* is the person in receipt of the whole or part of the rents and profits of the property, or the person in occupation otherwise than as a tenant from year to year or for a lesser term. A tenant for more than a year of part of a house is an owner[18] and the term includes a long leaseholder who has sublet for a term longer than from year to year.[19] *The building owner* is an owner (as defined) who wishes to build or do work affecting a party structure. He, his servants, agents and workmen have powers of entry for the purposes of executing works under Part VI of the 1939 Act. In general, 14 days' notice of intention to enter must be given, and if necessary entry may be effected by breaking down doors and fences, provided a police officer is present.[20]

14. London Building Acts (Amendment) Act 1939, s. 4.
15. *Upjohn* v. *Seymour Estates, Ltd.*, [1938] 1 All E.R. 614 provides an example.
16. 1939 Act, s. 54.
17. See *Standard Bank of British South America* v. *Stokes* (1878), L.J.Ch. 554.
18. *Fillingham* v. *Wood*, [1891] 1 Ch. 51.
19. *Hunt* v. *Harris* (1859), 19 C.B. N.S. 13.
20. 1939 Act, s. 53.

2 RIGHTS OF OWNERS

Section 46 gives a building owner extensive rights to carry out works to *existing* party structures, either with the adjoining owner's written consent, or subject to the requisite notice being served. These provisions are not mandatory, but if they are not followed the building owner is left to fall back on his limited common law rights. The statutory rights are:[1]

(a) A right to make good, underpin, thicken or repair or demolish and rebuild a party structure or party fence wall, in any case where the work is necessary because of defect or want of repair.

(b) A right to demolish a timber or other partition separating buildings belonging to different owners which does not comply with the London Building Acts and byelaws, and to replace the same with a party wall conforming therewith.

(c) A right in relation to a building having rooms or storeys belonging to different owners intermixed to demolish such parts as do not comply with the London Building Acts and byelaws and to rebuild them in conformity therewith.

(d) Where buildings are connected by arches or structures over public ways or passages belonging to other persons, the right to demolish such structures or parts thereof as do not comply with the London Building Acts and byelaws and to rebuild them in conformity therewith.

(e) A right to underpin, thicken or raise any party structure or party fence wall which the Act allows to be underpinned, thickened or raised, or any external wall built against such a party structure or party fence wall, subject to making good any damage caused, and carrying up all flues and chimney stacks belonging to the adjoining owner.

(f) A right to demolish and rebuild a party structure which is of insufficient height for the purposes of any intended building of the building owner, subject to the same conditions as (e).

---

1. 1939 Act, s. 46. In *Gyle-Thompson* v. *Wall Street Properties, Ltd.*, [1974] 1 All E.R. 295, a BRIGHTMAN, J. held that the right to demolish and rebuild a party wall under s. 46 requires reconstruction to the same height. An award purporting to lower a party wall was held to be *ultra vires* and therefore invalid.

(g) A right to cut into a party structure subject to making good any damage caused.

(h) A right to cut away any footing or projection on or over the building owner's land in order to erect, raise or underpin any external wall or boundary wall or for any other purposes, subject to making good any damage caused.

(i) A right to cut away or demolish any parts of a wall or building overhanging the building owner's land as may be necessary to enable a vertical wall to be erected against that wall or building, subject to making good any damage caused.

(j) A right to execute any other necessary works incidental to the connection of a party structure with the premises adjoining it.

(k) A right to raise a party fence wall, to raise and use a party fence wall as a party wall, and to rebuild it as a party fence wall or as a party wall.

Before a building owner can execute any of these works he must serve written notice on the adjoining owner specifying the works proposed,[2] except where the adjoining owner has given his prior consent in writing or the work is necessary as the result of a dangerous structure notice. This is called a party structure notice and is normally accompanied by a drawing or plan although plans need only be served where special foundations are proposed, *i.e.*, those embodying steel beams or rods for spreading the load of a building.[3] The Royal Institute of British Architects publish appropriate blank party structure notices. Special foundations are not authorised in connection with existing party structures unless the adjoining owner gives his consent.[4] Two months' notice must be given, except in the case of a party fence wall or special foundations, in which cases a month's notice will suffice.

---

2. Section 121 provides that all notices are to be in writing. The method of service is governed by s. 124 and is generally by means of pre-paid post. If it is proved that the notice was received, it seems irrelevant that the precise statutory method was not followed: *Stylo Shoes, Ltd.* v. *Price's Tailors Ltd.*, [1960] Ch. 396; [1959] 3 All E.R. 901; *Moody* v. *Godstone Rural District Council*, [1966] 2 All E.R. 696. Section 47 of the 1939 Act deals with party structure notices.
3. 1939 Act, s. 44.
4. 1939 Act, s. 46 (3).

The work must then be commenced within six months after service, otherwise the notice becomes ineffective.[5]

The adjoining owner may serve counter-notice in writing within one month requiring the building owner to carry out additional works. Where special foundations are proposed, the counter notice must be served within 21 days. The counter notice can require the building owner to build chimneys, copings, breasts, jambs, flues, piers, recesses and so on, in or on the structure, for the convenience of the adjoining owner. Special foundations can be required to be of greater depth or strength.

The counter notice must include plans, sections and particulars of the works required, and the building owner must comply with the notice unless it would be injurious or unnecessarily inconvenient or delaying for him. The cost of works under a party structure notice is governed by s. 56; in general costs are to be defrayed by both owners in proportion, regard being had to the use to which each of them will put the works. The building owner bears the expense of works which are for his sole benefit, but this important right of contribution in the case of repair or other works for mutual benefit should not be overlooked. Section 56 refers to "expenses incurred", and these have been held to include the fees of architects, surveyors and district surveyors.[6] Before the works begin, the adjoining owner may require the building owner to give security for expenses in an agreed sum, settled in default of agreement by the county court.[7] Disputes are to be settled in accordance with the procedure prescribed by the Act, which is considered below.

Works carried out by the building owner must comply with the rules set out in s. 51 of the 1939 Act. In particular, the work must be carried out so as not to cause unnecessary inconvenience to the adjoining owner or occupier.[8] If any part of the adjoining property is laid open, the building owner must erect and maintain at his own expense proper hoarding and shoring for the protection of the adjoining land and the security of its occupier.

---

5. 1939 Act, s. 48.
6. *Fifoot* v. *Apperley* (1905), *Building News*, September 18th.
7. *Ibid.*, s. 57.
8. Noise and dust from building operations can seldom amount to a nuisance: *Andreae* v. *Selfridge & Co., Ltd.*, [1938] Ch. 1.

The Act does not authorise negligence, and its provisions relating to making good and compensation for disturbance leave untouched any common law claim for negligence or nuisance.[9] All work must be carried out in accordance with the London Building Acts and byelaws, and must follow any agreed plans or an award of the surveyors nominated by the parties.[10] Failure to make good damage caused to an adjoining property is an offence punishable on summary conviction with a maximum fine of £20, plus £5 a day for a continuing offence.[11] No opening can be made in a party wall without the consent of the local authority, although there is a saving in respect of openings in walls which replace existing walls containing openings.[12]

New party structures

The service of notice in connection with a new party structure is obligatory, and this applies where the boundary is not built on and an owner wishes to erect a party wall.[13] The adjoining owner may then give written consent to the proposed structure astride the boundary or wholly on the building owner's land. The notice must specify the position of the proposed wall. If consent is given, the wall will be a party wall or a party fence wall, and the costs of its construction will be shared between the adjoining owners in proportion to the use made of the wall.

If the adjoining owner refuses his consent, the building owner must erect the wall wholly on his own land, although he may project its footings and foundations below ground level in the adjoining property, paying compensation for any damage sustained. This right must be exercised not less than one month nor more than six months after service of the notice. No length of notice is prescribed, but in practice at least one month's notice should be given. The right to erect a party wall under this provision will not entitle the building owner to obstruct an easement of light.[14] Special foundations (*supra*) may not be placed under the land of the adjoining owner.

9. London Building Act 1930, s. 5.
10. 1939 Act, s. 55, deals with surveyor's awards and is considered below.
11. 1939 Act, s. 148 (2) (xix).
12. *Ibid.*, ss. 4 (1) and 17.
13. *Ibid.*, s. 45.
14. *Crofts* v. *Haldane* (1867), L.R. 2 Q.B. 194.

3 DISPUTES AND AWARDS

Where a party structure notice or counter-notice has been served, a difference is presumed if the recipient does not give his written consent to the proposals within 14 days of receipt of the notice.[15] The special machinery of the Act relating to differences then comes into operation. The difference must be settled by surveyors appointed and acting under s. 55. The owners may agree to the appointment of an "agreed surveyor" who will make an award upon the difference. The usual course, however, is for each party to appoint his own surveyor, who settle the difference by negotiation and make a joint award. The two nominated surveyors may select a third surveyor who acts as intermediary. This is very rare in practice.

When the award has been made it is executed in duplicate, and each copy is signed by the surveyors. The surveyors must be appointed in writing, and their award is declared to be conclusive and is not to be questioned in any court. The award may, however, be challenged by appeal to the county court within fourteen days. Under s.55(*k*) the award "may determine the right to execute and the time and manner of executing any work and generally any other matter arising out of or incidental to the difference". The award is important because no work can be commenced until it has been made. It also deals with costs.

The award may be challenged by appeal to the county court within 14 days. Alternatively, and provided that the sum involved (excluding costs) is £100 or more, and security approved by the county court is given, the matter may be taken to the High Court. Since this is an arbitration, and the court has power to set aside or remit such awards[16] there could be a direct reference to the High Court, *e.g.*, on the grounds of misconduct or excess of jurisdiction.

These provisions have worked extremely well in practice and their interpretation has seldom been before the Courts. Such decisions as there are have been on points of great import. In *Burlington Property Co., Ltd.* v. *Odeon Theatres, Ltd.*,[17] for example, the Court of Appeal held that the nominated surveyors have no power to make an award entitling the building owner to substitute for existing windows in the ground storey portion of the party wall wider openings coming down

15. 1939 Act, s. 49.
16. See *Re Stone and Hastie*, [1903] 2 K.B. 463.
17. [1938] 3 All E.R. 469.

to the ground level so as to admit of pedestrians passing through them to and from an adjoining public court, even though the award expressly provided that the ground storey portion of the wall should be constructed of sufficient strength to carry the upper part of the wall.

The most recent case is *Gyle-Thompson* v. *Wall Street (Properties), Ltd.*,[18] when BRIGHTMAN, J. had to consider what he described as "important points of law" arising out of the operation of the 1939 Act. The defendants obtained planning permission to develop a warehouse site in Chelsea. They wished to reduce the height of the party fence wall adjoining the plaintiff's premises in order to provide more light for the proposed new dwellings. Negotiations began between the parties and surveyors were appointed; agreement was not reached. A party structure notice was served on the plaintiff and, unusually, a third surveyor was appointed by the two acting surveyors as they could not agree. Unhappily, there were procedural defects, and the correct procedure was not followed throughout. In the event, there was an award made which purported to lower the height of the party structure, the statutory authority relied on being s.46(1)(*a*) and (*k*). The main point at issue was whether or not the award was valid. BRIGHTMAN, J. in a very careful reserved judgment, held that it was not. His lordship applied *Burlington Property Co., Ltd.*, v. *Odeon Theatres, Ltd.*[17] The two paragraphs in question did not give a building owner the right to demolish a party fence wall and rebuild it to a reduced height. In the absence of an express right to lower the party structure, the right to "demolish and rebuild" conferred on a building owner required reconstruction of the wall to the same height. There was no right to change the form of a party structure. "If the building owner has the right to reduce the height of a wall which belongs to him and his neighbour without his neighbour's consent, such a right would be, in effect, a right for the building owner to expropriate the property of his neighbour", said BRIGHTMAN, J. Of course, the fact that a structure *is* a party structure does not necessarily mean that it is jointly owned.[19] It seems that in the present case the wall was jointly owned, but in any event it is thought that BRIGHTMAN, J.'s interpretation is the correct one.

That is not the only importance of the case. The defendants contended, *inter alia*, that under s.55(*m*) and (*n*) the award was conclusive

18. [1974] 1 All E.R. 295.
19. See *per* FRY, J. in *Watson* v. *Gray* (1880), 14 Ch. D. 192, at 194.

against the plaintiff and could only be challenged by an appeal to the county court. The learned judge had no difficulty in dismissing this contention. "This submission is not correct", he said, "in relation to an award which is *ultra vires* and therefore not a valid award". Here the defendants had claimed a right which they did not have and the surveyors had made an award which they had no power to make. The award did not, therefore, "determine the right" of the defendants to execute the proposed works, and thus the plaintiff was not precluded by s.55(*m*) and (*n*) from bringing proceedings in the High Court to prevent unlawful interference with his property.[20]

Quite apart from these two points, BRIGHTMAN, J. held that the surveyors' award was, in any event, invalid on a number of procedural grounds, *e.g.*, one of the surveyors had not been appointed in writing by the plaintiff as his surveyor. Accordingly, that surveyor had no statutory authority to concur in the appointment of the third surveyor. The learned judge felt that the procedural objections were well-founded and meritorious because the 1939 Act gives a building owner a statutory right to interfere with the proprietary rights of the adjoining owner without his consent. The surveyors, he said, "are in a quasi-judicial position with statutory powers and responsibilities. It therefore seems to be important that the steps laid down by the Act should be scrupulously followed throughout, and short cuts are not desirable". Later in his judgment he pointed out that the surveyors' approach to the procedural requirements ought not to be casual.

It would seem, therefore, that those acting under s.55 of the 1939 Act will need to be much more scrupulously careful to observe all the formalities in the future. Thus, under s.55(*a*), unless a single surveyor is agreed upon by the parties to the dispute, each party must appoint a surveyor and the two appointed surveyors must select a third surveyor, s.55(*c*) empowers the other party to appoint one on his behalf. All appointments and selections *must* be made in writing: s.55(*h*).

Gyle-Thompson v. *Wall Street* (*Properties*), *Ltd.* emphasises the need for exact observance of the statutory provisions in all cases: a casual attitude will not do where there is an effective invasion of private rights.

---

20. See *Re Stone and Hastie*, [1903] 2 K.B. 463.

Chapter 9

BOUNDARY DISPUTES

"Certain it is that the whole of the costs of this litigation could have been saved if one or other party had used a few staples and a roll of wire. 'For the want of a nail a shoe was lost.' I need not complete the quotation." *Per* DIPLOCK, L.J. in *Jones* v. *Price*, [1965] 2 All E.R. 625, at 635.

In many cases boundary disputes arise out of imagined grievances between neighbours, but a litigious person may wish to assert his theoretical rights rather than compromise. It is frequently difficult to establish the ownership of a particular boundary fence, and generally the commonsense answer to an over-anxious client is to tell him to leave the matter to be resolved when trouble arises. If there is no evidence of ownership, and the need for repair is urgent, the best practical answer is for the contenders to agree that the fence is joint property, and for each of them to bear a proportionate part of the cost of repair. Even where a party wall is divided vertically[1] and is built exactly across the boundary, it is difficult to repair or rebuild one half without dealing with the other.

A sympathetic local authority may assist in some cases by serving notice to repair on both owners under some statutory provision, such as ss. 24 and 25 of the Public Health Act 1961, where a wall is in a ruinous condition. The vast majority of boundary disputes can and should be settled by amicable agreement, or by one party waiving his rights, and a lesson can be learned from DIPLOCK, L.J.'s trenchant observation quoted at the head of this chapter. Boundary disputes can give rise to the most expensive and protracted litigation, but unhappily this is not a point appreciated by lay clients, the more so in these days of legal aid.

Various boundary problems have been considered elsewhere in this book, and it remains only to summarise the position in four special cases.

---

1. See Chapter 8, *ante*, pp. 147–148.

1 VENDOR AND PURCHASER

Between vendor and purchaser boundary disputes are a matter of contract, and quite frequently there will be express terms as to boundaries. These will then govern the matter. The general position is well summarised in the following passage from Hunt:[2]

> "The vendor of land must avoid misleading the purchaser with respect to the boundaries of the property sold; and, to prevent any mistake on the part of the purchaser regarding the extent thereof, the vendor should, in all cases where there is any possibility of mistake, not only mark the boundaries on the plan (if any) but also in express words describe the boundaries in the particulars of sale, and in the event of the boundary not describing itself an intending purchaser should go and look at the property: in case no such description be given, the purchaser cannot be compelled to complete the purchase if deceived by the plan and particulars respecting the extent of the property which he intended to purchase."

Where the conditions of sale are silent as to the boundaries the purchaser *may* be entitled to rescind if the property differs *substantially* from what was contracted to be sold,[3] but there are strict limits to the right of rescission.[4] It should be noted that s.1(6) of the Misrepresentation Act 1967 now provides that where a person has entered into a contract after an innocent representation has been made to him, the fact that the contract has been performed does not impede any right of rescission available to him.[5]

The purchaser may insist on taking the conveyance at a reduced price instead of exercising his right to rescind. Misdescription, and the right to compensation are provided for in both the National and Law Society's Conditions of Sale.[6] Clause 13 of the Law Society's Conditions of Sale provides as follows:

> "13 (1) Measurements and quantities, if substantially correct, shall not be the subject of compensation, nor shall any compensation be

---

2. *Boundaries & Fences* (6th Edn.), pp. 2–3, citing *Denny* v. *Hancock* (1870), 6 Ch. App. 1.
3. *Jacobs* v. *Revell*, [1900] 2 Ch. 858; *Re Puckett & Smith's Contract*, [1902] 2 Ch. 258; Williams, *Vendor and Purchaser*, (4th Edn.), vol. 1, 437.
4. See Cheshire and Fifoot, *Law of Contract*, (8th Edn.), pp. 259 *et seq.*
5. *I.e.*, the so-called rule in *Seddon* v. *North Eastern Salt Co., Ltd.*, [1905] 1 Ch. 326 has been abolished.
6. National Conditions of Sale, 17th Edn., cl. 14 (1); Law Society's Conditions of Sale, 1973 Edn., cl. 13.

payable in respect of any mistake in a sale plan furnished for the purpose of identity: but, where an incorrect statement, error or omission, whether as to measurements, quantities or otherwise, materially affects the description of the property, nothing in this paragraph shall prevent the payment or allowance of compensation under the next paragraph.

(2) Subject as aforesaid, any error, omission or mis-statement in the contract or in replies to any enquiry oral or written made with respect to the property in the course of the negotiations leading to the contract (whether or not it materially affects the description of the property) shall not annul the sale, nor entitle the purchaser to be discharged from his purchase but shall entitle the purchaser or the vendor as the case may require, to compensation: Provided that the purchaser shall not be entitled to such compensation in respect of any matter of which he is deemed to have notice under Condition 3 (3) or 4 (2) where applicable.

(3) If any dispute arises between the parties as to the amount of such compensation, it shall be settled by arbitration by a sole arbitrator agreed by the parties, or, in default of such agreement, nominated by the President or other principal officer for the time being of the local law society in the area in which the property is situate, and the Arbitration Act 1950 shall apply accordingly.

(4) Nothing in these Conditions shall—

(*a*) entitle the vendor to compel the purchaser to accept or the purchaser to compel the vendor to convey (with or without compensation) property which differs substantially from the property agreed to be sold and purchased, whether in quantity, quality, tenure or otherwise, if the purchaser or the vendor respectively would be prejudiced by reason of such difference, or

(*b*) affect the right of the purchaser to rescind or repudiate the contract where compensation for a claim attributable to a material error, omission or mis-statement cannot be assessed."

In general there is no obligation on the vendor to prove the ownership of boundary features.[7] Difficulty may arise if the conveyancer simply takes the description of the parcels from that in the abstract. In case of doubt it is best to frame a new description and, as indicated earlier, to have a proper plan drawn up by a surveyor.[8] Great care should be taken where the vendor may be estopped from denying the boundary[9] or there is any question of adverse possession. If some qualifying phrase is used, the description should not be contradictory

7. National Conditions, cl. 12 (2).
8. See the specimen parcels and plan in Parker's *Modern Conveyancing Precedents*, pp. 108–110.
9. *Hopgood* v. *Brown*, [1955] 1 All E.R. 550.

with the rest of the parcels clause.[10] The same principles apply in registered conveyancing where the property is sold simply by reference to a title number.

2 LANDLORD AND TENANT

It has long been settled law that the tenant is bound to preserve the boundaries of the property demised to him[11] and to see that the boundaries do not become confused with land of his own. There is, as LORD ELDON remarked in *A.-G.* v. *Fullerton*,[12]

> "a common equity, that a tenant, having put his landlord's property and his own together, for his own convenience, in order to make the most of it during his tenancy, is bound to render up specifically the landlord's land, and if he cannot, that a commission shall issue from a court of equity to inquire what were the lands of the landlord, the court taking care, to the intent that the tenant may discharge his obligation, to do what is right as to possession in the meantime; and if the tenant has so confounded the boundaries, by sub-dividing the land by hedges and stones, and destroying the metes and bounds, so that the landlord's land cannot be ascertained, the court will inquire what was the value of the landlord's estate, valued fairly, but to the utmost against the tenant, who has himself destroyed the possibility of the landlord's having his own."

This obligation extends to each of several co-lessees.[13]

The landlord may apply to the Chancery division during the currency of the lease, where the tenant has confused the boundaries with those of adjoining lands. For his part, a landlord is not under any duty to erect a fence between land he lets and the land which he retains.[14] Similarly, a landlord is not bound to repair existing fences, unless he covenants to do so.[15] If a tenant in possession destroys existing fences, he will be liable to the lessor.[16]

---

10. *Eastwood* v. *Ashton*, [1915] A.C. 900. This is the danger of using some qualifying phrase like "as now in the occupation of the vendor"
11. *Ashton* v. *Lord Exeter* (1801), 6 Ves. 288; *A.-G.* v. *Stephens* (1855), 6 De G. & M.G. 111; *Brown* v. *Wales* (1872), L.R. 15 Eq. 142.
12. (1813), 2 Ves. & B. 263.
13. *Willis* v. *Parkinson* (1817), 2 Mer. 507.
14. *Erskine* v. *Adeane* (1873), 8 Ch. App. 756; *Wilson* v. *Newberry* (1871), L.R. 7 Q.B. 31.
15. *Cheetham* v. *Hampson*, (1791), 4 T.R. 318.
16. *Berriman* v. *Peacock* (1832), 9 Bing. 334.

3 REGISTERED LAND

Disputes involving the boundaries of registered land may come before the court, which may direct that the register be rectified under s. 82 of the Land Registration Act 1925, and this is often preferable to applying to the registrar for rectification. In *Re Freehold Land in Dances Way, West Town, Hayling Island*[17] the appellant applied to the Land Registry for rectification of the Register, and this was granted. It was held by the Court of Appeal (LORD EVERSHED, M.R., and UPJOHN, L.J., DIPLOCK, L.J. dissenting) that the Chief Land Registrar's decision did not give rise to *res judicata* on the construction of the conveyance in question. Therefore, despite the fact that the register has been rectified by the registrar, the court may place another construction on the conveyance in later proceedings between the same parties, and this does not make for certainty.

However, the registrar does have power to rectify the register on application in many cases, either by agreement between the parties, or else in cases of fraud, error or mistake.[18] The registrar may refer the matter for the court's decision[19] although he himself has the jurisdiction to determine any question, subject to appeal to the court.[20] However, it is provided by s. 82 (3) that:

> "The register shall not be rectified, except for the purpose of giving effect to an overriding interest, so as to affect the title of a proprietor in possession, unless—(a) such proprietor is a party or privy, or has caused or substantially contributed by his act, neglect or default to the fraud, mistake or omission necessitating rectification; or (b) the immediate disposition to him was void, or the disposition to any person through whom he claims otherwise than for value was void; or, (c) for any other reason it would be unjust not to rectify against him."[1]

A good example where rectification was ordered under s. 82 (3) (a) is *Re No.* 139 *High Street, Deptford*.[2] There, in 1948 the respondent bought property which was described simply as "No 139, High Street, Deptford" and there was no plan. Both he and his vendors thought that certain land adjoining the property was included in that description, but in fact it belonged to the applicants. On the plan annexed to the certificate of registration the disputed land was part

---

17. [1962] 2 All E.R. 42.
18. *Ibid.*
19. L.R.R., 1925, r. 298 (2).
20. *Ibid.*, rr. 298 (1), 299.
1. See *Re Leighton's Conveyance*, [1937] Ch. 149.
2. [1951] Ch. 884.

of the area for which registration was granted. The applicants applied to rectify the register so as to exclude the disputed land. WYNN-PARRY, J., held that the respondent had contributed to the mistake within the meaning of s. 82 (3) (a) by his description of the property in the application for registration, and that the register should be rectified accordingly.[3]

More recently, a claim for rectification came before PENNYCUICK, J. in *Re Sea View Gardens*, *Claridge* v. *Tingey*,[4] where the disputed plot of land had been conveyed to the plaintiff in 1936. In 1964 a large area of land, of which the disputed plot was a small part, was comprised a transfer to the defendant, who was ignorant of the plaintiff's title to the disputed plot. The defendant began to erect a building partly on the disputed plot, having lodged the transfer at the registry. The encroachment came to the plaintiff's notice in March 1965 when she visited the place for the first time for several years and saw the building. She issued a summons claiming relief under s. 82 in August 1965.

PENNYCUICK, J. held that while the defendant had not known that the inclusion of the disputed plot in the transfer was in error, he had, for the purpose of s.82(3)(a) substantially contributed to the registrar's mistake in registering the defendant as proprietor of it, because he had lodged the transfer at the land registry. Accordingly s. 82(3)(a) did not preclude rectification of the register. In the event the matter was adjourned for further evidence.

Referring to the defendant's argument that the registered proprietor is not a party to the mistake for the purposes of the subsection, merely by putting forward a conveyance or transfer which incorrectly describes the land, the learned judge agreed that this would appear to be so on the facts in *Re No.* 139 *High Street*, *Deptford.* But, he said,

> "on a proper reading of the judgment, that is not the grounds for WYNN-PARRY, J.'s reasoning. He bases his reasoning, quite clearly, on the view that, where a registered proprietor lodges with the land registry a document which contains a misdescription of the property, then he has caused or substantially contributed to the mistake."

PENNYCUICK, J. emphasised that where the true owner, having learnt that the registered proprietor is doing work on the land, stands

3. See also *Chowood, Ltd.* v. *Lyall* (2), [1930] 2 Ch. 156.
4. [1966] 3 All E.R. 935.

by and allows the work to be done before intervening to apply for rectification of the register, it may well be that it would not then be just to order rectification. This is, of course, merely an extension of the principle of estoppel as applied to registered land.[5]

Thus for the purposes of s. 82 (3) (a) the registered proprietor is party or privy to the mistake and has caused or substantially contributed to it merely by putting forward a conveyance or transfer which contains incorrect particulars of the plot. This is so whether the land is shown on a plan or set out in a verbal description. This merely exemplifies, in the context of registered land, what we have said about the need for a precise definition of boundaries and a full and accurate description of the property, if necessary based on a survey of the site. In theory the solicitor ought to inspect the property which his client is purchasing, but this can rarely, if ever, be achieved. But where the position is doubtful the boundaries ought to be checked by a surveyor.

Where rectification is ordered, the dispossessed proprietor may have a claim for indemnity under s. 83 of the Act, and this will be so even though he contributed to the mistake, provided there was no fraud.[6] If the applicant wishes, the registrar may determine whether a claim for indemnity has arisen and award payment, subject to appeal to the court.[6]

On first registration, there is provision for the making and hearing of objections by the registrar, subject to an appeal to the Chancery Division.[7] The application to the High Court is by way of originating summons, but in practice most disputes of this sort are settled by the registrar.[8] By s. 83(5) no indemnity is payable where the applicant has himself caused or substantially contributed to the loss by his fraud or derives title, otherwise than under a registered disposition for valuable consideration, from a person so committing fraud. By s. 1(4) of the Land Registration Act 1966 no indemnity is payable where the loss has been caused or substantially contributed to by any act, neglect

---

5. Variation of boundaries by estoppel was discussed in Chapter 2, *ante*, p. 21.
6. This happened in *Re No.* 139 *High Street, Deptford*, [1951] Ch. 884: see (1952), 16 *Conveyancer* (N.S.) 363.
7. Land Registration Act, 1925, s. 13; L.R.R., r. 288 and r. 289. See (1956), 20 *Conveyancer* (N.S.) 194 as to the procedure and *Re Freehold Land in Dances Way*, [1962] 2 All E.R. 42, and *Re Gilbert's Application*, [1961] 2 All E.R. 313.
8. But note its limitations, *ante*, p. 169.

or default of the applicant or the person through whom he derives title otherwise than for value. Sections 82 and 83 of the Land Registration Act 1925, as amended, are reproduced as Appendix 4.

4 CROWN AND DUCHY OF CORNWALL LANDS

As a result of the Crown Estate Act 1961, the former special provisions relating to the settlement of disputes concerning Crown lands have been abolished. Crown lands are therefore in the same position as other property, and s. 1 of the 1961 Act gives the Crown Estate Commissioners wide general powers of management. In practice Crown lease contain a provision for the settlement of boundary disputes which may arise by the Commissioners.

Special provisions still relate to Duchy of Cornwall lands. With the previous consent of the Treasury, the Duke of Cornwall may make any necessary arrangement to settle boundary disputes affecting Duchy lands.[9] Any agreement must be enrolled within six months of its date at the Duchy of Cornwall office. If the terms of the agreement itself are in dispute, the matter may be referred to arbitration by His Royal Highness, with the consent of the Treasury, and the arbitration award needs to be similarly enrolled. After enrolment the agreement or award is final and binding on all interested parties.[10]

---

9. During the minority of the Duke of Cornwall, the Sovereign or whoever else acts on his behalf has the same powers.
10. The Duchy of Cornwall Office is at Buckingham Gate, London, S.W.1.

Chapter 10

MISCELLANEA

"The fundamental assumption of modern statute law is that the landowner holds his land for the public good." Sir Ivor Jennings in 49 Harv. L.R. 426 at p. 436.

In previous chapters reference has been made to various statutory provisions touching fencing. Here we shall be concerned with some important legislative provisions affecting the private landowner and his fences from the point of view of planning and building law. Finally, reference will be made to some relevant provisions of the criminal law.[1]

PLANNING AND BUILDING LAW

1 WALLS AND FENCES

By s. 23 (1) of the Town and Country Planning Act 1971, planning permission is required for development. "Development" includes all building operations which are defined as including rebuilding, structural alterations and additions to a building, and other operations normally undertaken by a builder.[2] Boundary walls and fence structures are buildings and thus within the meaning of "development" requiring planning permission.

However, in general no application for planning permission need be made to the local planning authority before erecting a wall or fence structure. This is because of the operation of the Town and Country Planning General Development Order 1973,[3] which grants planning permission for over twenty classes of development, set out

1. No further consideration will be given to statutory duties to fence imposed *e.g.*, by s. 68 of the Railways Clauses Consolidation Act 1845.
2. Town and Country Planning Act 1971: s. 22 (1) defines "development"; s. 290 defines "building operations". The building of ordinary boundary walls will not normally require approval under the Building Regulations 1972, as amended.
3. S.I. 1973 No. 31, as amended by S.I. 1973 No. 273 and S.I. 1974 No. 418. The amending orders are not material for present purposes.

in its first Schedule. Class II thereof allows the erection of gates, fences, walls and other means of enclosure not exceeding 1 metre in height if abutting on a highway used by vehicular traffic or 2 metres in height elsewhere, as well as their maintenance, improvement and alteration, subject to standard conditions specified in art. 3:

(1) The permission does not authorise any development which involves the formation, laying out or material widening of a means of access to a trunk or classified road.
(2) No development shall be carried out which creates an obstruction to the view of persons using any highway used by vehicular traffic, at or near any bend, corner, junction or intersection so as to be likely to cause danger to such persons.

Where a direction restricting permitted development has been made,[4] this will be revealed by the standard inquiries before contract, which accompany local land charges searches to local authorities. Article 11 (2) (i) of the General Development Order provides that the local planning authority must observe restrictions on the grant of planning permission affecting trunk and allied roads, and this may involve consultation with the Secretary of State for the Environment.[5]

The maximum permitted height for boundary walls or fences is, therefore, 1 metre or 2 metres as appropriate. Whether or not a structure abuts on to a highway is a question of fact, but it seems that there should be some physical contact with the highway.[6] Those wishing to erect walls and fences above the permitted maxima must apply for express planning permission in the normal way. In view of the first condition imposed by the General Development Order it necessarily follows that no break may be made in an existing boundary wall or fence to give access to a trunk or classified road unless express planning permission is sought. Moreover, by s. 18 of the Highways Act 1959, a special road authority (as defined in s. 11) may stop up any private means of access to special roads, such as motorways, and provide new means of access to the premises in question. A hedge growing

4. Permission granted by the General Development Order may be excluded in any particular area by a direction made under article 4 thereof.
5. Article 11 sets out special provisions as to permission for development affecting trunk and special roads.
6. *Barnett* v. *Covell* (1903), 90 L.T. 29. It is an offence under s. 122 of the Highways Act 1959, to erect a fence in a carriageway.

from year to year would not come within the phrase "other means of enclosure" for planning purposes. However, the heights prescribed in Schedule 1, Class II of the General Development Order 1973 can be taken as the maximum height for all purposes.[7]

2 WALLS AND BUILDINGS AT CORNERS

Section 81 of the Highways Act 1959 empowers highway authorities to prohibit the erection of any building or wall on land near any corner or bend in a highway maintainable at the public expense, which would be likely to cause obstruction to the view of users of the highway. The highway authority have further power to serve a notice on the owner or occupier[8] of land at or near any corner or bend in the highway, requiring him to alter the height or character of a wall, fence, hoarding, paling, tree or shrub. This power does not apply to walls forming part of the structure of a permanent edifice.

The person on whom the notice is served may object thereto within 14 days of service, as to any specified requirement or restriction imposed by the notice. The matter is then determined by a single arbitrator appointed by agreement between the parties, or in default by the county court. There is a right to compensation for injurious affection, and the owner or occupier may recover from the authority the expenses reasonably incurred in carrying out the directions contained in the notice.[9]

The provisions of s. 81 do not apply to walls belonging to statutory undertakers, and the consent of the Secretary of State for the Environment is needed if the wall forms part of an ancient monument or building of archaeological interest. The penalty for non-compliance with a s. 81 notice is a maximum fine of £5 and a further daily fine of up to £2 for a continuing offence. Wall is defined by s. 81 (14) as including: "any partition of whatsoever material constructed, and any bank."

3 ACCESS TO MAIN ROADS

The General Development Order 1973 makes it necessary to obtain express planning permission for any development involving the formation, laying out or alteration of any means of access to a trunk

7. An enforcement notice can not be served where a four year period has elapsed from the date of development: Town and Country Planning Act 1971, s. 87 (3).
8. Defined in the Highways Act 1959, s. 295.
9. See further (1966), *New L.J.* 1345 as to compensation for consequential loss.

or classified road. The local authority (or the Minister) may close any unauthorised means of access by fencing, by virtue of s. 85 of the Highways Act 1959, even though the time for serving an enforcement notice under s. 87 of the Town and Country Planning Act 1971 may have expired. Section 85 gives highway authorities general power to fence highways, although in doing so they must not interfere with any public right of way, fence or gate required for agricultural purposes, or obstruct any means of access for which planning permission has been granted.[10]

4 CROSSINGS OVER FOOTWAYS

By s. 155 of the Highways Act 1959 the local authority may by notice require the construction of an adequate carriage-crossing, where the occupier of any premises with access to a highway maintainable at the public expense, habitually takes a horse, horse-drawn or mechanically-propelled vehicle across a grass verge or kerbed footway in the road. There is a saving in respect of motor-cycles and other vehicles with a cylinder capacity not exceeding 250 c.c.

A person aggrieved by such a notice may appeal to the magistrates' court. The authority may construct the carriage-crossing and recover the expenses involved from the occupier. Any occupier may by notice require the council to carry out such works at his expense, and once the estimated amount of the costs has been deposited, the local authority must execute the necessary works.[11]

CRIMINAL DAMAGE

There are important provisions of the criminal law relating to fences, and in an age of increasing vandalism these protections are of importance.

By s. 1 of the Criminal Damage Act 1971[12] it is an offence to destroy or damage any property belonging to another, without lawful excuse,

---

10. Section 85 (3) (d) provides that in the exercise of their powers the authority may not obstruct any means of access existing before 1st July, 1948, *unless* it was constructed in contravention of ss. 1 and 2 of the Restriction of Ribbon Development Act 1935. Local byelaws may prohibit outward opening doors: ss. 132, 133 of the 1959 Act.
11. Note also the provisions of s. 55 of the Public Health Act 1936, under which the local authority must reject plans submitted for the erection of a new house unless they show a satisfactory means of access to the street for the removal of refuse and faecal matter.
12. Replacing s. 25 of the Malicious Damage Act 1861.

intending to destroy or damage any such property or being reckless as to whether any such property would be destroyed or damaged. This prohibition extends to fences, walls and other boundary features because s. 10(1) defines "property" so as to include any property of a tangible nature, whether real or personal, although it excludes "foliage of a plant growing wild on any land". This would, therefore, exclude a self-set hedge, but not one planted by the owner or occupier. Section 1 creates the two main offences of the Act, namely, the simple offence of destroying or damaging another's property and the aggravated offence of destroying or damaging any property intending to endanger the life of another, or being reckless in that regard. Where the offence is committed by destroying or damaging property by fire it is to be charged as arson. It is also an offence to threaten to destroy or damage property.[13] The accused must act "without lawful excuse" if he is to be convicted under s. 1. Under the former law, it was held in *Evison* v. *Marshall*[14] that a person who, in asserting a claim to a right of way, threw down more of a fence than was necessary to assert his right could not be convicted of malicious damage to the fence. Conversely, in *R.* v. *Clemens*[15] it was held that if more damage is wilfully done than is necessary to assert a *bona fide* claim or right, the action is malicious.

Section 5 provides for certain special lawful excuses, and also preserves any existing defences.[16] These are (a) an honest belief that the owner of the property concerned has consented to its destruction or damage, or would have consented had he known the circumstances; and (b) an honest belief that it was reasonable to destroy or damage property to protect property belonging to oneself or another, or to protect a right or interest (as defined in subsection (4)) which was or was believed to be vested in oneself or another. The provisions of s. 5 are set out at length:

> "(1) This section applies to any offence under section 1 (1) above and any offence under section 2 or 3 above other than one involving a

13. See s. 2.
14. (1868) 32 J.P. 691.
15. [1898] 1 Q.B. 556.
16. The operation of the section does not extend to the aggravated offence under s. 1 (2), or to the offence of threatening under s. 2, or to the possession with intent offence under s. 3 (*b*), where the threat or the intention relates to destruction or damage of property in a way which the offender knows is likely to endanger the life of another.

threat by the person charged to destroy or damage property in a way which he knows is likely to endanger the life of another or involving an intent by the person charged to use or cause or permit the use of something in his custody or under his control so to destroy or damage property.

(2) A person charged with an offence to which this section applies shall, whether or not he would be treated for the purposes of this Act as having a lawful excuse apart from this subsection, be treated for those purposes as having a lawful excuse—

(*a*) if at the time of the act or acts alleged to constitute the offence he believed that the person or persons whom he believed to be entitled to consent to the destruction of or damage to the property in question had so consented, or would have so consented to it if he or they had known of the destruction or damage and its circumstances; or

(*b*) if he destroyed or damaged or threatened to destroy or damage the property in question or, in the case of a charge of an offence under section 3 above, intended to use or cause or permit the use of something to destroy or damage it, in order to protect property belonging to himself or another or a right of interest in property which was or which he believed to be vested in himself or another, and at the time of the act or acts alleged to constitute the offence be believed—

(i) that the property, right or interest was in immediate need of protection; and

(ii) that the means of protection adopted or proposed to be adopted were or would be reasonable having regard to all the circumstances.

(3) For the purposes of this section it is immaterial whether a belief is justified or not if it is honestly held.

(4) For the purposes of subsection (2) above a right or interest in property includes any right or privileges in or over land, whether created by grant, licence or otherwise."

Finally, it may be noted that s. 8 provides generally for the ordering of compensation for the destruction or damage to property after conviction of the accused.

APPENDIX 1

LAND SURVEYING ASPECTS OF BOUNDARY DISPUTES

Every four years land surveyors from all over the Commonwealth and from some other countries meet at Cambridge for the Commonwealth Survey Officers Conference when a wide range of subjects is discussed. These include the survey of property boundaries—cadastral survey as it is called. This session always proves to be very controversial.

At the 1967 Conference Mr S. R. Simpson, formerly Land Tenure Adviser in the (then) Ministry of Overseas Development, said "The English system makes it quite clear where the parcel is situated and on the ground there will be no uncertainty as to where the boundaries are".[1] In trying to achieve this state of affairs countries like Australia and South Africa require surveyors with considerable training to take measurements to less than a centimetre. The measurements must be fully checked in the field and the records (which are numerical rather than graphical) are examined by officials in a surveyor general's office. In England at its simplest (and worst) it is possible, even today, to transfer land on the basis of a layman's unchecked measurements to the nearest foot. The record is almost always graphical.

Even in its most elaborate form the English survey system is far simpler than the numerical systems of countries like South Africa and Kenya, and with which the writer is familiar. As a surveyor he set out to discover whether Mr. Simpson's claims for the English system were justified. What follows are the results of the evidence then gathered.

To a surveyor used to a numerical system the procedure adopted by some of the major property development companies is interesting. As prudent prospective purchasers of development land they do not rely on the land registry map and the evidence on the ground. They usually prepare an accurate 1/500 plan of the site in which they are interested then agree the boundaries with the adjoining owners. This can be a long and delicate process and is never necessary in a numerical system.

An interesting feature of registered property is the note found on many filed plans in England. "The boundaries shown by dotted lines have been plotted from the deed plan and are subject to revision on survey." This occurs when there is no physical feature defining the whole of the boundary.

---

1. Conference of Commonwealth Survey Officers 1967—Report of Proceedings, Part I, Paper F.2, "The Role of Maps and Boundaries in Land Registration", para. 16.

There is then no check whatsoever that the deed plan accurately represents what is thought to have been bought and sold. It seems strange that any system of land registration should allow such a note. The following are recent examples of boundary disputes. Case 5 below illustrates graphically why a purchaser should be wary when the "subject to revision" note appears on the filed plan.

CASE 1

A purchaser bought a piece of land and the filed plan showed the shaded area (Fig. A) which went to AB beyond an existing feature CD, AC being about 8 metres and BD about 4 metres. The purchaser then bought the land

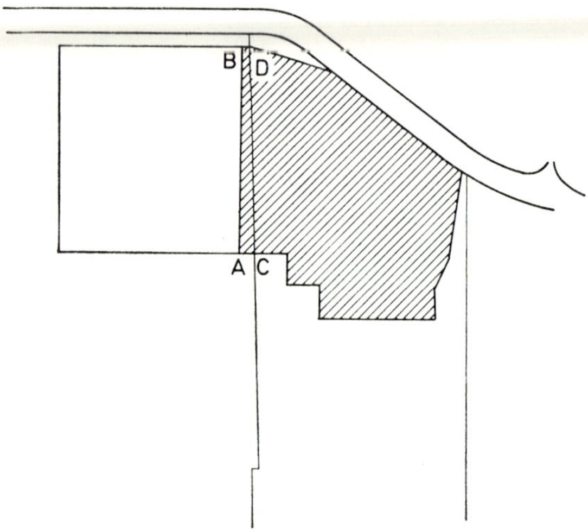

Figure A

adjacent to AB and prepared a conveyance up to AB. The Registry claimed that after resurvey it issued a revised filed plan for the first purchase up to CD. The purchaser claimed he never received the revised plan. The Registry wanted the purchaser to approach the vendor and prepare a conveyance for the land omitted.

CASE 2

A purchaser, X, bought the shaded portion ACDF from Y who kept the remainder (Fig. B). Lines EBG were pegged according to conveyance dimensions to allow a one metre maintenance strip so Y would be allowed to attend to any fence which might be erected on FAC. Dimensions for this line were given from existing detail. X then actually fenced EBG, not his true boundary FAC. Y then sold to Z. A defined boundary was shown on Z's filed plan as Z's boundary with X when in fact the boundary was an undefined line FAC one metre his side of the existing fence. Z claimed up to the fence and a one metre maintenance strip beyond it. X's surveyors and registry surveyors had to go on the ground together to re-establish the boundary from the conveyance dimensions and X's surveyors were proved correct from detail outside the original ownership.

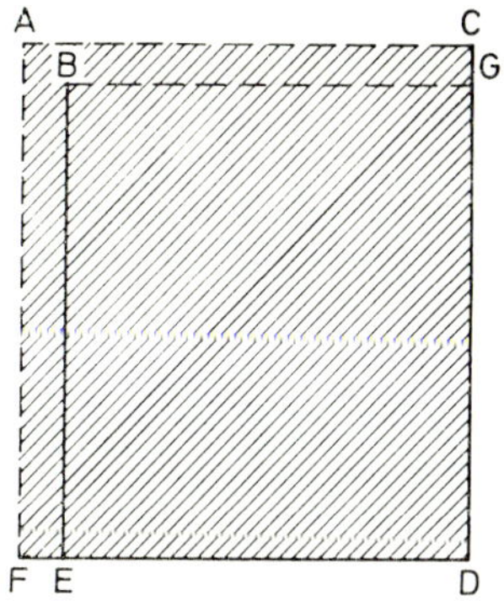

Figure B

CASE 3

The filed plan was based on the 1/2500 "County Series" mapping which the Ordnance Survey admit to being unsatisfactory. There were differences of up to 2.4 metres between the true found position and the detail shown on the plan. One boundary had nothing on the ground to indicate its position. The position given by the filed plan depended on which detail was matched to the true ground position. It was impossible to be certain whether one house had access of half a metre or three metres down one side.

CASE 4

An owner had a chicken house towards the end of his garden. There was chicken wire behind it (AB in Fig. C overleaf). The true boundary of the property was CD but when an estate was developed adjacent to this, registry surveyors included the portion ABCD in the title of one plot. The owner of the chicken house plot wisely engaged a solicitor and after considerable delay was paid £200 plus expenses from the insurance fund. The strip was about 2 metres wide.

An understanding of the normal procedure when a building estate is being developed is desirable in order to appreciate Case 5. This procedure is described in "Development of Registered Building Estates", Practice Leaflet for Solicitors No. 7, and may be summarised briefly.

Before the first transfer of a plot is likely to be lodged, the developer should send two copies of an accurate layout plan to the district land registry. After approval, one copy is retained in the registry and the duplicate is returned to the developer. Transfers are then usually prepared on the basis of the approved layout plan. As soon as the Land Registry receive an estate layout plan they ask the district office of Ordnance Survey to provide an up-to-date survey of all development on the estate. The request receives top priority and the updated plan is usually sent to the registry within two weeks. On a large estate surveys are carried out at frequent intervals until the estate is complete. The Land Registry filed plan is prepared after matching the estate layout plan with the Ordnance Survey map. Only details surveyed by Ordnance Survey are shown in firm lines. Boundaries with no physical feature are platted from the estate layout plan and shown dotted and the "subject to revision" note is usually added.

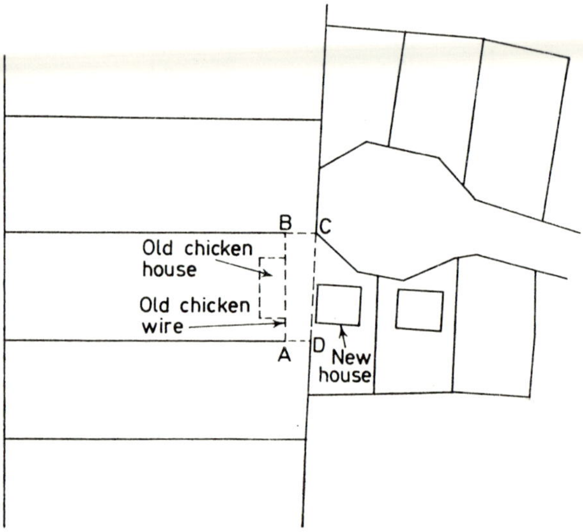

Figure C

As the practice leaflet remarks, "It sometimes happens that the developers depart from the approved estate layout without informing their solicitors or the Land Registry. Their solicitors then prepare transfer plans based on these out of date layout plans and, when the error comes to light, either when the transfers are lodged for registration or at some later date when a survey is made, confusion and delays are inevitable." The departure from the approved layout plan frequently results, as in Case 5, from mistakes in the layout survey. Any delay in submitting a transfer for registration would mean a delay in checking the transfer plan. If the filed plan shows a dotted line there can be a very long delay before a check is made.

Case 5

A developer bought a piece of land but the northern limits of it had no substantial feature or marker on the ground. An estate layout was prepared (Fig. D) and the plan showed that houses bordering on this limit were to have

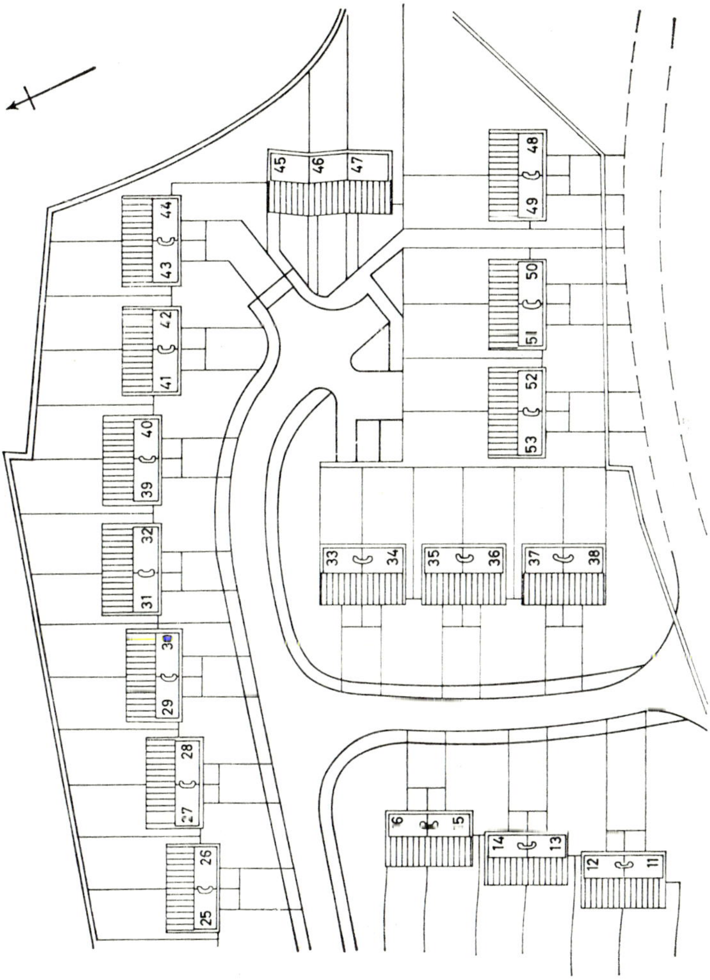
45
46
47
48
49
43
44
50
51
41
42
52
53
39
40
31
32
33
34
35
36
37
38
29
27
28
25
26
6
5
14
13
12
11

Figure D

back gardens of 12 metres. (Front gardens were open plan.) Following normal practice this plan was used for transfer of subdivisions until the Ordnance Survey had produced their maps of the area.

There was a mistake in setting out and houses were built about 6 metres nearer the northern boundary than they should have been. However, plots were still pegged out giving 12 metre back gardens and so including land not in the developer's title. Plot purchasers bought the properties under the impression that there would be 12 metre back gardens. A year after some of the people moved in, Ordnance Survey surveyors uncovered the mistake. Nevertheless at least one owner (plot 32) had a filed plan showing the full 12 metre back garden though with the note "the boundaries shown by dotted lines have been plotted from the deed plan and are subject to revision on survey". The adjoining owner had a filed plan showing a 6 metre back garden. The two are shown on the same plan (Fig. E).

Figure E

It seems the developer in fact realised the mistake soon after it occurred and thought he had a verbal agreement to acquire the extra land but later there was uncertainty on this. Probably only expensive litigation could establish the whole truth. Certainly by 1972 nothing had been resolved and plot owners 31 and 32 still had the filed plans they had in 1968. Their northern fences are colinear on the ground.

One interesting point is that the filed plan for the whole estate also has the same note about being plotted from the deed plan and being subject to revision on survey. This is the shaded boundary on the plan (Fig. E) and the only dimensions given for the undefined boundaries are those shown. It is not surprising that two different surveyors attempting to relocate them arrived at positions over a metre apart.

Having boundaries neither adequately surveyed nor adequately marked seems to be asking for trouble. There were about forty houses in the whole development each selling at about £4,700, and the following figures may prove of interest:

Total cost of houses	£18,800	These figures are approximate
Estate Agents' fees	£5,200	
Land Registration fees	£480	
Solicitors' fees (not less than)	£3,200	
Cost of recorded survey (not more than)	£2	

A surveyor from the Greater London Council, Mr. A. W. Whitehouse, was critical of the state of affairs when he spoke at a meeting of chartered land surveyors in April 1972. He deplored the fact that new boundaries can be created without a requirement for plans good enough to locate their position on the ground without dispute:

> "Often this produces inaccuracies which come to light later resulting in adjustment of the title originally registered, further property transactions which would otherwise be avoided and sometimes considerable hardship because encroachment deprives adjoining owners of land and perhaps amenities. . . . The problem is particularly acute with regard to large development. Here the field is left wide open for indiscriminate positioning of boundaries where adjoining owners on the perimeter may not even be aware of any encroachment until too late in the day. Those who are particularly watchful, however, can create costly delays to development whilst the disputed boundary is sorted out."

The Consumers' Association gave statistics on boundary disputes from 6000 transfers during the three years up to 1970. The percentage of snags or disputes concerning boundaries and rights of way on registered and unregistered land was 3.2% during conveyance and 0.9% after completion. Taking new houses only the figure after completion was 1.7% which is a most damaging statistic. The sample did not distinguish between registered and unregistered land. All that the Consumers' Association were able to say was that the position on registered land is "better but not perfect". Although some of the disputes had nothing to do with survey many certainly had and all the examples quoted above were on registered property. To a surveyor trained on a numerical system the number of disputes is enormous. Under a good numerical system any boundary uncertainty can be settled by a surveyor from information in the surveyor-general's office without risk of dispute with either adjacent owners or other surveyors.

Many improvements have been made in the English system but even in areas of compulsory registration where there is always up to date large scale mapping there are difficulties. The Chief Land Registrar, speaking at the Royal Institution of Chartered Surveyors, said, "On newly developed building estates almost invariably the fencing is subcontracted and that is where you get the trouble because the subcontractor puts up a fence in the wrong place and does not thereafter resurvey." Later he agreed with a speaker that the Torrens (*i.e.* numerical) system has merits. "For some years now", he said, "I have been trying to persuade the Law Commissioners in this country to adopt one or two of the ideas of Torrens particularly connected with ... errors that creep in on unfenced properties and building estates."

The Law Commission working paper No. 45 ("Land Registration 3rd paper") published in July 1972 contains a section on Identity and Boundaries but concludes (para. 34) that no reforms are needed.

The arguments for general or numerical boundaries are not, of course, as clear cut as might at first appear. It must be admitted that boundaries in England are usually well marked and if this is so dispute is much less likely. On registered land Ordnance Survey surveyors do provide a check on plans. However, firstly, in many cases this is after the completion date and it is too late to prevent a dispute and secondly the system is not as error free as that of the best numerical systems. Also it is only a check to within the limits of the scale of the plan and certainly not to better than 0.5 metres on a scale of 1/1250 or 1 metre on a scale of 1/2500. (On county series it may be much less accurate but this is gradually being superseded.) Of course the numerical system is more costly in surveyors' time and in the time of checking staff though it saves lawyers' time particularly when it comes to describing the parcel.

Very different circumstances have given rise to the two systems. Registration of title only became feasible in England after an attempt to define existing boundaries very accurately had been abandoned in favour of general boundaries. The numerical systems usually started off in areas like South Africa and Australia where no boundaries existed. Where boundaries do exist and properties are being put on the register for the first time two major problems face the authorities. They have to discover who the owners are and they have to discover exactly what they own. They have to adjudicate as to ownership and also as to boundaries. This is a common problem in the developing countries today and it is exactly the problem that England faces as property is gradually brought onto a compulsory registration system.

When registration in England started (as a voluntary system) in 1862, an owner who wished to put his property on the register had to agree on the precise position of the boundaries. This immediately aroused suspicion where none had existed before. The insistence on precise definition was a major barrier to the successful introduction of registration of title. The later Acts from 1875 onwards allowed general boundaries and this certainly contributed to the success registration now enjoys. But it has meant that precise adjudication of the boundaries has never been carried out. It is not a practical proposition to carry it out and general boundaries have to be accepted for this reason alone on all existing parcels. Better definition of the boundaries usually follows by mutual agreement and without serious dispute where features have existed for a long time. Whether the concept of general boundaries should still extend to new boundaries is more debatable.

It is worth while studying what the numerical system entails and whether it could have applications in reducing the number of problems in England. The survey principles are simple. The whole country is covered with a network of points fixed to one part in 30 000 or better, *i.e.* the distance between any two points say 3 kms. apart would be known to about 0.1 metres. On shorter lengths the proportional 1/30 000 is not maintained by the distance between points say 200 metres apart should never be wrong by more than about 4 cms. The positions are defined by co-ordinates in an homogeneous system. England has such a network already. The density varies but is generally adequate for the amount of development.

In a numerical system boundaries are defined by pegs at turning points and their position is determined in relation to the network. The boundary pegs themselves become additions to the network and useful for fixing later boundaries.

The amount of work involved in fixing boundaries on the network depends mainly, of course, on the network density but also very much on the instruments employed. Recent inventions have reduced the labour enormously and measurements over any distance or in busy areas would not be done with chain or tape but with optical or electronic devices. With a typical electrical instrument, distances up to two miles can be measured in under two minutes to better than a centimetre.

The computation of the measurements to determine co-ordinates has also been speeded up enormously. Using electronic desk calculators computation can now be done in ten minutes that not long ago would have taken an hour.

An essential feature of this system is that co-ordinates of the network are available for any surveyor to use. There is usually no charge except to cover the cost of copying and the co-ordinates are issued for many purposes other than cadastral survey. Unfortunately the Ordnance Survey charges include a "value to user" element which makes them expensive and compared with other countries the co-ordinates are rarely used other than by Ordnance Survey themselves.

There are undoubtedly drawbacks to the numerical system. The major objections it meets in England is that boundaries under it are imaginary lines between obscure (and often insecure) markers instead of being well recognised physical features. (A specific point of a physical feature such as the corner of a building can of course easily be co-ordinated and this is frequently done.) Another objection to a numerical system is that it requires a considerable organisation and detailed regulations and is considered by many to be cumbersome and unjustifiably expensive. The cost is, however, not great compared to other fees and occurs only on the initial sale unlike that of estate agents, solicitors and the Land Registry which are incurred with every resale.

There is no reason why selective or modified use should not be made in England of the numerical system. It should certainly be considered where a new boundary is not substantially marked or where the existing mapping is not able to provide the required accuracy. Turning points in the boundary should ideally then be connected directly to control points. No amount of development can obliterate the means of accurate relocation. Less expensive and almost as good would be fully checked connections from a survey of the boundaries to at least three well defined points unlikely to be disturbed which appear on the large scale Ordnance Survey map. The map itself would then act only as a locater to marks used in the boundary survey and a competent surveyor could relocate the boundary should dispute arise. Of course, if the marks are destroyed the survey loses much of its merit but accurate dimensions are worth a great deal.

An alternative is to have accurate plans at a much larger scale than the Land Registry provide—at least 1/500 in built up areas. The accuracy then approaches that of a numerical system. A good plan should then be accurate to 0.3 metres. Nowadays field records would be punched and fed direct to computers which would produce accurate plots direct.

Much can be learnt from up to date mapping of the Ordnance Survey. At present 1/1250 sheets covering all towns and urban areas with a population of about 20 000 and over can be obtained. They show grid lines of the National Co-ordinate system. Sheets at 1/2500 cover the whole of Great Britain apart from areas of mountain and moorland. Ordnance survey local offices do not sell these maps but they will be able to state who the local agents are. Costs stated in the 1972 map catalogue are:

1/1250	£1.10 per sheet
1/2500 National Grid (small sheet)	£1.10 per sheet
1/2500 National Grid (large sheet)	£1.65 per sheet
1/2500 County Series	88 per sheet

The "County Series" is a series originally surveyed before the National Grid network existed and has only later been adjusted into it. The National Grid Series is all from post 1945 surveys. There is a programme of continuous revision for all mapping. 1/2500 mapping shows areas in hectares to three decimal places on the new maps and in acres on the new and old.

In their annual report for 1979/70 the Ordnance survey had this to say on the accuracy of their maps: "The accuracy of a map may be defined in terms of a statistical quantity known as the 'standard error'. A comparison is made between the 'true' positions of a large number of points on the sample sheets as determined by a higher order method of survey and their positions on the map. The difference between the two values for each point may be regarded as an error on the map. These errors are for the most part random in nature and will vary in magnitude and direction from point to point. The 'standard error' is a measure of the random errors and therefore indicates the accuracy of the map detail. Broadly speaking, two thirds of all the errors are likely to be smaller than the standard error, the remainder being larger. The chance of an error occurring with a magnitude of more than three times the standard error is less than one in three hundred. The accuracy tolerance of Ordnance Survey maps are as follows:

1:1250 (new survey)	—	standard error not greater than 0.4 m. (=1′ 3″)
1:2500 (old County Series 'Overhauled')	—	standard error not greater than 2.4 m. (=8′ 2″)"

Whatever plan is used precautions must be taken before completion to ensure that the plan reflects accurately the position on the ground. In at least one of the big land development companies it is standard practice for a 1/500 survey to be made of all development before completion of the transfer. There are then never any boundary disputes. Surveyors in the Greater London Council are similarly involved and no disputes occur. This should be standard practice everywhere.

M. M. Barrett,
M.Sc. (Land Surveying), A.R.I.C.S.

APPENDIX 2

LAND REGISTRY PRACTICE NOTES RELEVANT TO IDENTITY AND BOUNDARIES

No. 5. Filed Plan—Colouring.
" 6. Attachment of Plan on Conveyance or Transfer to Land Certificate.
" 12. Filed Plan—Field numbers and areas.
" 13. Boundaries—"Hedge and ditch" rule.
" 27. Registration with general boundaries.
" 29. Colour References on Filed Plans.
" 34. Covenants and Declarations as to Ownership of Fences: "T" Marks.
" 42. Developing Building Estates: Preliminary arrangements with the vendor.[1]
" 43. Developing Building Estates: Verifications and searches by purchasers.[1]
" 45. Plans "for the purpose of identification only".
" 46. Plans of flats.
" 51. Official Search of Filed Plan: (C.146 (Building Estates) Procedure)
" 52. Metrication.
" 59. Boundary discrepancies on leasehold building estates.
" 60. Official searches of the public index map—supply of plan to searcher.

---

1. Incorporated in Land Registry Practice Leaflet No. 7.

APPENDIX 3

SOME RELEVANT PRACTICE NOTES

12. *Filed Plan—Field numbers and areas*

Field numbers and areas are not shown on the filed plan. The reasons why the Chief Land Registrar will not agree to this being done are as follows:—

(*a*) A survey over the whole of the country is being carried out by the Ordnance Survey on the National Grid. This will introduce completely new co-ordinates, which will render obsolete the field numbers shown on existing ordnance survey maps.

(*b*) The parcels shown on the 6-inch ordnance maps do not contain area measurements and these maps may be used in case of mountain or other undeveloped land.

(*c*) The area measurements shown on one edition of the ordnance survey maps differ from those shown on another edition. Areas stated in deeds are sometimes inaccurate, but any area measurements shown on the filed plan would naturally be assumed to be correct.

(*d*) For field numbers and areas to be shown, the Land Registry would have to consider not only the area measurement shown on a parcel in the ordnance survey, but also the extent of a part of that parcel, where it has been sub-divided. In such a case there might not even be any physical boundaries.

13. *Boundaries—"Hedge and ditch" rule*

The boundaries shown on the filed plan or general map are only general boundaries and follow the ordnance survey map through the centres of hedges. In the case of agricultural land, this is frequently incorrect, having regard to the "hedge and ditch" rule. The explanation of the Registry's practice is to be found in Rule 278 in cases where the boundaries have not been fixed.[1]

---

1. For further information and as to the history of this rule, see paragraph 45 of the Report of the Royal Commissioners (1870) appointed to inquire into the operation of the Land Transfer Act; the Fourth Report of the Acquisition and Valuation of Land Committee (the Scott Report, 1919), page 18, and the article in *Current Legal Problems*, 1953 (Stevens), entitled "The State and Title to Land".

34. *Covenants and Declarations as to Ownership of Fences: "T" marks*

It is the practice of the Registry to make an entry on the register in respect of a declaration as to the ownership of fences and other boundaries contained in a transfer of registered land. A positive covenant to erect or maintain a fence is not entered directly on the register but particulars of positive covenants in transfers are sewn up in the land certificate. (See Practice Note 21.)

If a conveyance or transfer contains restrictive covenants intermingled with positive covenants relating to the maintenance of boundaries and the covenants are set out in the register, then the "T" marks referred to in the deed will also be shown on the filed plan, or described by a marginal note in the register. If the covenants are not so set out, an office copy of the deed, including its plan, will be bound into the land certificate.

"T" marks may be shown on a deed plan where there is no covenant, declaration of ownership or other reference to them in the body of the deed and their presence is sometimes relied upon as evidence of the ownership of boundary structures. Whatever convention there may be as to the meaning of such "T" marks, it appears that they have no legal significance and for that reason alone it was not the practice, prior to 1962, to reproduce them on the filed plan. Since then, however, the Chief Land Registrar, in deference to the express wishes of solicitors, has agreed that even when there is no fencing covenant or other provision, "T" marks shown on a deed plan will be reproduced on the filed plan in the following circumstances:—

1. The applicant for first registration must specially request this to be done because he regards it as important in the interests of his client.
2. The "T" marks will be those shown on the plan to the deed inducing first registration or, if there is no plan on that deed, in the latest preceding deed containing a plan of the land being registered.
3. A note will be added to the filed plan that "The 'T' marks were reproduced from the plan on a deed dated . . . but are not otherwise referred to in that deed."

APPENDIX 4

LAND REGISTRATION ACT 1925, SECTIONS 82 AND 83

(AS AMENDED BY THE LAND REGISTRATION AND LAND CHARGES ACT 1971)

82. (1) The register may be rectified pursuant to an order of the court or by the registrar, subject to an appeal to the court, in any of the following cases, but subject to the provisions of this section:—

(*a*) Subject to any express provisions of this Act to the contrary, where a court of competent jurisdiction has decided that any person is entitled to any estate right or interest in or to any registered land or charge, and as a consequence of such decision such court is of opinion that a rectification of the register is required, and makes an order to that effect;

(*b*) Subject to any express provision of this Act to the contrary, where the court, on the application in the prescribed manner of any person who is aggrieved by any entry made in, or by the omission of any entry from, the register, or by any default being made, or unnecessary delay taking place, in the making of any entry in the register, makes an order for the rectification of the register;

(*c*) In any case and at any time with the consent of all persons interested;

(*d*) Where the court or the registrar is satisfied that any entry in the register has been obtained by fraud;

(*e*) Where two or more persons are, by mistake, registered as proprietors of the same registered estate or of the same charge;

(*f*) Where a mortgagee has been registered as proprietor of the land instead of as proprietor of a charge and a right of redemption is subsisting;

(*g*) Where a legal estate has been registered in the name of a person who if the land had not been registered would not have been the estate owner; and

(*h*) In any other case where, by reason of any error or omission in the register, or by reason of any entry made under a mistake, it may be deemed just to rectify the register.

(2) The register may be rectified under this section, notwithstanding that the rectification may affect any estates, rights, charges or interests acquired or protected by registration, or by any entry on the register, or otherwise.

(3) The register shall not be rectified, except for the purpose of giving effect to an overriding interest, so as to affect the title of the proprietor who is in possession

(*a*) unless such proprietor is a party or privy or has caused or substantially contributed, by his act, neglect or default, to the fraud, mistake or omission in consequence of which such rectification is sought; or

(*b*) unless the immediate disposition to him was void, or the disposition to any person through whom he claims otherwise than for valuable consideration was void; or

(*c*) unless for any other reason, in any particular case, it is considered that it would be unjust not to rectify the register against him.

(4) Where a person is in possession of registered land in right of a minor interest, he shall, for the purposes of this section, be deemed to be in possession as agent for the proprietor.

(5) The registrar shall obey the order of any competent court in relation to any registered land on being served with the order or an official copy thereof.

(6) On every rectification of the register the land certificate and any charge certificate which may be affected shall be produced to the registrar unless an order to the contrary is made by him.

83. (1) Subject to the provisions of this Act to the contrary, any person suffering loss by reason of any rectification of the register under this Act shall be entitled to be indemnified.

(2) Where an error or omission has occurred in the register, but the register is not rectified, any person suffering loss by reason of such error or omission, shall, subject to the provisions of this Act, be entitled to be indemnified.

(3) Where any person suffers loss by reason of the loss or destruction of any document lodged at the registry for inspection or safe custody or by reason of an error in any official search, he shall be entitled to be indemnified under this Act.

(4) Subject as hereinafter provided, a proprietor of any registered land or charge claiming in good faith under a forged disposition shall, where the register is rectified, be deemed to have suffered loss by reason of such rectification and shall be entitled to be indemnified under this Act.

(5) No indemnity shall be payable under this Act in any of the following cases:—

(*a*) Where the applicant or a person from whom he derived title (otherwise than under a disposition for valuable consideration which is registered or protected on the register) had caused or substantially contributed to the loss by fraud or lack of proper care;

(*b*) On account of any mines or minerals or of the existence of any rights to work or get mines or minerals, unless a note is entered on the register that the mines or minerals are included in the registered title;

(*c*) On account of costs incurred in taking or defending any legal proceedings without the consent of the registrar.

(6) Where an indemnity is paid in respect of the loss of an estate or interest in or charge on land the amount so paid shall not exceed—

(*a*) Where the register is not rectified, the value of the estate, interest or charge at the time when the error or omission which caused the loss was made;

(*b*) Where the register is rectified, the value (if there had been no rectification) of the estate, interest or charge, immediately before the time of rectification.

(7) (*Repealed*).

(8) Subject to subsection (5)(*c*) of this section, as amended by section 2(2) of the Land Registration and Land Charges Act 1971—

(*a*) an indemnity under any provision of this Act shall include such amount, if any, as may be reasonable in respect of any costs or expenses properly incurred by the applicant in relation to the matter; and

(*b*) an applicant for an indemnity under any such provision shall be entitled to an indemnity thereunder of such amount, if any, as may be reasonable in respect of any such costs or expenses, notwithstanding that no other indemnity money is payable thereunder.

(9) Where indemnity is paid for a loss, the register, on behalf of the Crown, shall be entitled to recover the amount paid from any person who has caused or substantially contributed to the loss by his fraud.

(10) The registrar shall be entitled to enforce, on behalf of the Crown, any express or implied covenant or other right which the person who is indemnified would have been entitled to enforce in relation to the matter in respect of which indemnity has been paid.

(11) A liability to pay indemnity under this Act shall be deemed a simple contract debt; and for the purposes of the Limitation Act, 1623, the cause of

action shall be deemed to arise at the time when the claimant knows, or but for his own default might have known, of the existence of his claim:

Provided that, when a claim to indemnity arises in consequence of the registration of an estate in land with an absolute or good leasehold title, the claim shall be enforceable only if made within six years from the date of such registration, except in the following cases:—

(*a*) Where at the date of registration the person interested is an infant, the claim by him may be made within six years from the time he attains full age;

(*b*) In the case of settled land, or land held on trust for sale, a claim by a person interested in remainder or reversion, may be made within six years from the time when his interest falls into possession;

(*c*) Where a claim arises in respect of a restrictive covenant or agreement affecting freehold land which by reason of notice or the registration of a land charge or otherwise was binding on the first proprietor at the time of first registration, the claim shall only be enforceable within six years from the breach of the covenant or agreement;

(*d*) Where any person interested is entitled as a proprietor of a charge or as a mortgagee protected by a caution in the specially prescribed form, the claim by him may be made within six years from the last payment in respect of principal or interest.

(12) This section applies to the Crown in like manner as it applies to a private person.

INDEX

C

I

J

L

M

N